Department of Health

The Prevention of Suicide

organised by the
Faculty of Public Health Medicine,
General Practitioners
College of Psychiatrists

Sian Griffiths, Ian Wylie,
Morgan and André Tylee

London: HMSO

Contents

"Keep up your patients' spirits by music of viols and ten-stringed psaltery or by forged letters describing the death of his enemies or by telling him that he has been elected to a bishopric, if a churchman."

Henri de Mondeville, 1350

"You and I ought not to die before we have explained ourselves to each other."

John Adams, letter to Thomas Jefferson, 1813

Foreword

It is right to work to reduce the number of suicides and attempts at suicide. In 'The Health of the Nation' (1992), mental illness was selected as a key area for development with an overall objective 'to reduce the morbidity and mortality caused by mental illness'.

If this mortality is to be reduced, reduction in suicide rates amongst severely mentally ill people and the general population is of central importance.

Targets for achievement specify reductions against an overall picture of a suicide rate which has been relatively stable over the past two decades. However this apparent stability conceals changes of profound significance such as the divergence between male and female rates, with the former rising and the latter dropping.

The target of reducing overall suicide rates by 15% by the year 2000 represents a clear commitment to change within a timescale which allows for research, strategy development, and implementation. The contributions assembled together here provide a valuable background to the understanding of what is currently known about suicide and what can be done about it.

Suicide is a difficult topic to discuss. It is usually the culmination of intense distress and, so often, leaves further distress behind it. It is understandable that for so long it has been relatively neglected as an area on which preventative efforts can be focussed. And yet, suicide is clearly significant as a cause of death, now numerically surpassing road traffic accidents. The remarkable success of prevention in reducing deaths from road traffic accidents despite the massive increase in the number of vehicles on the road makes an illuminating and perhaps inspiring contrast. That prevention programme has, over the years, involved a coordinated programme of research, improvement in accident and emergency services, development of safety measures and, especially important, public education. Likewise suicide prevention must involve a multifaceted programme across government, health and social services, local authorities, voluntary agencies, the private sector and the media. The contributions here cover many of these areas and provide a wide-ranging examination of the wealth of research and experience about suicide that exists in this country and internationally.

This expert analysis reviews the changing epidemiology of suicide and the circumstances in which it occurs. Insights are provided into the assessment of suicide and of specific high risk groups such as young men in prisons. Psychological autopsy studies gave valuable information, twenty to thirty years ago, about the high proportion of those committing suicide who were suffering from mental disorders and who had had contact with primary and specialist services. The passing of time requires re-examination of these and such studies are documented here. International experience of prevention strategies, in the Netherlands, Scandinavia and the USA, may have lessons for England although different suicide rates and patterns mean that caution is needed in any comparisons. The description of programmes in schools and in primary and secondary care illustrate the variety of approaches that are worth consideration and research in England. The impact of the media is also highlighted.

Training in risk assessment and management by the range of professionals who meet people at high risk of suicide can improve their skills. The Samaritans have a long established tradition of providing a ready and accessible response to those at risk. Audit can inform practice – nationally through the Confidential Enquiry into Homicides and Suicides by Mentally Ill People and locally in primary and secondary care.

Policy across government can make an impact and must complement efforts made by individuals working within health and social services.

There remain many widespread misconceptions about suicide, for example, that people who talk about it never do it, which research long ago demonstrated to be incorrect. There is also the fatalistic belief that if someone is going to seriously attempt suicide, there is not much you can do to stop them going through with it.

Depression and the other mental disorders which usually precede it has been eminently treatable for many years. Suicide rates are affected by social circumstances. These need to be taken into account in setting targets in any prevention strategy but, as the conference on which this book is based clearly demonstrated, whilst there is still much to learn there is much that can be done.

People who are now joining together in "Healthy Alliances' with those who have worked and researched so assiduously over the years in this area, can reduce the suffering accompanying suicide and ultimately reduce the number of suicides occuring. I commend this book as a major contribution to that effort.

Virginia Bottomley
Secretary of State for Health
Whitehall
LONDON

Acknowledgements

The editors are grateful to Mr. Derek Flannery for his detailed and careful work collating and arranging the texts, and wish to thank the following who have kindly given permission for the use of copyright material:

World Health Organisation, Geneva, and Drs. Dechering and Kerkhof for Fig. 1, Chapter 3, taken from *World Health Statistics Annual 1989,* pp. 222–354, also Drs. Dechering, Kerkhof and Kunst for Fig. 2, source, Central Bureau of Statistics, The Hague; and Drs. Kerkhof and Kunst for Table 2.

The Editor, British Medical Journal and Dr. John Horder for Figure 1, Chapter 6, taken from *British Medical Journal, 1983: vol. 286* pp. 191–194, – 'Alma Ata Declaration'.

The Samaritans, for the poster in Chapter 11.

List of Contributors

Simon Armson
Chief Executive
The Samaritans

Douglas Beaton, Charge Nurse
Psychiatric Acute Care Crisis Intervention Team
300, Ivydale Road, Nunhead SE15

Virginia Bottomley, MP
Secretary of State for Health

Dr W D Boyd
Director, Confidential Inquiry into Homicides and Suicides by Mentally
Ill People

Dr W F G Dolman
Her Majesty's Deputy Coroner for the Southern District and the Inner
West District of London

Dr Enda Dooley
Director of Prison Medical Services
Department of Justice, Dublin

Karen Dunnell
Head of Health Statistics, OPCS

Dr Sian Griffiths
Regional Director of Public Health and Health Policy
South West Thames Regional Health Authority

Dr David Gunnell
Senior Registrar in Public Health Medicine
Somerset Health Authority

Dr Keith Hawton
Consultant Psychiatrist and Clinical Lecturer
Department of Psychiatry, University of Oxford

Dr Rachel Jenkins
Principal Medical Officer and Honorary Senior Lecturer
Department of Health and Institute of Psychiatry

Dr Sonia Johnson
Project Co-ordinator
Maudsley Continuing Care Study, Institute of Psychiatry

Rose Jones
Principal Clinical Psychologist
Culverhay Community Mental Health Team
South Devon Health Care Trust

Dr Michael Kerfoot
Senior Lecturer
Department of Psychiatry, University of Manchester

Dr Ad Kerkhof
Associate Professor in Clinical Psychology
Rijks Universiteit, Leiden, The Netherlands

Dr Anton Kunst
Department of Public Health
Erasmus University, Rotterdam, The Netherlands

Dr John Lambourne
Consultant Psychiatrist
South Devon Health Care Trust

Dr Paul Lelliott
Deputy Director
Research Unit, The Royal College of Psychiatrists

Professor Alan Maynard
Centre for Health Economics
University of York

Dr Jeremy Metters
Deputy Chief Medical Officer
Department of Health

Professor Gethin Morgan
Department of Mental Health
University of Bristol

Professor Eugene Paykel
Department of Psychiatry
University of Cambridge

Professor Denis Pereira Gray, OBE
Department of General Practice
University of Exeter

Dr Stephen Platt
Director of Development and Evaluation
Health Education Board for Scotland

Professor David Shaffer
Professor of Child Psychiatry
University of Cambridge

Professor A C P Sims
President, The Royal College of Psychiatrists

Dr Hilary Stirland
Director of Public Health
Wandsworth Health Authority

Dr Geraldine Strathdee
Consultant Psychiatrist
Maudsley Hospital, Camberwell

Dr Graham Thornicroft
Senior Lecturer
Institute of Psychiatry, University of London

Dr Christopher Vassilas
Consultant Psychiatrist
West Suffolk District General Hospital

Ann Watts
Nunhead Sector Service Manager
300, Ivydale Road, Nunhead SE15

Joy Wiltshire
Manager and Community Psychiatric Nurse
Culverhay Community Mental Health Team
South Devon Health Care Trust

Part 1

Setting the Scene

1   The Health of the Nation

Rt Hon Virginia Bottomley, MP, Secretary of State for Health

There are few worse things for parents, for work colleagues, for others to face than the suicide of a colleague, of a neighbour, of a relative, because of all the associated feelings of guilt of the taboos, of the questions that should or shouldn't have been asked. Of all the areas of activity for the health service, a suicide is almost a contradiction: if you are a doctor, a nurse, a physiotherapist, if you are in any of the caring professions, a suicide is a particular affront to cope with. It is not only the loss of life for the individuals involved, the avoidable loss of life, but the enormous difficulties of equipping people to cope with suicide and to develop their skills.

As we well know, one of the ways of coping with enormously difficult tasks is to put your mind elsewhere and try not to think about it at all. It's one of the reasons that I was determined that amongst our targets in The Health of the Nation the reduction of suicide should be one. This is a brave target and, as a Department of Health and across the Government – because health strategy is owned by all departments of government – we cannot avoid this target as we go forward to the end of the century. This conference is a very important first step.

Our health strategy we believe, is a model for others to follow. We have presented this to the World Health Organisation showing how it was agreed by government. The task now is not only to get ownership, across central and local government departments, but to begin to measure and record our success. I think many of you will have seen the handbook produced by the Department of Health on mental illness and the targets there. That, I believe, was a very important step in drawing together expertise and knowledge.

I am determined, to see substantial improvements in mental health care. That means understanding and commitment as well as resources. There have been substantial increases in resources, but we have to think about how those resources are deployed. The inclusion of mental illness, not only in the Health of the Nation, but as a key area in introducing community care means, we must now integrate our efforts and give mental health the priority it deserves. I am not convinced we have completed that transition in thinking from the old days of out-of-sight, out-of-mind in institutions to services in the community that are effective in meeting the needs of those who are most in need of services.

The key areas in The Health of the Nation strategy for mental illness are threefold. Firstly, to improve significantly the health and social functioning of mentally ill people. Secondly, to reduce the overall suicide rate by at least 15%. Thirdly, to reduce the lifetime rate of suicide in people with severe mental illness by at least one third. Of all the targets we chose this was the area with which we had some of the greatest difficulties. In the Green Paper we had talked about a target in terms of people no longer being in institutions, but this was not the right thing to be measuring at this particular moment. That first target of improving significantly the health and social functioning of mentally ill people is the only one of all the many targets in The Health of the Nation that is of a general qualitative kind as opposed to one that can be precisely measured. It was because we were so determined to address this issue as well as to improve our measures of effectiveness in this important area.

Let me say more about suicide. It is an avoidable form of mortality, accounting for about 1% of deaths annually. While suicide rates have been going down overall, there has been a worrying increase in the rate among young men, and more people now are dying from suicide than are killed in road traffic accidents. People understand the importance of reducing the loss of life from road traffic accidents. Do we yet have that common commitment to reducing loss of life from suicides? I will not be content until people can regard that campaign as quite as valuable and relevant as the campaign to avoid traffic accidents.

The other aspect to reducing suicides is improving the treatment and care of people with a mental illness. Mental illness affects most people at some stage in their life, either directly or through somebody they know closely. It is as common as heart disease: and three times as common as cancer. I wish everybody I saw shaking a tin for cancer charities was also involved in shaking a tin for mental health charities. I well know that once you shake a tin for a subject you begin to think about it, begin to understand it, begin to recognise it. As many as nine out of ten people who take their own lives are likely to have some form of mental disorder – Depression, alcoholism, schizophrenia – all relatively treatable.

To reduce the level of suicide we must improve our level of understanding and care for people with mental illness. And it is particularly important to understand that everyone has a part to play. The development of health alliances is fundamental to a great number of the key areas of The Health of the Nation, but nowhere more so than for targets on suicide. The mental illness handbook, which I referred to earlier, is addressed jointly to the NHS and local authority social service departments. It recognises that the causes and treatments of mental illness are social as well as medical. It underlines the close cooperation between those agencies and others that is essential if we are to ensure effective care for people with mental illness. Thus tackling suicide is very similar to the campaign to address the issues around children killed from non-accidental injury. It was only when the agencies began to see that this was not just a social services problem, nor just a health visitor's problem, nor just a GP and school's problem. Loss of life through non-accidental injury can only be addressed where there is a real recognition that there are partners in preventing avoidable death. Suicide is very similar. It is when all the agencies turn round and acknowledge that they can only succeed when they work together that there is real progress.

The care programme approach is, I believe, a real example of where building partnerships is fundamental. The implementation of the care programme approach, is still patchy. The programme is being evaluated at the moment and I think there will be some sharp lessons to be learnt – of course we always want the complete product when we've only just started, but we must have a view about moving forward and becoming more effective. It is the ready availability of a key worker which is so often the vital link, someone who notices a changing mood, an emerging danger and can pass on those concerns and see that necessary action is taken. We must focus our care on the needs of the individual. That means making our services local, comprehensive, sensitive, assessing what local needs really are, what users actually want, and ensuring that services respond effectively.

Developing community supervision orders is sometimes posed as an alternative to making services more responsive to users. It isn't. What is very important, is that we try and try again really to listen to what the users of the services are saying, and to listen to the way in which services sometimes have not been acceptable. We must listen to what's being said by users and be relentless, I believe, in making mental health services ever more appropriate.

Voluntary organisations have a particular pivotal role. They have made a particular contribution in the development of a great range of services in this country. They are innovative, they are flexible, they tend to be user-friendly, and less threatening than many of the services provided by governments, by health, and social services departments. Because of their independence from the mainstream they are much more in tune with grass roots opinion. Acting as advocates for service users, they are agents for change.

The NHS does have a clear responsibility to take the lead in developing broader alliances as well. With Social Service Departments above all; with employers and Trade Unions to improve the management of workplace stress, with voluntary organisations, Women's Institutes, schools, housing departments, Working Men's Clubs.

But over and above all these, over and above those of us who are paid to do our jobs let us think for a moment about the people who are not paid to have anything to do with mental illness, the general public. Until we can combat the stigma and the taboo around mental illness, we will not make the progress that we want. If your brother commits suicide is it as easy to tell your friends as if your brother or father dies of cancer? I fear it's not. I fear that people still do not want to tell others that they are off work for a mental illness. They do not worry about telling people they are off work because they have a heart condition: that is a question of public information and education.

We must continue to challenge the out-of-sight, out-of-mind syndrome. It is unenlightened and prejudiced attitudes that make it so much harder for people to settle and get the support they need in the community. Suicide is so often plagued with popular misconceptions. It is *our* job to explode those myths. And a key part of the discussion about the prevention of suicide must involve primary care. Where do people go now when they're troubled? As often as not it is the GP. And of course the way in which general practitioners handle people with mental health problems is of the greatest significance. The easiest thing to do when somebody comes into the surgery who feels depressed is not to ask him or her about it. People very often come in presenting with some sort of other problem and it is much easier not to turn the conversation to an area you are not confident you could do anything about.

The multidisciplinary audits of suicide across primary and secondary health care and in conjunction with social services department can give pointers that will help improve service delivery and prevent future suicides Many audits are being set up locally, and nationally the confidential enquiry into homicides and suicides by mentally ill people will shortly begin gathering information on suicides. The knowledge we already have about circumstances that contribute to suicide can assist in developing focus strategies. The OPCS report confirms what we already know that the risk of suicide is higher among particular occupational groups (doctors, vets, farmers, pharmacists) and this is related to the easy access those groups have to the means to commit suicide.

It's targeted initiatives such as the Citizens Advice Bureau, National Farmers' Union and The Samaritans focussing on suicide in rural communities, which bring together different players in alliances for health that will indeed have a major impact.

Another group where suicide rates are high is, of course prisoners. I am pleased that the Home Office prison service is developing suicide prevention measures. Including the use of listeners, an innovative scheme where fellow prisoners, supported by the Samaritans, can give support in times of need. Improving communication and cooperation between staff such as prisoner officers, health care staff, chaplains, probation officers, as well as the training of prison officers and health care staff in the recognition and the assessment of suicidal risk.

You also know that limiting access to common acceptable means to commit suicide can create the time to deal with underlying problem and prevent suicide occuring. We know what happened in the population when we moved over to natural gas. Similarly the introduction of catalytic converters, which reduce carbon monoxide levels by at least 80% became a requirement for all new cars from the beginning of this year. And there will be many other public health measures which we can and should persue. One area of interest at the moment being considered is the link to paracetamol.

There is much that can be done to reduce the number of suicides. We are indeed determined that this is one of the key areas in the Health of the Nation, where we can challenge the loss of life, where a partnership across government departments, across local authority and other agencies can make a real impact. I look forward to learning the outcome of some of your debates.

2 Epidemiology and Trends in Suicide in the UK
Karen Dunnell

This talk was based on two recent articles in Population Trends which are reproduced below.

Trends in suicide deaths in England and Wales

John Charlton, Sue Kelly, Karen Dunnell
Health Statistics, OPCS
Barry Evans
Communicable Disease Surveillance Centre
Rachel Jenkins, Ruth Wallis
Department of Health

Reprinted from *Population Trends 69*

Population Trends is the journal of the Office of Population Censuses and Surveys. It is published four times a year in September, December, March and June. In addition to bringing together articles on a variety of population and medical topics, *Population Trends* contains regular series of tables on a range of subjects for which OPCS is responsible.

Trends in suicide deaths in England and Wales

John Charlton, Sue Kelly, Karen Dunnell
Health Statistics, OPCS
Barry Evans
Communicable Disease Surveillance Centre
Rachel Jenkins, Ruth Wallis
Department of Health

This article, the first of two, describes recent trends in suicide rates and the methods used. For the first time since 1911, male suicide rates have been rising at a time when female suicide rates have been falling. The age distribution of suicides has also changed, to the extent that males aged under 45 are now more at risk than older males, whose rates have fallen. There is evidence of both cohort and period effects.

Introduction

This article, the first of a series of two, updates previous *Population Trends* articles on suicide trends. [1, 2] This article describes the trends in suicide rates and methods used, while the second article will consider factors that may be associated with the trends. Although accounting for only 2 per cent of all male deaths and 1 per cent of female deaths, suicide and undetermined deaths are significant when premature deaths are examined. They account for 8.5 and 3.8 per cent of years of life lost before age 65 among males and females respectively.

Definition of suicide

Two different definitions of 'suicide' have been used in this article:

(a) *recorded suicides:* 6th ICD E970–E979; 7th ICD E970–E979, 8th ICD 950–E959; 9th ICD E950–E959 (as used in *Population Trends 35*[2]); and

(b) *suicides & undetermined* (from 1968 onwards only): as (a) above plus E980–E989, excluding E988.8 after 1978.

When choosing a definition it is useful to consider how suicide deaths are certified. The coroner investigates every case where violent or unnatural death is suspected, and sudden deaths of unknown cause. The verdicts that may be recorded are homicide, accidental death, suicide, and open verdict. A verdict of suicide should only be recorded if there is clear evidence that the injury was self-inflicted and that the deceased intended to kill him/herself. If there is any doubt about the intentions of the deceased either an accidental or an open verdict should be recorded. There is thus some under-recording of suicide deaths in the recorded suicide figures, and it is likely that most open verdicts among adults are cases where suicide occurred but was not proven. In cases where the coroner needs to adjourn the inquest when someone has been charged with an offence in connection with the death, or the case is under police investigation, OPCS has used the code E988.8 from 1979 onwards for non-transport incidents, to accelerate the registration (accelerated registrations). Nearly all these cases that are resolved turn out to be homicides. Thus E988.8 has been excluded from our wider definition of suicide. Transport incidents are coded initially as traffic accidents.

Figure 1 shows the number of recorded suicides since 1911 for men and women separately, based on a 3-year moving average. The reduction in the number of suicides during the First and Second World Wars and the rise in the inter-war Depression, peaking in 1932, are striking. After the end of the Second World

Fig 1 Number of suicide deaths* by sex, 1911-1990, England and Wales

War the number of deaths due to suicide rose to a peak for both sexes in 1963. The increase up to 1963 was more pronounced for women than for men. The introduction of the Suicide Act 1961, which abolished the criminal aspect of suicide, was followed by a small temporary increase in rates, but since 1963 women's suicides have continued to fall. Men's suicides fell until the early 1970s since when they have been rising. This is the first time since 1911 that male and female suicide trends have moved in opposite directions.

Figure 1 also shows the trends for suicides and undetermined deaths (definition (b)), and how the trends for the two definitions follow the same pattern over time (open verdicts were only counted for individuals aged 15 and over). Platt *et al*[3] have shown that the main difference between open verdicts and recorded suicides is in the method of killing, with passive methods such as drowning less likely (54 per cent) to be given a suicide verdict than active methods such as hanging (98 per cent). Definition (b) was chosen for the more recent time trends in order to include deaths the majority of which would be suicides. For longer term time trends, definition (a) was used because the category 'undetermined' did not exist prior to 1968.

Suicide Trends 1946–90

Trends in age-specific death rates for recorded suicides, 1946–90

Trends are shown in Figure 2 by 5-year age-groups for men and women, using 5-year average death rates. Since the early 1970s the rates for men aged 45 and over have fallen, while the rates for men under 45 have risen to such an extent that they currently exceed the rates for the older age-groups, apart from men aged 75 and over, who still have the highest rates. All age-groups had converged to similar rates by 1986–90, apart from ages 15–24 where, although the rates have risen, they are still substantially lower than those of older age-groups.

For women the rates for all age-groups, apart from those aged under 25, have fallen, with all age-groups having shown a peak in the period 1956–65. This peak is much more pronounced than the peak around the same time for men. Thus suicide rates for the age-groups under age 45 remained lower than those for the older age-groups. Convergence of suicide rates for different age-groups is again evident although, unlike the case for men, ages 45 and over still experienced higher suicide rates by 1986–90.

Trends in suicide and undetermined death rates, 1968–90

These trends were very similar to the recorded suicide trends shown in Figure 2 above. Figure 3 shows how suicide and undetermined death rates have become very similar for each age-group under age 75 by 1986–90. The rates for men aged 45

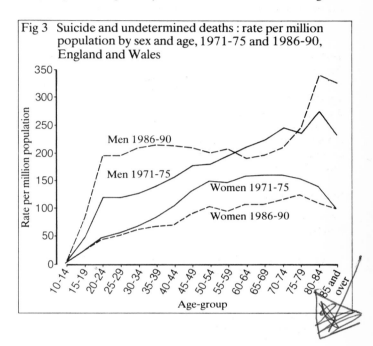

Fig 3 Suicide and undetermined deaths : rate per million population by sex and age, 1971-75 and 1986-90, England and Wales

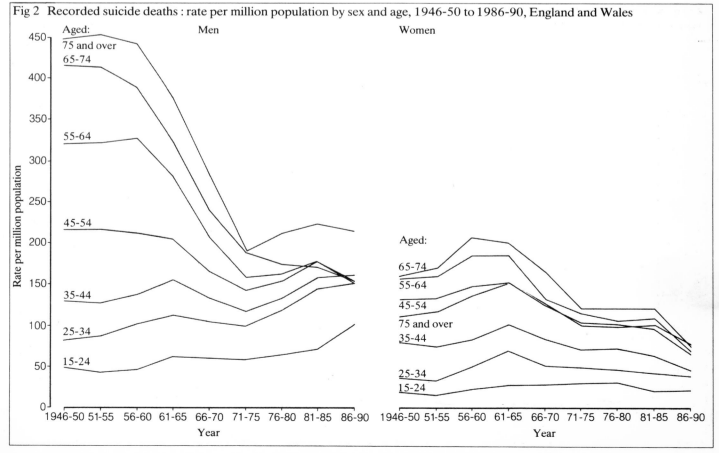

Fig 2   Recorded suicide deaths : rate per million population by sex and age, 1946-50 to 1986-90, England and Wales

and over have fallen, while those for men under 45 have risen. Women's rates for all ages have fallen, with the greatest falls occurring in those aged 45 and over, but the suicide rates for women aged under age 45 still remained lower than those for the older age-groups.

Is the change in suicide rates a cohort effect?

Figure 4 shows recorded suicide rates by age for successive birth cohorts of men and women. The birth cohorts are identified on the graphs by the central year of birth: each cohort includes individuals who could have been born 4 years either side of the central year.

For men, it can be seen that more recent cohorts have higher age for age mortality than earlier ones: that is, the 1966 cohort has higher mortality than the 1956 one, which has higher mortality than the 1946 one. The 1971 cohort (single point on graph) has a mortality rate at ages 15–19 of 52 per million, which is significantly higher than that for all earlier cohorts at this age. The suicide rates in the cohorts born after 1946 may not yet have peaked, in which case we might expect the suicide rates of the under 45 age-group to continue to rise for some years to come. The earlier cohorts displayed a different pattern. The 1916 cohorts had a pronounced peak at age 45–49 (the 1960s peak). The 1936 and 1962 cohorts had peaks at age 45–49 and 55–59 respectively that corresponded to deaths in the early 1980s.

For women aged 45 and over it can clearly be seen how successive birth cohorts experienced lower age for age suicide mortality: that is, the 1936 cohort had lower rates than the 1926

cohort which in turn had lower rates than the 1916 cohort. Below age 45 the picture is similar apart from the influence of the 1960s increase on the cohort curves – the 1966 cohort had lower rates than the 1956 cohort which had lower rates than the 1946 cohort.

There is thus evidence of both cohort and period effects on suicide rates of men and women. It is possible that suicide rates among young men may continue to rise as these cohorts grow older, while female suicide rates may continue to fall. The recent rise in suicide rates among the youngest women may, however, later extend into older age-groups.

Access/method

The probability of committing suicide will depend to some extent on the ease of access to effective means. The method used will depend on availability, ease of use, and 'fashion'. Figure 5 shows trends in recorded suicide rates for the main methods. The trends for the different age-groups are very similar, and hence are not generally shown in this article. In 1948–50, poisoning by domestic gas accounted for 41 per cent of recorded suicides in men and 60 per cent of recorded suicides among women. By 1968–70, poisoning by solid or liquid substances had become the most used method, particularly amongst women, where nearly two thirds of recorded suicides were this method. Poisoning by solid or liquid substances remained the most commonly used method for women in 1988–90 (43 per cent of all recorded suicides). For men, however, poisoning by other gases (principally motor vehicle exhaust fumes) became the most used method, accounting for nearly a third of all recorded suicides. In 1948–50, recorded suicides among men from hanging and suffocation accounted for 20 per cent of suicides, rising to 31 per

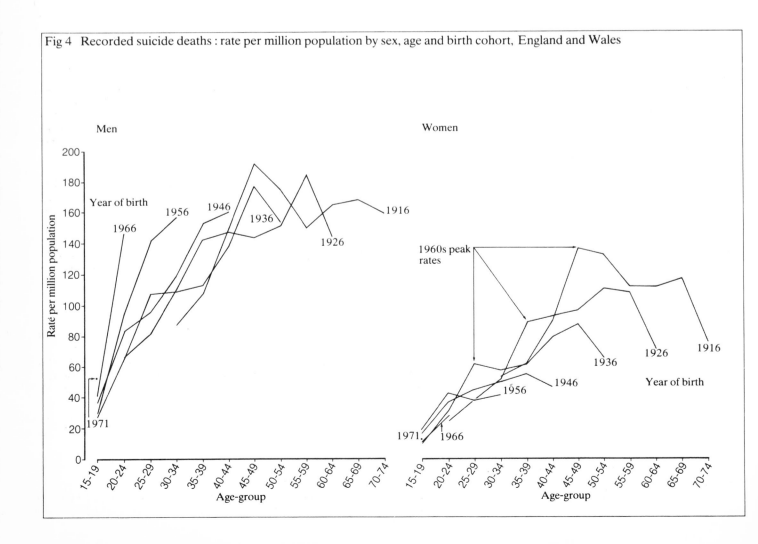

Fig 4 Recorded suicide deaths : rate per million population by sex, age and birth cohort, England and Wales

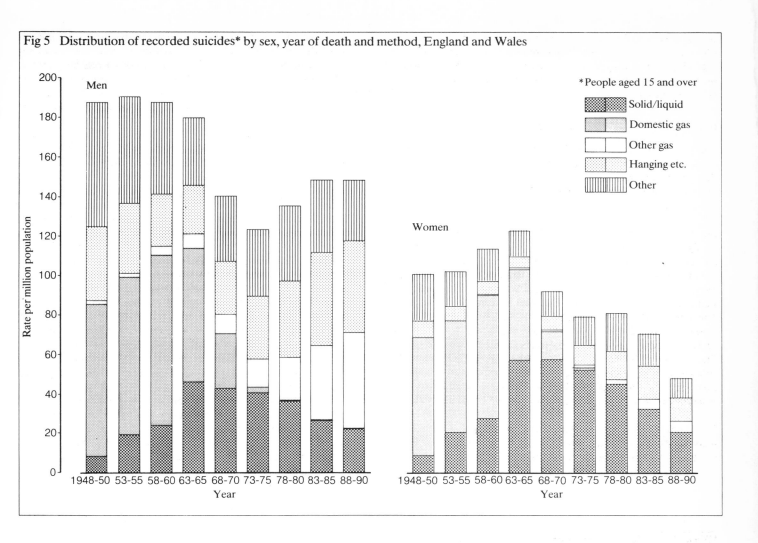

Fig 5   Distribution of recorded suicides* by sex, year of death and method, England and Wales

cent by 1988–90. The corresponding proportions for females were 8 and 25 per cent.

From 1968 to 1990, the distribution by method for suicide and undetermined deaths was similar to that for recorded suicides. Other methods accounted for a higher proportion of suicide and undetermined deaths than of recorded suicides.

Domestic gas

The graph shows the disappearance of domestic gas as a method of self-poisoning by the late 1970s, and the emergence of other (mainly motor vehicle exhaust) gas as the modern self-poisoning method. However, this switch is much more evident for males than females. The decline in suicide rates from poisoning by domestic gas paralleled the reduction of the carbon monoxide content of the domestic gas supply.[2]

Other gases

Rates for poisoning by other gases have increased from a very low level in 1948–50 to become one of the most common methods of suicide in 1988–90. Unlike the other methods, these suicide rates were lowest amongst those aged 65 and over. Those in the age-group 45–64 had the highest rates up to 1983–85, but by 1988–90 the 15–44 age-group exceeded these.

During the 1980s, over 90 per cent of recorded suicides from this method were due to motor vehicle exhaust gas. There has been a rapid rise in car registrations over the period, although the increase since the early 1980s has been more modest. There have been suggestions that the recent rise in these suicides could be due to the increase in hatchback cars since 1983 – these require a

shorter hose pipe. In 1983 hatchbacks (i.e. 3 and 5 door saloons) formed 26 per cent of the total cars registered and, in 1989, 51 per cent. Another possible reason may be the increased use of this method following publicity of such cases in the media. For suicide and undetermined deaths, the trends in death rates from poisoning by other gases followed the patterns for the recorded suicides very closely.

This method has always been far more common among men than women. Poisoning by other gas is now the most common method of suicide for males. For women, poisoning by other gas is the only suicide method for which death rates are increasing, but the rates for this method are only the fourth highest among women. The introduction of catalytic converters which reduce the emission of poisonous gases from cars may reduce these fatalities in the future.

Poisoning by solid and liquid substances

Recorded suicides by poisoning (solid or liquid substances) increased for all age-groups from 1948–50 to 1963–65, since when they decreased, particularly for those aged 45 and over. For this method, the highest death rates are in the oldest age-groups. In the mid–1960s peak, the death rate in the 65 and over age-group was more than double that in the 15–44 age-group. Suicide rates by this method have generally been higher among women than men, the only cause of suicide deaths for which this is true.

Hanging and suffocation

Figure 6 shows how the age distribution has changed between 1981–5 and 1986–90. The increase in the youngest men (below age 30) is particularly striking. Death rates for recorded suicides by these methods have in the past been highest in the older age-groups. For men aged 45 and over, rates for suicides by hanging and suffocation were at a peak in 1948–50, decreasing to a minimum in 1963–65, before increasing steadily until 1983–85. Between 1983–85 and 1988–90, they fell sharply. For men aged 15–44 the rates decreased slightly between 1948–50 and 1963–65, before rising continuously to reach a peak in 1988–90 which was only slightly below the rate for the 45–64 age-group. By comparison, women's rates were fairly stable from 1948–50 to 1968–70, when they started to rise, steeply in the case of women aged 45 and over. Recently rates for women aged under 25 have started to rise. As for men, rates for women aged 45 and over decreased between 1983–85 and 1988–90. The trend in suicide and undetermined death rates is very similar to that for recorded suicides, for both sexes.

The distribution of suicides between the categories in this group of methods is different for men and women, with plastic bags being more commonly used by women. During the 1980s nearly 90 per cent of recorded suicides in men in this group were due to hanging. For women the proportion was much lower, averaging just over 50 per cent, but rising to over 60 per cent in 1989 and 1990. Most of the remaining suicides among women are due to suffocation by plastic bag. The recent increase in the use of plastic bags is most marked in men aged 80 and above (Figure 6).

Other methods

The highest proportion of suicides (and undetermined deaths) in this category have been coded as 'suicide by other unspecified means'. There are also sizeable contributions from suicide by jumping from a high place (both sexes, younger age-group), suicide by firearms and explosives (men), and suicide by drowning (both sexes, ages 45 and over).

For recorded suicides in 1948–50, 'other methods' accounted for 34 per cent of all suicides in men and 24 per cent of all women's suicides. By 1988–90 these sex differences had narrowed to 21 per cent for men and 20 per cent for women. By comparison, the

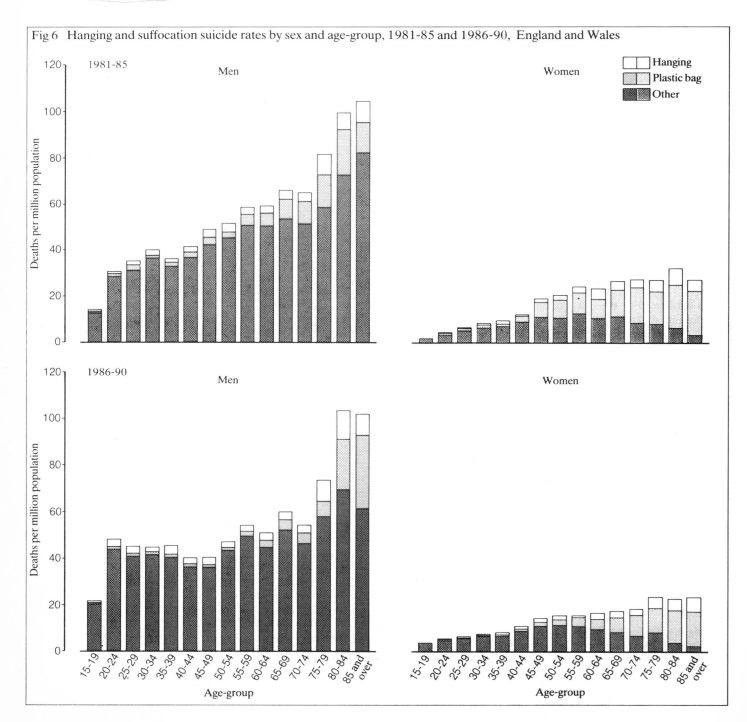

Fig 6   Hanging and suffocation suicide rates by sex and age-group, 1981-85 and 1986-90, England and Wales

1988–90 proportions of suicide and undetermined deaths from other methods were 28 per cent for males and 27 per cent for females.

The proportion of deaths due to each cause are summarised in Table 1.

Regional analysis

Figure 7 compares regional changes in rates of recorded suicides, and of suicides and undetermined deaths, for men and women aged 15–44. This is the age-group where suicide rates have risen for men and fallen less than other age-groups for women (the 'undetermined' data include E988.8). The comparison is of two periods, 1979–83 and 1985–89, periods for which the data were readily available. Regional rates for 1985–89 are given in Table 2.

The two definitions of suicide yield broadly similar results. Using the broader definition of suicide, South East Thames, North Western, and East Anglian RHAs have the highest male suicide rates – 225, 218, and 209 deaths per million population, respectively. Oxford, North East Thames, Wessex, Mersey, and Yorkshire have the lowest rates at around 160 per million. Suicide rates in young men increased in all RHAs between the two periods. By far the largest increase occurred in East Anglia – 58 per cent. There were also increases greater than 25 per cent in North Western, Oxford, and Trent RHAs. The smallest increases occurred in North East Thames and North West Thames, 3 and 4 per cent respectively.

Table 1   *Distribution of 'other' methods*

Method	1948–50	1988–90
Men	%	%
Drowning	35	14
Firearms	21	27
Cutting instruments	20	10
Jumping	9	16
Other	15	33
Women		
Drowning	60	33
Firearms	3	5
Cutting instruments	10	9
Jumping	15	23
Other	13	30

Women aged 15–44 in South East Thames and North Western RHAs have the highest suicide rates, 85 and 71 deaths per million population respectively. These regions also have the highest rates for young men. However, the lowest suicide rates for females are in Trent (47) and Wales (48). All regional rates for women have decreased except three: South East Thames, East Anglia, and Oxford. North West Thames RHA had the largest decrease at 29 per cent, followed by Wales at 17 per cent.

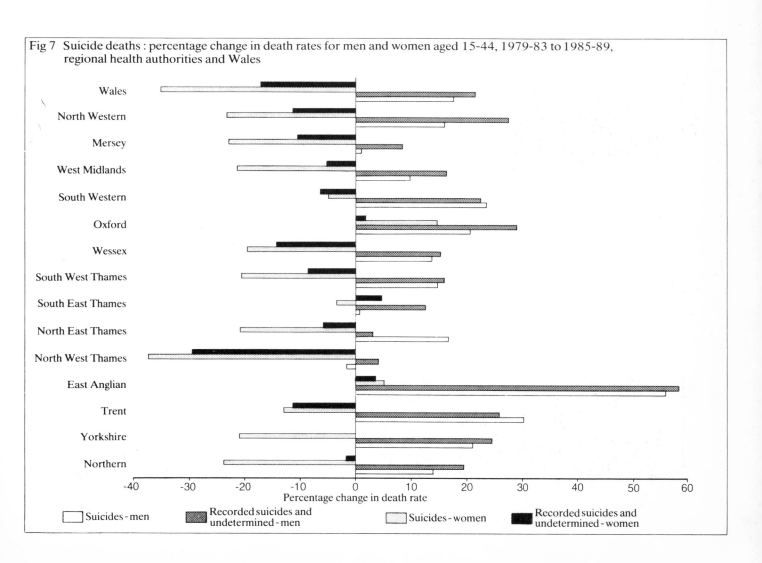

Fig 7   Suicide deaths : percentage change in death rates for men and women aged 15-44, 1979-83 to 1985-89, regional health authorities and Wales

Table 2 *Suicide rates per million population 1985–89 by regional health authority, and Wales*

Regional health authority	Recorded suicides		Suicide and undetermined	
	Males	Females	Males	Females
Northern	131	29	190	58
Yorkshire	115	34	167	64
Trent	132	27	180	47
East Anglian	162	41	209	57
North West Thames	117	35	204	67
North East Thames	132	38	165	65
South East Thames	141	55	225	85
South West Thames	124	35	174	63
Wessex	133	41	166	60
Oxford	117	39	160	57
South Western	142	39	190	60
West Midlands	123	33	170	55
Mersey	113	27	166	51
North Western	152	43	218	71
Wales	133	24	180	48

Conclusion

This article has described the trends for different age and sex groups nationally, and for people aged 15–44 regionally. A further article will describe trends in various factors that may be associated with increased risk of suicide.

References

[1] Adelstein A, Mardon C. Suicides 1961–74. *Population Trends*, 3, HMSO (1975) 13–18.

[2] Bulusu L, Alderson M. Suicides 1950–82. *Population Trends*, 35, HMSO (1984) 11–17.

[3] Platt S, Backett S, Kreitman N. Social construction or casual ascription: distinguishing suicide from undetermined deaths. *Social Psychiatry and Psychiatric Epidemiology*, 23 (1988) 217–221.

Suicide deaths in England and Wales: trends in factors associated with suicide deaths

John Charlton, Sue Kelly,
Karen Dunnell
Health Statistics, OPCS
Barry Evans
Communicable Disease Surveillance
Centre
Rachel Jenkins
Department of Health

Following a previous article which described changes that are occurring in suicide rates, this article examines trends in different factors known to be associated with suicide mortality in an attempt to gain a better insight into the reasons for the changes. In particular we hypothesise that for young men the increasing numbers remaining single or becoming divorced may explain about half of the increases observed between the early 1970s and late 1980s. This age-group of men has also been affected by high unemployment rates, exposure to armed combat, increasing risk of imprisonment, and an increase in the misuse of alcohol and other drugs. There is little evidence of a rise in the prevalence of mental illness. Further research is needed to improve our knowledge about the impact of these and other factors on suicide rates.

Introduction

A previous article in *Population Trends*[1] described trends in suicide rates among men and women and made comparisons between regional health authorities. For men under age 45, successive birth cohorts had higher age-for-age suicide mortality. Period effects were also found, a major one being increases in rates for men aged under 45 and for women of all ages from just after the Second World War until the mid-1960s.

This article examines some factors known to be associated with suicide mortality and the effect of any changes on recent trends. It also compares suicide rates in England and Wales with those in other EC countries, and the USA. Unless otherwise stated, the term 'suicides' in this article refers to 'suicides and undetermined deaths' (see Box 1).

The likelihood of a person committing suicide depends on several factors including:

- **illness:** mental (including alcohol and other drug misuse, and effects of behaviour-altering drugs) or physical (including painful, life threatening, or disabling illness);
- **personal factors:** for example level of social support, attitude to suicide;
- **stressful life events:** loss of job, divorce, widowhood, imprisonment, migration, diagnosis of threatening illness, traumatic shock, involvement in war;
- **changes in the wider cultural environment:** economic climate, cultural attitudes, etc; and
- **access to means of committing suicide:** for example the change from carbon monoxide to natural gas for cooking.

Population level data on the prevalence of risk factors such as unemployment, mental disorders, alcohol and other drug misuse may give clues to reasons for changes in national suicide trends. However, these data are limited in the extent to which they can 'explain' the trends in suicide rates. The probability of an individual committing suicide will depend on the combination of many risk and protective factors acting on him/her around and before the time of the event. With aggregate data the changes in different risk factors at the individual level may be masked by the level of aggregation. It is nevertheless still of value

to monitor trends in risk factors at the population level, especially those which could be changed.

Some of the factors related to suicide risk have not changed significantly during the period in question. However, since they are important in explaining differences between population groups, we will cover them first before examining trends in some of the other risk factors.

Gender

Suicide is four times as common in England and Wales in men as in women. The previous paper has shown that trends for men and women are different. These differences have to be borne in mind when considering the trends. Ideally, we need to be able to explain why some factors influence men to a greater extent than women, and what factors protect women. In practice we have found it easier to account for the increases in suicide rates in young men than for the decreases in women.

Occupation, social class, and unemployment

Occupation

Using data on occupation collected at death registration for the years 1979-90 the proportional mortality ratios (PMRs) for men aged 16-64 have been calculated. The PMR gives an indication of how a particular occupation's mortality from a specific cause

---

Box 1   Definition of suicide

In this and the previous article (*Population Trends 69*), two different definitions of 'suicide' have been used:

(a) *recorded suicides*

ICD6 Codes E970-E979, ICD7 Codes E970-E979, ICD8 Codes E950-E959, ICD9 Codes E950-E959; and

(b) *suicides and undetermined deaths* (from 1968 onwards only)

Recorded suicides as (a) plus ICD Codes E980-E989, excluding E988.8 after 1978.

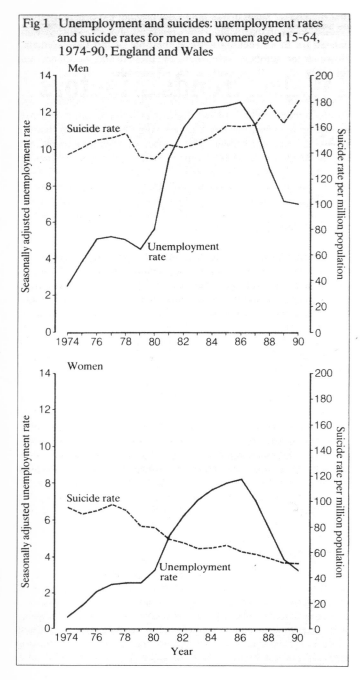

Fig 1 Unemployment and suicides: unemployment rates and suicide rates for men and women aged 15-64, 1974-90, England and Wales

contracting, and transport. Several manual occupations are also listed.

Social class as defined by occupation

Does the existence of relatively high mortality from suicide among small occupational groups in medical and allied professions mean that suicide is generally more common among the professional classes? Evidence from two analyses of mortality and social class is summarised in Table 2.

The data from the Longitudinal Study (LS) are for men aged 15-64 at entry to the study. Men were classified using their occupation at the 1971 Census when the study was set up. SMRs have been calculated using all deaths to study members from 1971 until 1985. Men in Social Classes II and III had below average SMRs. Men in Social Class I had an SMR of 110, those in Class V – 127. This analysis also gives values for those unoccupied at census and those whose occupations were inadequately described. Both these groups had higher SMRs – 168 and 304 respectively.

The second analysis, by PMRs, is for all male deaths in the age-group 16-64 for the years 1979-90. The results, based on

Table 1 *Suicides by occupation, male deaths at ages 16–64, 1979–90.*
The ten highest and lowest PMRs

Occupation	Suicides and undetermined deaths	
	PMR	No. deaths
Vet	364	35
Pharmacist	217	51
Dental practitioner	204	38
Farmer	187	526
Medical practitioner	184	152
Therapist n.e.c.	181	10
Librarian, information officer	180	30
Typist, secretary	171	16
Social and behavioural scientist	170	11
Chemist scientist	169	70
Civil Service, Executive Officers	44	17
Drivers, motormen, etc, railways	43	24
Bus inspectors	42	5
Managers in building and contracting	38	34
Civil Service administrators HEO–Grade 6	37	14
Transport managers	36	31
Glass and ceramics furnacemen	34	4
Machine tool setter operators	29	5
Education officers, school inspectors	15	1
Physiotherapists	0	0

differs from that of the whole age-group. Thus, a PMR of 200 suggests a doubling of the death rate where 100 is the value for the whole age-group being compared (see Box 2 overleaf).

Table 1 gives the PMRs and the number of deaths for the ten occupations with the highest and lowest PMRs. As can be seen, vets have the highest value, with three times the expected number of deaths. Pharmacists, dentists, farmers, and medical practitioners are next with around twice the expected mortality. The existence of these professional groups in the high mortality category suggests that easy access to drugs which can be used for suicide is an important factor. They may also be high stress occupations. Farmers may have easy access to chemicals, drugs, and firearms. There is also evidence that in recent years this group has experienced particular financial difficulties. Farmers and vets are part of a culture where very sick or distressed animals are killed. This may lead them to consider suicide more readily than other people.

Occupations with relatively low suicide rates include administrators and managers in the Civil Service, education, building and

Table 2 *Deaths from suicide among men in different social classes*: SMRs and PMRs*

Social class	Longitudinal Study– males aged 15-64 at entry – deaths 1971-85		All male deaths, ages 16-64, 1979-90	
	SMR	Observed deaths	PMR	Observed deaths
I	110	22	116	1,319
II	88	62	99	5,202
IIIN	99	44	102	3,083
IIIM	82	122	87	9,004
IV	102	67	100	5,649
V	127	35	111	3,582
Armed forces	. .	. .	76	311
Inadequately described	304	17	149	504
Unoccupied	168	37	126	3,885

* Social class as defined by occupation: I Professional, II Intermediate (lower professional and executive), III Skilled (manual and non-manual), IV Partly skilled, V Unskilled. The data from the LS include accidental poisoning.

a much larger sample of deaths, show a similar pattern to the LS data. The only difference is that Social Class I has a higher PMR than Social Class V. This is probably due to the different methods used to calculate SMRs and PMRs. The higher Social Class I PMR indicates that a greater proportion of all cause mortality in Social Class I, than in Social Class V, is due to suicide.

Traditionally occupational mortality analysis has mainly been carried out using information from men's death certificates. There are two main reasons for this. First, women tend to have less exposure to a particular occupation because they move in and out of occupations during the family life cycle. Second, occupation is recorded for women on death certificates only if they were in paid employment for most of their working life. Thus analyses for individual occupations comparable with Table 2 are not routinely available.

Unemployment

Fox and Shewry[2] reviewed findings from the OPCS Longitudinal Study looking at mortality in the years following the 1971 and 1981 Censuses. Mortality among those unemployed and seeking work was higher after both censuses. They conclude,

> 'In both periods some of the observed excess mortality can be explained in terms of socio-economic factors, but not all. There is also similarity in the pattern of SMRs by cause of death; deaths after the 1981 Census point to suicides, other accidents, lung cancer and ischaemic heart disease as causes with the highest and most significant SMRs.'

In particular, those men unemployed and seeking work at census were at 2-3 fold greater risk of suicide death than the average. Moser et al[3] conclude that 'excesses in mortality were apparent both for men aged 15-64 who were seeking work in 1971 and for the wives of such men.' Although the numbers of suicides reported in the study were small, the SMR suggests

---

Box 2   Proportional mortality ratios (PMRs)

The PMR enables the impact of a disease upon an exposed population to be examined. In this paper we are interested in PMRs for suicide amongst men aged 16-64 in different occupations and social classes. The PMR is calculated as follows:

$$PMR = \frac{\text{Observed deaths from suicide}}{\text{Expected deaths from suicide}} \times 100.$$

The expected deaths are computed by applying the proportion of total deaths due to suicide in the comparison or general population (in this case, all men aged 16-64) to the total deaths in the occupation group or social class of interest.

Thus a PMR of 200 indicates that the proportion of deaths attributable to suicide was twice as great among the specific occupation group as among a comparable England and Wales population, that is all men aged 16-64.

Care should be taken when interpreting PMRs since the relative frequency of other causes of death can affect the proportional mortality for the cause of interest. As a result, an observed excess for one cause of death in the exposed group may represent a true increased risk, but may also simply represent a deficit of deaths from other causes.

---

that the risk of suicide was about double that expected. Analysis of deaths occurring in the 1980s suggests that the same pattern existed for those seeking work at the time of the 1981 Census.[4] However the numbers were small, and these deaths would account for only a small proportion of all suicides.

Most unemployment is short term (under six months), and unemployment totals are net figures at a fixed point in time, so unemployment rates never give a complete picture of distress caused by unemployment. The impact of unemployment may depend on the chance of becoming re-employed. Unskilled people, and those in manual occupations, are more likely to be made redundant and less likely to find alternative work than those with skills or in non-manual occupations. The effect of unemployment may be less in times of mass unemployment than in times of low unemployment.[5]

Having established that suicide is one of the possible consequences of unemployment we need to ask whether changes in the levels of unemployment can be related to changes in suicide rates. Charlton et al,[6] examined aggregate data for counties in England and Wales which described the different geographic trends in unemployment and suicides. They were unable to show any association between change in unemployment and change in suicide rates. Crombie performed a similar analysis on Scottish data, and again found no relationship.[7,8]

Nationally unemployment increased substantially at the end of the 1970s, stayed high until the mid-1980s, and then started to decline until the late 1980s, rising again in the early 1990s. Figure 1 shows trends in seasonally adjusted unemployment, alongside the suicide trends. Unemployment figures have been calculated on a consistent basis throughout the period. Thus in the 1981-90 period, male suicide rates were highest at the time when unemployment rates were lowest. If there is any relationship it is likely to be a lagged one, and the mechanism would be complicated.

Marital breakdown

It has been found that higher rates of emotional problems in adulthood are experienced by those whose childhoods were characterised by poverty, insecure housing, and separated and divorced parents.[9] These social problems are of course correlated with one another and it is difficult to separate out the effects of each. Nevertheless it is worth speculating whether increasing rates of marital breakdown during the 1960s and 1970s may be responsible for some of the increase in suicide rates observed among young men during the 1980s. If this were the case we would need to explain why it affected young men and not young women. Such explanations are difficult with the information available for analysis here. We need to wait for longer term results from cohort and linkage studies.

Another question is the extent to which the increase in divorce has affected the rate of suicide among men aged 15-44. Figure 2 shows the trends in suicide rates for men in different marital status groups. Divorced and widowed men have the highest rates. Widowed men have somewhat higher suicide rates than divorced men in each age-group. They have been grouped together here for simplicity. Also, nearly all the divorced and widowed men aged 15-44 are divorced. At given ages *single men have suicide rates that are almost as high as those for divorced men*. In general in each ten-year age-group, apart from the 15-24 year olds, single, widowed, and divorced men have suicide rates which are about three times greater than those of married men. This could suggest a protective effect of marriage for men. Alternatively, it may be because men who may be prone to suicide are more likely to remain single or become divorced at a given age than other men.

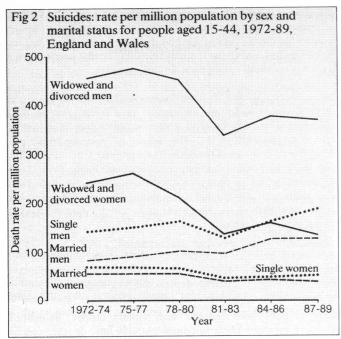

Fig 2   Suicides: rate per million population by sex and marital status for people aged 15-44, 1972-89, England and Wales

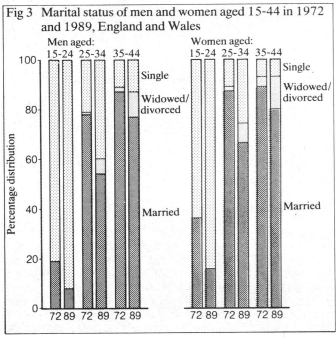

Fig 3   Marital status of men and women aged 15-44 in 1972 and 1989, England and Wales

Between 1972-74 and 1987-89 suicide rates among married men aged under 45 increased. Those for all age-groups of divorced men decreased whilst rates for single men, except those aged 15-24, generally stayed the same. However, the marital status distribution of the population changed quite dramatically during the period of interest. Among men aged 15-44 the proportion of single and divorced increased in each of the 10 year age-groups. Figure 3 shows the changes between 1972 and 1989 for both men and women.

To what extent are the changes in marriage and divorce patterns related to the increase in suicide? In 1972-74 the suicide rate for men aged 15-44 was 115 per million. By 1987-89 it had risen to 186 per million. Using the marital status distribution and suicide rates in ten-year age-groups we have calculated the suicide rate in 1987-89 assuming that there had been no changes in the proportions of men in different marital status groups. It would have been 149 per million. Thus we suggest that one half of the increase in rates in young men may be due to the smaller proportions who are married. These calculations take no account of the increases in cohabiting among single men during the period. Death statistics do not record cohabitation as a marital status.

Figure 2 also shows the trends in suicides among women in different marital status groups. All of them show decreases over the last 20 years. The declining pattern of change for widowed and divorced women aged 15-44 is very similar to that of men. It is possible that as divorce becomes more common and there are many more divorced people in the community less stress is associated with this marital status. It is unclear, however, why suicide rates for single and married women are falling whilst those for single and married men have been increasing.

Alcohol, drug misuse, and mental illness

Alcohol and drugs

The relationship between alcohol and other drug misuse and suicide is well established. First, the same risk factors may be involved in their aetiology. Second, it is known that a high proportion of people who committed suicide were alcoholics. Adelstein and White,[10] in a cohort study of over 2,000 hospital patients with a diagnosis of alcoholism, found significantly raised suicide levels in both men (SMR = 320) and women (SMR = 230). Miles[11] and Hawton[12] have suggested that 15 per cent of alcoholics may eventually commit suicide. Kessel and Grossman[13] have shown that male alcoholics are at greater risk than female alcoholics. Alcohol may also be used frequently both immediately before and during suicide attempts. This may make successful suicide more likely.[14]

The risk of suicide among drug addicts is also known to be very high. James[15] suggested that the risk of suicide among heroin addicts is approximately 20 times that of the general population.

Data are available for deaths from drug misuse and alcohol-related causes. Figure 4a shows trends in acute alcohol-related deaths (excluding cirrhosis of the liver). Figure 4b includes deaths from cirrhosis, which takes longer to kill. For the acute causes, men aged 25-44 showed the largest increase in rates (more than four fold), followed by men aged 15-24. Rates for younger women also rose, but the levels remained substantially lower than those for men of the same age. When cirrhosis deaths are included the differences between men and women widen, but there was a growth in cirrhosis deaths among women aged 25-44 that led to their rates steadily increasing over the period. In the 45-64 age-group the death rates more than doubled for both sexes. If these rises reflect increases in alcohol misuse nationally, this would explain to some extent the increase in male suicide rates.

Since 1968 there has been a six-fold increase in drug-related deaths among males aged 15-24 and a five-fold increase for males aged 25-44. For women there were also substantial increases, but from a much lower base – differences between male and female rates have widened substantially (Figure 4c). If these rises reflect increases in drug misuse rather than an increased tendency to report cause of death more accurately, this, too, would explain to some extent the increase in male suicide rates. Among young people, especially those under age 20 and male, volatile substance abuse (for example glue and lighter fuel sniffing) has increased greatly since 1971.[16] Deaths from these causes will be the subject of a future article in *Population Trends*.

Mental illness

The two most common forms of mental illness thought to be related to suicide are schizophrenia and depression. Hawton estimates that between 10 and 15 per cent of people with schizophrenia and 15 per cent of people with affective psychosis commit suicide.[14] Miles found similar rates.[11]

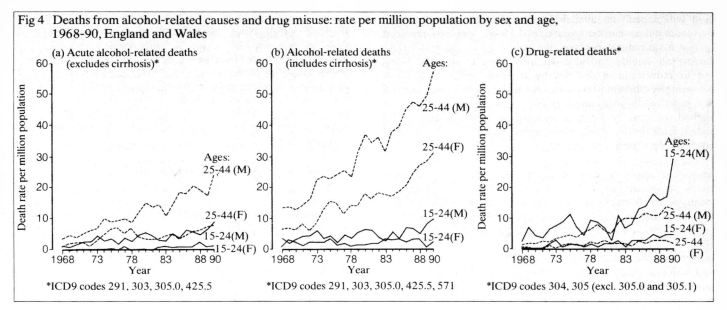

Fig 4 Deaths from alcohol-related causes and drug misuse: rate per million population by sex and age, 1968-90, England and Wales

(a) Acute alcohol-related deaths (excludes cirrhosis)*
*ICD9 codes 291, 303, 305.0, 425.5

(b) Alcohol-related deaths (includes cirrhosis)*
*ICD9 codes 291, 303, 305.0, 425.5, 571

(c) Drug-related deaths*
*ICD9 codes 304, 305 (excl. 305.0 and 305.1)

We have shown that the prevalence of alcoholism has probably increased, but what about other forms of mental illness? Murray suggests that the incidence of schizophrenia has not increased and may well have fallen.[17] While we have information on changes in inpatient admissions and discharges, these are influenced by hospital-related factors, and are very limited in their usefulness as a monitor of trends in mental illness generally. More useful are local surveys of mental illness in the general population which, until now, do not indicate any significant increase in the prevalence of mental illness. However, there has been an increase in the number of mentally ill people being cared for in the community rather than in hospital, and without careful attention to the assessment and management of suicidal risk this may increase vulnerability, exposure to risk factors, and access to means of suicide.

Prisons

Table 3 shows the changes that have occurred in the prison population and the number of prison receptions since 1981. The number of prison suicides (as recorded by Coroners) per year has also risen considerably, from around 15 per year in 1961 to around 40 per year in 1988-90. Forty suicides a year in the late 1980s represents about 2 per cent of all suicides in the 15-44 age-group of men. Having increased from only about 15 in the early 1970s, the extra 25 per year represents about 4 per cent of the increase in the young male suicide rate between the early 1970s and late 1980s. Most of these suicides involve young (under 45) male remand prisoners. This is illustrated by Figure 5 which contains data provided by the Home Office. Lloyd has reviewed the aetiology of prison suicide.[18] The most striking finding is the high rate among the remand population. Remand prisoners who commit suicide are more

likely to have been charged with violent crimes. Sentenced prisoners are more likely to commit suicide later on, the reasons for this are complex and not clear cut. Dooley[19] examined 300 prison deaths over the period 1972-87. Case notes were available for 295 of these. During this period the prison suicide rate per 1,000 receptions increased by 80 per cent. Part of the

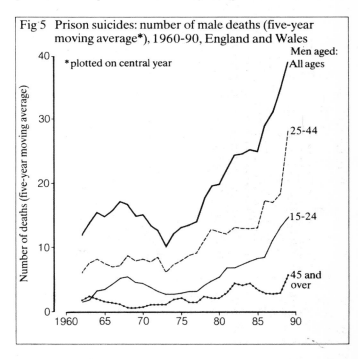

Fig 5 Prison suicides: number of male deaths (five-year moving average*), 1960-90, England and Wales

*plotted on central year

explanation may be due to the fact that the proportion of remand prisoners increased. Another explanation may be overcrowding, leading to less supervision and support. Prisons also contain an excess of men with known risk factors for suicide, such as previous psychiatric history, self injury, alcohol/drug misuse, social isolation, and marital disruption. Dooley showed these factors to be predictive of suicide as well.[19] He ascribes 40 per cent of prison suicides to the prison environment, 15 per cent to outside pressures, 12 per cent to guilt feelings for the offence, and 22 per cent to already diagnosed severe mental disorders.

Access and method

The probability of committing suicide will depend to some extent on the ease of access to effective means. The method

Table 3 *Receptions into prison establishments and population in custody, England, Wales and Northern Ireland*

thousands

	1981	1986	1988	1989	1990
Average population					
Males	44.5	47.1	49.0	48.5	45.2
Females	1.5	1.6	1.8	1.8	1.6
Remand prisoners	7.4	10.3	10.8	10.7	9.8
Receptions	49.6	57.7	59.8	60.6	54.4

Source: Social Trends no. 22

used will depend on availability, ease of use, and 'fashion'. For example, as carbon monoxide domestic gas was replaced by non-toxic natural gas over the period up to the mid-1970s, the overall suicide rate also declined, most of this fall being due to reductions in suicides by domestic gas. Since 1948, poisoning by other (mostly motor vehicle exhaust) gas has emerged as a popular self-poisoning method, becoming the most popular method for men by 1990, accounting for nearly a third of all male suicide deaths.[1] During this period the number of registered cars has increased considerably.

Another example of how access to methods relates to their use is shown in Figure 6, which shows GP prescriptions for sedatives and tranquilisers; and for sedatives, tranquilisers, and hypnotics (data provided by the Office Health Economics). These are Prescription Pricing Authority grouping of drugs, which include psychotropic drugs such as fluphenazine hydrochloride, lorazepam, phenobarbitone, prochlorperazine, and promazine hydrochloride. Since 1966, prescriptions for drugs in the barbiturate group have been falling steadily, from 189 million in 1966 to 0.2 million in 1990. GP prescribing of these groups of drugs rose up to 1975 and then fell. The graph also shows

trends in age-standardised rates for suicides by self-poisoning (suicide and undetermined deaths, ages 15 and over). Suicide mortality from this cause fell steadily for males and females from 1968-70 until 1983-85 (somewhat predating the decline in GP prescribing), since when female mortality has continued to fall but male mortality has not changed.

Figure 7 gives a breakdown of the number of deaths from self-poisoning among men aged 15-44. It can be seen that analgesics are the largest group of substances, followed by tranquilisers and other psychotropic agents. The numbers of deaths by these drugs has increased considerably over the decade, while deaths from barbiturates and other sedatives and hypnotics have declined. It is not always appreciated that a relatively small overdose of paracetamol will cause fatal liver damage, and public health measures should be focused on limiting these deaths.

Other factors

We also looked at various other factors which might be associated with suicide mortality, but none of these greatly affected overall suicide rates.

HIV/AIDS

AIDS was first described in 1981, and testing blood for antibody to human immunodeficiency virus did not come into widespread use until late 1984.

The all cause mortality rate for men aged 15-44 began to rise in 1985. A detailed examination of this excess mortality[20] showed that the causes were concentrated in suicides, open verdicts, and AIDS. McCormick has shown that maybe only 30 per cent of AIDS deaths are recorded in mortality statistics as AIDS/HIV deaths.[21] AIDS may therefore be implicated in a proportion of the excess suicides and open verdicts recorded since 1984.

However, when age-specific rates were examined by regional health authority the increases in suicides since 1984 did not correlate with the areas most affected by the HIV epidemic. NW Thames and NE Thames regions have the largest numbers of AIDS case reports and reports of HIV infected individuals. These regions showed the smallest increases in suicide rates in males aged 15-44. This may be another example where the

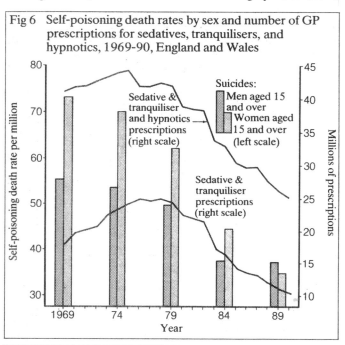

Fig 6   Self-poisoning death rates by sex and number of GP prescriptions for sedatives, tranquilisers, and hypnotics, 1969-90, England and Wales

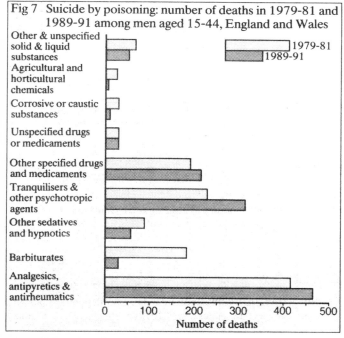

Fig 7   Suicide by poisoning: number of deaths in 1979-81 and 1989-91 among men aged 15-44, England and Wales

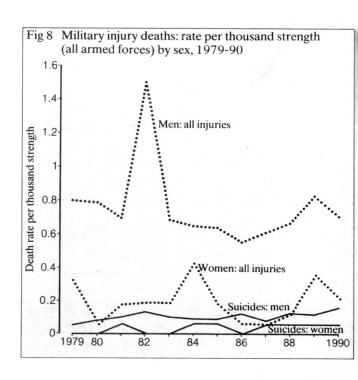

Fig 8   Military injury deaths: rate per thousand strength (all armed forces) by sex, 1979-90

Fig 9 International comparisons of recorded suicide rates for men and women aged 25-44, 1969-91

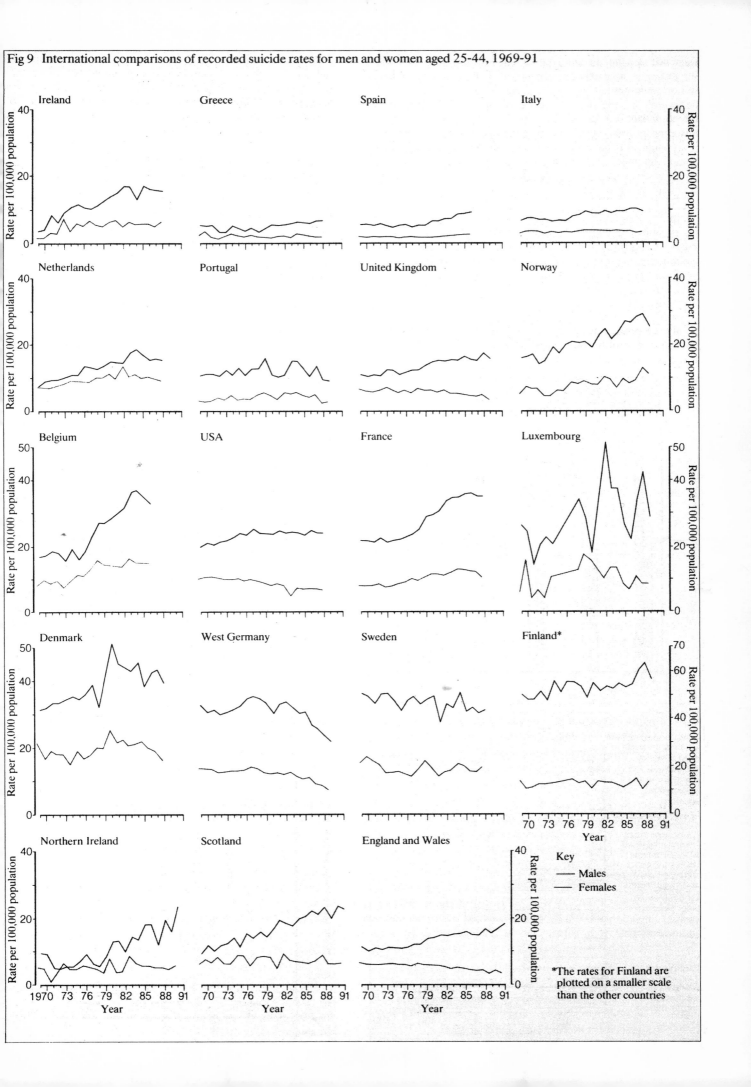

*The rates for Finland are plotted on a smaller scale than the other countries

Key
— Males
— Females

existence of other people in a similar situation provides social support or a lessening of stigma which may lead to a lower risk of suicides.

Effects of war

Health statistics from the Ministry of Defence[22] have been used to calculate suicide rates for serving members of the armed forces, since it has been suggested that the effects of war may increase the risk of suicide. These are shown in Figure 8 (see page 39), where the same patterns are observed as in the general population. Rates for men have doubled from 70 per million in 1979-81 to 140 per million in 1988-90. However, those suffering post traumatic psychological stress may leave the forces before committing suicide, and be excluded from the MoD figures. Data from follow-up of ex-armed forces personnel are difficult to obtain.

International comparisons

Figure 9 compares the EC countries, Scandinavia, and the United States in terms of recorded suicide rates among men and women aged 25-44.

Cross-cultural comparisons of suicide rates should only be made with extreme caution, since different meanings and attitudes will be associated with suicide in different cultures. These graphs only show recorded suicides, taken from WHO Annuals.[23] Some societies may be more likely to cover up suicides, for example by classifying them as 'accidental' or 'undetermined whether accidentally or purposely inflicted', while others may be more open to accepting a suicide verdict. Hence official statistics of different countries will reflect varying degrees of the true rate. However, the trends within country are more likely to reflect changes that are occurring.

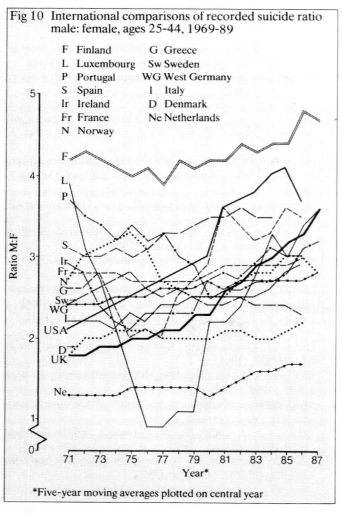

Fig 10 International comparisons of recorded suicide ratio male: female, ages 25-44, 1969-89

F Finland	G Greece
L Luxembourg	Sw Sweden
P Portugal	WG West Germany
S Spain	I Italy
Ir Ireland	D Denmark
Fr France	Ne Netherlands
N Norway	

Five-year moving averages plotted on central year

The trends for males aged 25-44 are by no means similar in the different Western countries. For example, West Germany has experienced a substantial decline, the USA rates have been level since 1978, and the rates in France have risen even more steeply than those in the UK.

The trends for females have in general followed those for the males, except in the UK and USA, where they have fallen by around 30 per cent. Within the UK female rates in Northern Ireland have risen (by 47 per cent), perhaps to some extent reflecting the 253 per cent rise in female suicide in Ireland between 1969-71 and 1986-88. Figure 10 illustrates how the male to female suicide ratio has risen in the UK and USA, compared with the other Western countries.

Only in the UK and the United States do we observe trends for the different sexes that are moving in opposite directions. Within the UK, Scotland and Northern Ireland have higher suicide rates than England and Wales.

Table 4 compares the levels of recorded suicide in the different countries. Generally southern countries have lower rates than northern ones, but there are exceptions. It can be seen that the rates in the UK are by no means the highest or lowest. The use of the undetermined category may vary from country to country according to coroners' conventions, however, which could alter the recorded suicide rates.

It is interesting to note how the ratio of male to female rates varies from country to country. Finland has exceptionally high male rates; but women's rates, at one sixth of the men's, are close to the average. The Netherlands has the most equal male and female rates.

Conclusions

Changes in suicide rates are related to a complex set of social, economic, and other changes. As other commentators have found, it is extremely difficult to pinpoint clear relationships. This is partly because some of the changes are difficult to measure, partly because the changes are related to one another and partly because there are probably relevant factors as yet unidentified. Nevertheless, we have looked systematically at some of the factors thought to be related in an attempt to see to what extent they may explain the changes in suicide patterns.

The main puzzle is why rates of suicide are increasing among young men but not among women. Further work is needed to explore this.

For men, particularly young men, we suggest that the increasing numbers of men remaining single or becoming divorced may explain up to one half of the increase in suicides observed between the early 1970s and late 1980s. This age-group of men have also been affected by high unemployment rates, exposure to armed combat, increasing risk of imprisonment, an increase in misuse of alcohol and other drugs, and the HIV virus. There is little evidence of a rise in the prevalence of mental illness.

In July 1992, the Government produced *The Health of the Nation* White Paper,[24] a strategy for health in England, which focuses on five 'key areas', of which mental illness is one. Two of the three targets in the mental illness key area are related to suicide, one being to reduce overall deaths from suicide by the year 2000, and the second being to reduce deaths from suicide in people with a severe mental illness by the year 2000. The findings in the paper give some pointers to possible preventive strategies.

Table 4 *Reported suicide rates per 100,000 population in Western Europe and USA, ages 25–44*

Country	Sex and M:F ratio	Averages 1969–71	Averages 1986–88	Percentage change	Country	Sex and M:F ratio	Averages 1969–71	Averages 1986–88	Percentage change
Denmark	Males	32	41	30	United Kingdom	Males	11	16	50
	Females	18	18	0		Females	6	5	−24
	M:F ratio	2	2	29		M:F ratio	2	4	95
France	Males	21	36	67	England and Wales	Males	11	15	43
	Females	8	11	48		Females	6	4	−28
	M:F ratio	3	3	13		M:F ratio	2	4	100
Greece	Males	5	6	21	Scotland	Males	10	22	112
	Females	2	2	−29		Females	6	7	13
	M:F ratio	3	4	51		M:F ratio	2	3	91
Ireland	Males	5	16	192	Northern Ireland	Males	8	17	115
	Females	2	5	253		Females	3	5	47
	M:F ratio	4	3	−18		M:F ratio	4	3	−18
Italy	Males	7	10	35	USA	Males	20	24	18
	Females	3	3	− 3		Females	10	6	−36
	M:F ratio	2	3	39		M:F ratio	2	4	85
Luxembourg	Males	21	33	56	Finland	Males	49	59	20
	Females	8	9	11		Females	12	13	9
	M:F ratio	4	4	4		M:F ratio	4	5	11
Netherlands	Males	8	15	83	Norway	Males	16	28	73
	Females	6	9	45		Females	6	10	63
	M:F ratio	1	2	26		M:F ratio	3	3	5
Portugal	Males	11	11	4	Sweden	Males	35	31	−12
	Females	3	4	38		Females	16	13	−16
	M:F ratio	4	3	−21		M:F ratio	2	2	5
Spain*	Males	5	9	63					
	Females	2	2	44					
	M:F ratio	3	4	12					
West Germany	Males	31	25	−19					
	Females	13	9	−30					
	M:F ratio	2	3	15					

* 1986–88 figures for Spain not available, 1984–86 used instead.

Acknowledgements

We gratefully acknowledge help and advice from Steve Platt, at the Medical Research Council's Medical Sociology Unit and colleagues in OPCS and other government departments.

References

[1] Charlton J *et al*. Trends in suicide deaths in England and Wales. *Population Trends* 69, HMSO (1992).

[2] Fox and Shewry. New longitudinal insights into relationships between unemployment and mortality stress medicine. vol 4, 1988, 11-19.

[3] Moser *et al*. In: Goldblatt P (ed). *Longitudinal Study. Mortality and social organisation*. LS no. 6, OPCS (1984) chapter 5.

[4] Moser KA, Goldblatt P, Fox AJ, Jones DR. Unemployment and mortality: comparison of the 1971 and 1981 longitudinal study census samples. *Br Med J 294*, 1987, 86-90.

[5] Warr P. Economic recession and mental health: a review of research. *Tijdschrift vor Sociale Gezondheidszorg 62*, 1984, 298-308.

[6] Charlton JRH, Bauer R, Thankore A, Silver R, Aristidou M. Unemployment and mortality: a small area analysis. *J of Epidemiol and Comm Health 41*, 1987, 107-113.

[7] Crombie IK. Trends in suicide and unemployment in Scotland 1976-86. *Br Med J 298*, 1989, 782-4.

[8] Crombie IK. Can changes in the unemployment rates explain the recent changes in suicide rates in developed countries. *International J of Epid 19*, no. 2, 1990, 412-6.

[9] Wadsworth. *The Imprint of Time*. 1991.

[10] Adelstein A, White G. Alcoholism and mortality. *Population Trends* 6, HMSO (1976) pp 7-13.

[11] Miles. Conditions predisposing to suicide: a review. *Journal of Nervous and Mental Diseases 164*, 1977, 231-46.

[12] Hawton. Assessment of suicide risk. *Br J of Psychiatry 150*, 1987, 145-53.

[13] Kessel and Grossman. *Br Med J 2*, 1961, 1671-72.

[14] Hawton K, Fagg J, McKeown. Alcoholism, alcohol, and attempted suicide. *Alcohol and Alcoholism* vol 24, no. 1, 1989, 3-9.

[15] Pierce-James I. Suicide and mortality amongst heroin addicts in Britain. *Br J of Addiction* vol 62, no. 3, 1967, 391-8.

[16] Wright SP, Pottier ACW, Taylor JC, *et al. Trends in deaths associated with abuse of volatile substances 1971-89*. Department of Public Health Sciences: St George's Medical School (Report no. 4) (London 1991).

[17] Murray R. Is schizophrenia disappearing? *Lancet 335*, 1990, 513-516.

[18] Lloyd C. Suicide and self-injury in prison: a literature review. *Home Office Research Study* no. 115, HMSO (1990).

[19] Dooley E. Prison suicide in England and Wales 1972-87. *Br J of Psychiatry 156*, 1990, 40-45.

[20] Dunnell K. Deaths among 15-44 year olds. *Population Trends* 64, HMSO (1991).

[21] McCormick A. Unrecognised HIV related deaths. *Br Med J 302*, 1991, 1365-1376.

[22] MoD. Statistical tables on the health of the Army Navy and Air Force (various years).

[23] WHO. *World Health Statistics Annuals*. WHO (Geneva) (1970-1990 volumes used).

[24] DH. *The Health of the Nation. A strategy for health in England*. HMSO (London 1992).

3 A European Perspective on Suicidal Behaviour

Ad Kerkhof and Anton Kunst

Introduction

The stability of differences in suicide rates between European countries, and within one particular country, The Netherlands, between different regions, has been associated with social correlates. Religious and family integration as well as education seem to be important to understand differences in suicide mortality. Secularization and individualization are held responsible for increases in suicide rates in The Netherlands among the young.

Epidemiology of suicide in Europe

In the European countries there has always been a remarkable stability in the rank order of suicide rates. Differences between nations have been fairly stable throughout this century. Increases and decreases of suicide rates after World War 2 have left unaffected the geographical pattern of suicide in Europe. Table 1 shows the suicide rates for the different European nations expressed per 100,000 of the population, adjusted for age. The data were obtained from the 1989 WHO Annual Statistics (pp. 390-395), concerning the latest available statistics from the reporting countries (from 1985 to 1988). Roumania and Albania did not report on suicide over these years, and in this table the suicide rates of Germany concern the former West German republic.

It can be seen that there are a number of countries with relatively low suicide rates, among which are the United Kingdom and Ireland, The Netherlands, Poland and Portugal. The Mediterranean countries, Spain, Italy and Greece, have the lowest suicide rates.

One may wonder whether these differences are true differences or artefacts because of differences in certification procedures and reliability of suicide statistics. The WHO, based on a number of studies, stated that European national suicide mortality statistics can be assumed to be a valuable source of data on which to base comparative epidemiological studies (WHO, 1982). Although some authors question the validity of these data for studying differences between countries (Platt, 1988), there is the fact that consistent differences in national suicide rates have been recorded over very long periods of time, differences that persist even after changes in ascertainment procedures have taken place. We therefore assume that the rank order of national suicide rates reported to the WHO reflects approximately the true rank order of these suicide rates.

Below the mean there are countries like Iceland, Norway, Germany and Bulgaria, followed by a middle range of countries like Sweden, Czechoslowakia, the former Yugoslavia, and Luxembourg. In the group with relatively high suicide rates one can find Belgium, France, Switzerland, Austria and the USSR. Very high suicide rates can be found in Denmark and Finland, and highest of all is Hungary. Male suicide rates show a similar geographical pattern. The Austrian male suicide rate is relatively high, as is

Table 1 Age standardized suicide rates in Europe 1985-1988.

Age Standardized Suicide Rates per 100,000 of the Standard Population (European Region)
Latest years available 1985-1988

COUNTRY	Total	Male	Female
Hungary	39.9	59.6	23.1
Denmark	26.8	35.3	18.9
Finland	26.7	43.6	11.4
Austria	22.6	35.6	11.6
Belgium	21.0	30.1	13.3
France	20.9	31.7	11.6
USSR	20.7	35.2	9.3
Switzerland	20.7	30.8	11.5
Yugoslavia	18.4	27.2	10.8
Czechoslovakia	18.1	28.5	9.0
Luxembourg	17.3	27.4	7.9
Sweden	17.3	24.8	10.2
Iceland	16.1	27.2	4.9
Bulgaria	16.0	24.6	8.5
Germany (West)	15.5	23.5	8.9
Norway	15.4	23.2	8.0
Poland	13.0	22.3	4.5
Scotland	11.4	17.6	6.2
Netherlands	10.8	13.8	8.2
Northen Ireland	10.1	16.1	4.4
England and Wales	8.0	12.1	4.1
Ireland	7.9	12.0	3.9
Portugal	7.9	13.4	3.4
Italy	7.6	11.8	4.3
Spain	6.6	10.4	3.4
Greece	3.7	5.8	1.8
Malta	2.3	4.1	0.5

Source: WHO Annual Statistics 1989

the Finnish male suicide rate. Hungary ranks highest again. Female suicide rates reflect a slightly different pattern. The Finnish female suicide rates are in the middle ranges; Belgium, France, Switzerland and Austria are to be found in the higher ranks, while Denmark and Hungary rank highest.

Most of the differences in suicide rates between the European nations have been fairly stable throughout this century, despite increases and decreases in national rates. There has been a decline in the suicide rates in England and Wales in the sixties (Sainsbury, Jenkins, and Levey, 1980), but that did not affect the low position of England and Wales in the European rank order. The Finnish suicide rates however, have increased dramatically between the two World Wars, so that Finland became one of the countries with the highest suicide rates. For 16 selected countries suicide rates have been compared over the last century. While the average rate for these countries has gone up, the variation around the mean as well as the rank order has stayed roughly the same (Diekstra, 1993).

Explanations of differences

The first question that arises is of course the reason why these differences exist. This question has bothered scientists for more than a century. Durkheim, nearly a hundred years ago, postulated that suicide varies inversely with the extent of social integration in family, religious, political and economic life (Durkheim, 1987). Without going into details one can say that there has been quite substantial support for Durkheim's views in the

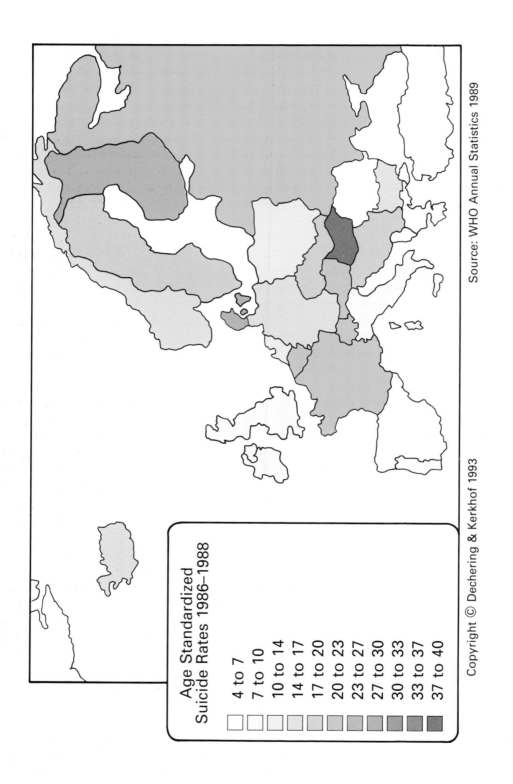

Age Standardized
Suicide Rates 1986–1988

4 to 7
7 to 10
10 to 14
14 to 17
17 to 20
20 to 23
23 to 27
27 to 30
30 to 33
33 to 37
37 to 40

Source: WHO Annual Statistics 1989

Copyright © Dechering & Kerkhof 1993

Figure 1

24

way that especially religion and divorce have been empirically related to differences between countries and different rates within countries over different points in time.

Religion

Catholicism can be seen as a form of collective community that provides greater social integration than other religious denominations (Breault, 1986; Trovato, 1992). Pescosolido and Georgianna proposed that organized religion serves as the basis for individuals to form social networks, and the more enduring and meaningful the interactions among members, the lower the risk of suicide (Trovato, 1992). Being detached from religion (atheists) or being too immersed in the religious life (cults) poses a heightened risk of suicide for the individual. Pescosolido convincingly showed that for many major religious groups the effect of religious affiliation on suicide vary across geographical areas. A geographical religious network approach appears to be fruitful for the study of suicide. Returning to our maps of Europe, one can see that in the Catholic countries such as Spain, Italy, Portugal, Greece, Ireland and Poland the suicide rates are fairly low. In the Netherlands, only the southern part is Roman Catholic, and in England one may wonder whether the Anglican Church has a similar preventive power as the Catholic church. Of course, there are Catholic parts in Europe where suicides rates are relatively high, such as in France, but one may wonder how strict French catholics are in adhering to religious traditions. And in many other parts of Europe the boundaries between the religious denominations are not the same as the boundaries between nations.

Family integration

Disruptions in family life, or in domestic integration, have been considered to have strong relationships with suicide. Divorce has been used as proxy for Durkheim's concept of declining family integration many times (Sainsbury, 1955; Breault, 1986; Stack, 1980, 1982, 1990; Trovato, 1987, 1992; Wasserman, 1984). Another proxy successfully related to suicide is the percentage of one person households in the region (Ashford and Lawrence, 1976). Increased divorce rates repeatedly showed up as a strong predictor for increases in suicide rates. However, this relationship mainly has been found within countries. To my knowledge few studies, except that of Sainsbury, Jenkins and Levey from 1980, and that from Barraclough, 1988, have addressed international differences in suicide rates. They found a strong correlation between suicide rates and divorce rates in 18 European countries the early sixties (and for other measures of family integration as well). There is the possibility that divorce has become more common in the last decades, and that therefore the disintegrating force might have become weaker. Indeed, as in the Netherlands, the suicide rates among the divorced, which invariably are higher than the rates of widowed, married, or unmarried people, tend to stabilize or decline.

Unemployment

Economic crises and booms were considered significant sources of disruption of the social order. Unemployment has been studied intensively in its relation to suicide. The literature concerning this relationship revealed that unemployed persons are more suicidogenic than those who are employed. But that does not mean that societies with high unemployment rates have higher suicide rates. This relationship has been found to be inconsistent or statistically insignificant (Boor, 1982, Dooley, et al., 1989a 1989b; Platt, 1984; Stack, 1981; Van Houwelingen, 1984, Breault, 1986; Pritchard, 1990). On the maps of Europe one cannot see obvious relationships here. The UK, despite massive unemployment, does not belong to the countries with the highest suicide rates. Industrialization, that is the change from rural societies to westernized modernization, is held responsible for increased suicide rates in Finland and Hungary (Osvath, 1988), but empirical evidence for this is lacking.

Trends

There is another way of looking into the social correlates of suicide in Europe, and that is to study relative increases and decreases in suicide rates between the European countries, and to relate these to changes in social indicators of well being, anomy or whatever can be associated with suicide rates. I refer to the well known study of Sainsbury, Jenkins and Levey, published in 1980. Without going into details, I will refer here to their most important conclusions: that trends in suicide are being determined by social factors whose effects are age and sex specific. The social variables which appeared to be having most effect in determining changes in the incidence of suicide in the period 1961 to 1974 are first, those relating to the changing status of women, then those indicative of increasing anomy and finally, socio-economic change (Sainsbury, Jenkins and Levey, 1980, p. 52-53). Three principal indicators of the changing status of women, the marriage rate, female education, and females in employment, contributed most to the discrimination. This suggests that the changing role of women in society, or stated in other words, the changing relationships between men and women, were related to increases in suicide rates in quite a number of European countries in the sixties and early seventies.

Regional analysis

The relationships presented so far have been studied mostly on a national scale. But, the national boundaries need not coincide with natural boundaries between the religions, or between regions with different cultural identities. For example in Hungary there are two regions with very different suicide rates. The western and northern parts are characterized by low indexes (Ozsvath, 1988). In Belgium regional differences in suicide mortality have been reported. (Moens, 1983, 1990). In The Netherlands, a distinct geographical pattern has been observed for many years. Let us now turn to the study of regional differences in suicide rates in The Netherlands and to possible explanations, and keep in mind that every country in Europe would need a separate analysis.

Epidemiology of suicide in The Netherlands 1900-1949

In 1960 Kruijt, a famous Dutch sociologist, studied regional suicide rates for the first half of the century (1900-1949), based on municipalities, and controlled for the sex and age distribution of the population. He found a distinct pattern that did not change during those fifty years. There was a large region in the northern part of The Netherlands where the suicide rates were particularly high. Then there was a part in the east of the Netherlands, and a high suicide density in the northern part of the province of Holland, and in the very south on some of the islands of Zeeland. Kruijt was of course very impressed by the stability of this picture and he went on to relate these regional differences to simultaneous sociocultural

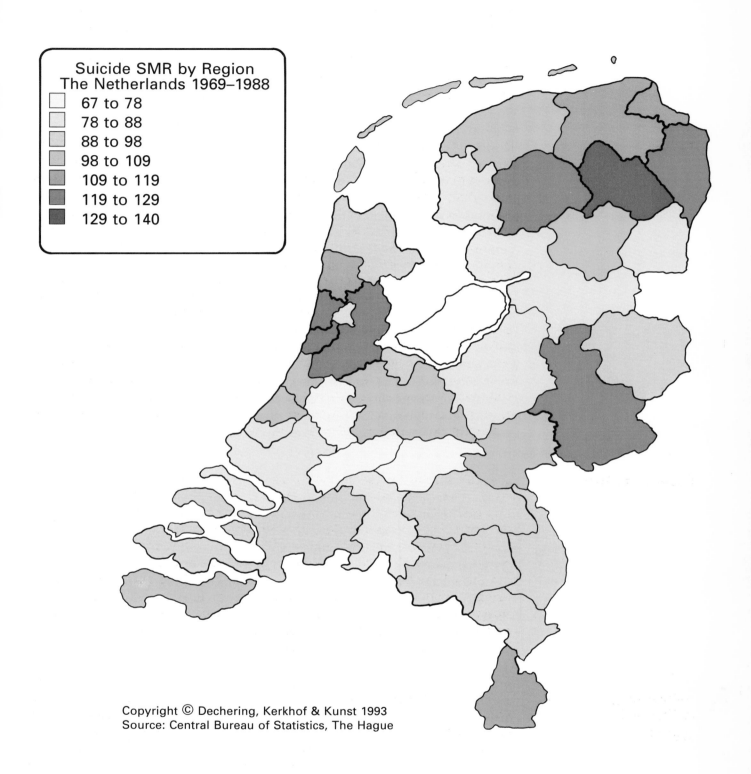

Suicide SMR by Region
The Netherlands 1969–1988

- 67 to 78
- 78 to 88
- 88 to 98
- 98 to 109
- 109 to 119
- 119 to 129
- 129 to 140

Copyright © Dechering, Kerkhof & Kunst 1993
Source: Central Bureau of Statistics, The Hague

Figure 2

27

characteristics and developments, in the tradition of Durkheim. He found a strong relationship between religion and suicide mortality: in the Catholic regions low suicide rates and in the protestant regions much higher rates, except in those regions that had large populations of so-called orthodox Christians, communities that very strictly adhered to biblical prescriptions of behaviour and community life.

1969-1988

When we look at the present situation we can observe a strikingly similar pattern. We used Standardized Mortality Ratios for suicide (corrected for regional differences in age and sex distribution) over the period 1969-1988 (Kunst en Kerkhof, 1993), calculated for so-called COROP regions. This distribution in regions has been made for the purpose of gathering relevant comparative data for socio-economic development. The geographical pattern of suicide in The Netherlands shows a distinct pattern that resembles the pattern for the first half of the century: a cluster of regions with high suicide rates in the nothern provinces of The Netherlands, a region of high suicide rates in the eastern part of the country, and a region around Amsterdam. The main conclusion to draw is that there is a remarkable stability in this pattern. Even more remarkable is this stability when we look at the geographical distribution of suicide rates for older males (In the observation period the demarcation of suicides by 50 years of age splits the total number of suicides exactly in two halves). This cluster of regions with high suicide rates still dominates the picture. The other regions with comparatively high suicide rates reappear as well: The nothern part of North-Holland, the region in the eastern part, and one of the islands in Zeeland. For those who know The Netherlands it will be clear that all of the regions with high suicide rates are rural areas. The Netherlands is very peculiar in this respect: nowhere in the world has this phenomenon been described. Note that older males in The Netherlands do show exactly the same pattern of suicide as their parents did as well as their grandparents did. Despite two world wars, economic change and changing cultural developments, nothing has changed in this geographical pattern. But it has to be stressed that this applies for older males. How about older females? The female suicide rates for the older age groups show some similarity and some dissimilarity with the older male geographical pattern. Again there appears the nothern and eastern cluster, but not so predominantly. But here we see a cluster of regions around Amsterdam with a high suicide density. This is a highly urbanized region. One may wonder why this region produces many suicides among older females, while it does not among older males.

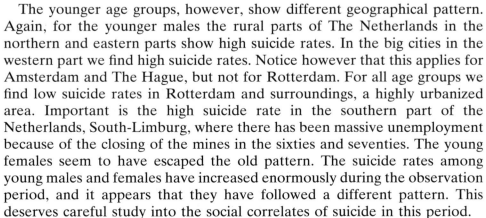

The younger age groups, however, show different geographical pattern. Again, for the younger males the rural parts of The Netherlands in the northern and eastern parts show high suicide rates. In the big cities in the western part we find high suicide rates. Notice however that this applies for Amsterdam and The Hague, but not for Rotterdam. For all age groups we find low suicide rates in Rotterdam and surroundings, a highly urbanized area. Important is the high suicide rate in the southern part of the Netherlands, South-Limburg, where there has been massive unemployment because of the closing of the mines in the sixties and seventies. The young females seem to have escaped the old pattern. The suicide rates among young males and females have increased enormously during the observation period, and it appears that they have followed a different pattern. This deserves careful study into the social correlates of suicide in this period.

Relations between suicide mortality and characteristics of regions

Standardized mortality ratios were related to the following characteristics of regions:

1 Urbanization – the percentage of inhabitants in large cities,

2 Religion – the percentage of roman catholics,

3 Religion – the percentage of orthodox Christians,

4 Education – mean number of years of education,

5 Economic life – the percentage of male unemployed,

6 Family life – the divorce rate.

The method used was a multiple regression analysis in which confounding interactions between variables could be controlled. The standardized regression coëfficients can be compared to one another in the strength of their relationship to suicide. (They stand for the absolute increase in SMR when there would be an increase of one standard deviation in the independent variable). See Table 2.

Table 2 Relations between suicide mortality and characteristics of regions

Standardized Regression Coefficients

Characteristic	Single		Multiple			
	Both Sexes all Ages	Both Sexes all Ages	Young Males ≤49	Old Males ≥50	Young Females ≤49	Old Females ≥50
% Inhabitants Large Cities	−.11	−.42■■	−.29■	−.61■■	.13	−.23
% Roman Catholics	−.11	−.38■	−.20	−.57■■	.18	−.40■
% Orthodox Christians	−.43■■	−.60■■	−.44■■	−.46■■	−.33■	−.65■■
Mean Years of Education	.31■	.27	.50■■	−.10	.42■■	.13
% Male Unemployment	.11	.12	.21	.18	−.08	−.05
Divorce Rate	.42■■	.37	.37■	.29	.20	.17
% Variance Explained		56.2	65.1	57.9	61.0	38.6

■ : p < .05
■■ : p < .01

copyright © A.J.F.M. Kerkhof and A.E. Kunst

When we look at the second column of this table, we see that for both sexes and all ages there are significant negative regression coefficients for the relationship between regional suicide rates and urbanization and religion. This means that rural areas in The Netherlands tend to produce more suicides than urban areas. Likewise, those areas with large Roman Catholic communities, as well as those areas with comparatively large orthodox protestant communities tend to produce less suicides than areas with low numbers of both religious affiliations. The two religious variables alone account for 36% of the explained variance. There is a positive relationship between divorce and regional suicide rates, as we would expect.

When we turn to the separate age and sex groups we see that the regression coefficients are different. We see that the rural suicidogeneous effect applies only to males, and not to females. Especially the older males are affected by this factor. The preventative power of the Roman Catholic religion only applies to the older age groups (males and females) but not any longer to the younger age groups. The preventive power of the existence of large communities of orthodox protestants holds for all age and sex groups. Remarkably is the result that higher education has a strong relationship with regional suicide rates for the young (males and females) and not for the old. Unemployment shows a positive but not significant relationship with the regional pattern of suicide rates among males. Divorce, finally, does have a relationship with regional suicide rates only for young males.

Discussion

The finding of Sainsbury et al. (1980) that social correlates of suicide must be age and sex specific have been confirmed by this study. The protective power of religion appears to be very strong, even for those that live in a religious environment without being themselves very religious. The suicidogeneous effect on males of rural life might be a specific Dutch effect, which might not be generalized to other countries. New is the finding that higher education in a region is associated with higher suicide rates among the young. Although this finding has never appeared before in empirical analysis, the prediction of this relationship dates back to Durkheim, who predicted that higher levels of education would lead people to regulate their own lives more individually, and would make people less inclined to adhere to collectivistic values and traditions. The sixties and seventies were indeed an epoque in which young people in The Netherlands in great numbers benefitted from much better education facilities. Because of better education facilities young people in The Netherlands, in large numbers, left their parental homes to study in other cities, living on their own. This was indeed a time of increased individualization, approved by many who felt restrained by their family and local community traditions.

The results of this study suggest that the increase in suicide rates among the young in the sixties and seventies in The Netherlands has something to do with individualization, with secularization, the loss of religious values, the loss of religious network ties, which according to Durkheim, reflects the degree of anomy in society. Especially the decline of the Roman Catholic religion in The Netherlands over the last decades can be associated with increasing suicide rates among the young. During the last seven years, however, there has been a reversed trend in suicide rates in The Netherlands: suicide rates have dropped by 10% since 1984. It might not be coincidental that in the last ten years a kind of religious revival can be observed, especially among the orthodox protestant youth.

Conclusions

Suicide rates are age and sex-specific and in each and every regional community influenced by social factors such as religion, education, divorce, the changing status of women in society, i.e. the changing roles of men and women towards each other. Unemployment may play a role, but presumably in a limited way. And there may be other, very stable cultural attitudinal factors as well, such as in the Northern part of The Netherlands.

The most important conclusion is that suicide rates tend to vary across regions within countries, that within each region they tend to be very stable, and that when they change this is a very gradual process, reflecting a decline in social cohesion, or a decline in social integration and regulation, which affects men and women, old and young differently. The protective power of collective moral values and religion against suicide sems to be greatly neglected. Even for those who are not religiously oriented, religion provided throughout the centuries a structure in society which enables individuals to give meaning to their lives. The influence of Christianity in Western European culture is obvious. My teacher in cultural psychology, Han Fortman, told me that it would be as difficult to teach a goldfish what the meaning is of water as it is to teach people what the meaning is of culture: we are so deeply immersed in it.

As to the topic of this conference, the prevention of suicide, I would conclude that fundamental changes in suicide mortality cannot be expected from improvements in health care facilities alone, but that fundamental changes in the social integration of a regional community or a society as a whole are needed as well. Suicide prevention therefore is also a political issue, in the sense that the political debate may respect and improve the moral values and social cohesion of the community, or it may contribute to further disintegration. The cultural values that tie an individual to his community need to be looked at very carefully.

References

Ashford J R and Lawrence P A (1976). Aspects of the epidemiology of suicide in England and Wales. *International Journal of Epidemiology, 5,* 133.

Barraclough B (1988). International variation in the suicide rate of 15-24 year olds. *Social Psychiatry and Psychiatric Epidemiology, 23,* 75-84.

Boor M (1980). Relationships between unemployment rates and suicide rates in eight countries. *Psychological Reports, 47,* 1095-1101.

Breault K D (1986). Suicide in America: A Test of Durkheim's Theory of Religious and Family Integration, 1933-1980. *American Journal of Sociology, 92,* 628-656.

Cavan P S (1928). *Suicide.* New York, Russel and Russel.

Crombie I (1990). Can Changes in Unemployment Rates Explain the Recent Changes in Suicide Rates in Developed Countries? *International Journal of Epidemiology, 19,* 412-416.

Diekstra R F W (1933). *Suicide and Parasuicide: Epidemiology.* Leiden, Department of Clinical, Health and Personality Psychology Reports.

Dooley D, Catalano R, Rook K and Serxner S (1989). Economic Stress and Suicide: Multilevel Analyses. Part I: Aggregate Time-Series Analyses of Economic Stress and Suicide. *Suicide and Life-Threatening Behavior, 19,* 321-336.

Dooley D, Catalano R, Rook K and Serxner S (1989). Economic Stress and Suicide: Multilevel Analyses. Part 2: Cross-Level Analyses of Economic Stress and Suicide. *Suicide and Life-Threatening Behavior, 19,* 337-351.

Durkheim E (1897) *Le Suicide: Etude de Sociologie.* Paris. 1930. Nouvelle édition. Presses Universitaires de France.

Gibbs J P and Martin W T (1964). *Status Integration and Suicide.* Eugene: University of Oregon Books.

Houwelingen J van, Tazelaar F and Verbeek A (1984). Werkloosheid, Gezondheid, en Sterfte in Naoorlogs Nederland. *Sociologische Gids, 31,* 6-23.

Kerkhof A J F M (1985). *Suicide en de Geestelijke Gezondheidszorg.* Lisse: Swets & Zeitlinger.

Knippenberg H (1992). *De religieuze kaart van Nederland.* Assen: Van Gorcum.

Kruijt C S (1960). *Zelfmoord: Statistisch-Sociologische Verkenningen.* Assen: Van Gorcum & Co.

Kruijt C S (1962). Sociologische Aspecten van de Zelfmoord. *Huisarts en Wetenschap, 5,* 73-79.

Kruijt C S (1975a). Het Verloop van de Zelfmoordcijfers in de Westerse Wereld sedert de Tweede Wereldoorlog. *Demografie, Bulletin van het Nederlands Interuniversitair Demografisch Instituut, 15.*

Kruijt C S (1975b). *Sociale Spanningen in een Maatschappij van Overloed: Zelfmoord als Indicator.* Den Haag: Ministerie van Volkshuisvesting en Ruimtelijke Ordening: Studierapporten Rijksplanologische Dienst.

Kunst A E, Kerkhof A J F M (1993). Regionale verschillen in suicide sterfte in Nederland in 1969–1988. Samenhang met sociale, economische en culturele indicatoren. *Tijdschrift voor Sociale Gezondheidszorg* (submitted).

Kunst A E, Looman C W N and Mackenbach J P (1990a). Socio-Economic Mortality Differences in the Netherlands in 1950–1984: A Regional Study of Cause-Specific Mortality. *Social Science and Medicine, 31,* 141–152.

Kunst A E, Looman C W N and Mackenbach J P (1990b). *Regionale Sterfteverschillen en Sociall-Economische Indictatoren.* Rotterdam: Instituut Maatschappelijke Gezondheidszorg Erasmus Universiteit (ISBN 9072245-44-X).

Mackenbach J P, Kunst A E, Looman C W N and Beeck E F van (1990). *Regionale Sterfteverschillen.* Rotterdam: Instituut Maatschappelijke Gezondheidszorg Erasmus Universiteit (MGZ.90.01).

Moens G F G (1983). De Stijging van de Sterfte door Zelfdoding in België tussen 1979 en 1980. *Tijdschrift voor Sociale Gezondheidszorg, 61,* 979–983.

Moens G F G (1990). *Aspects of the Epidemiology and Prevention of Suicide.* Leuven, Leuven University Press.

Moens G F G, Baert A E and Voorde H van de (1984). Het verloop van de Nederlandse Suicide Sterfte tussen 1969–'71 en 1979–'81. *Tijdschrift voor Sociale Gezondheidszorg, 62,* 785–790.

Ozsvath K (1988). Epidemiology of Suicide Events in a Hungarian County. In: H J Möller, A Schmidtke & R Welz (Eds.). *Current Issues in Suicidology.* Berlin, Springer Verlag.

Pescosolido B A (1990). The social context of religious integration and suicide: Pursuing the network explanation. *Sociological Quarterly, 31,* 337–357.

Pescosolido B A and Georgianna S (1989). Durkheim, suicide and religion: Toward a network theory of suicide. *American Sociological Review, 54,* 33–48.

Platt S (1984). Unemployment and Suicidal Behaviour: A Review of the Literature. *Social Science and Medicine, 19,* 93–115.

Platt S (1988). Suicide trends in 24 European Countries, 1972–1984. In: H J Möller, A Schmidtke & R Welz (Eds.). *Current Issues of Suicidology.* Berlin, Springer (pp. 3–13).

Pritchard C (1990). Suicide, Unemployment and gender variations in the Western World 1964–1986. *Social Psychiatry and Psychiatric Epidemiology, 25,* 73–80.

Sainsbury P (1955). *Suicide in London: An Ecological Study*. London: Chapman & Hall.

Sainsbury P, Jenkins J and Levey A (1980). The Social Correlates of Suicide in Europe. In: R Farmer & S Hirsch (eds.). *The Suicide Syndrome*. London: Croom Helm, pp. 38–53.

Stack S (1981). Divorce and suicide: A third series analysis, 1933–1970. *Journal of Family Issues, 2,* 77–90.

Stack S (1982). Suicide: A decade review of the sociological literature. *Deviant Behavior, 4,* 41–66.

Stack S (1983). The effect of the decline in institutionalized religion on suicide, 1954–1978. *Journal for the scientific Study of Religion. 22,* 239–252.

Stack S (1985). The effect of domestic/religious individualism on suicide, 1954–1978. *Journal of Marriage and the Family, 47,* 431–448.

Stack S (1987). The Sociological Study of Suicide: Methodological Issues. *Suicide and Life-Threatening Behavior 17,* 113–150.

Stack S (1990). New micro-level data on the impact of divorce on suicide, 1959–1980: A test of two theories. *Journal of Marriage and the Family, 52,* 119–127.

Stack S (1990). The effect of divorce on suicide in Denmark, 1951–1980. *Sociological Quarterly, 31,* 359–370.

Trovato F (1987). A longitudinal analysis of divorce and suicide in Canada. *Journal of Marriage and the Family, 49,* 193–203.

Trovato F (1992). A Durkheimian analysis of youth suicide: Canada, 1971 and 1981. *Suicide and Life-Threatening Behavior, 22,* 413–428.

Wasserman I M (1984). A longitudinal analysis of the linkage between suicide, unemployment, and marital dissolution. *Journal of Marriage and the Family, 46,* 853–859.

World Health Organization (1982). *Changing Patterns in Suicide Behaviour.* Copenhagen, EURO Reports and Studies 74.

World Health Organization (1989). *Annual Statistics.* Geneva, WHO.

4 Causes and Opportunities for Prevention
Dr Keith Hawton

Introduction

This contribution provides an overview of some of the factors known or thought to contribute to suicide and highlights some targets and strategies regarding prevention. Several of these are covered in more detail by other contributors. Suggestions for further research are also included since, although we know a considerable amount about factors which contribute to suicide, more information is required in the light of recent changes in the patterns of suicide in the United Kingdom.

It is important to recognise that the major rises and falls that have occurred in rates of suicide this century have not been the result of specific preventive policies but of important social upheavals and other changes. These include the two World Wars, during which suicide rates fell very considerably, and the Depression of the late 1920s and early 1930s, which was accompanied by a significant rise in suicide rates. More recently a decline in suicide rates of almost a third occurred during the 1960s and early 1970s, which was almost certainly due to the gradual replacement of poisonous coal gas in domestic supplies by non-toxic North Sea gas (although other factors such as the reduction in use of barbiturate medication could also have contributed). These facts should engender a sense of realism when discussing the potential of preventive strategies, although the coal gas story also suggests possibilities for prevention.

When considering potential strategies it is important to take note of the changes in the age and sex patterns of suicide that have occurred recently in England and Wales and which are described in detail elsewhere in this volume. In summary, for the first time this century the rates of suicide for the two sexes have diverged, increasing substantially in males and decreasing in females. Suicide rates in people aged 45 years and over in both sexes have decreased markedly since the early 1960s. However, rates have increased dramatically in young males, especially in the past decade or so. Thus between 1980 and 1990 the rate (suicide and deaths due to undetermined cause) in males aged 25–44 years in England and Wales increased by approximately a third (the rate in 1990 exceeding that of men age 65 plus for the first time this century), and that in males aged 15–24 years increased by 85% (with a near doubling of the rate in 20–24 year-olds). By contrast the rate (suicide and undetermined cause) in young females has declined slightly. These changes clearly have relevance to prevention. Most importantly they highlight how little we know about the characteristics of young suicide and the factors that contribute to their deaths. A major investigation of this group, using the method of psychological autopsy (Schneidman 1981) is urgently required. When considering possible foci for prevention this area of relative ignorance must be borne in mind.

Psychiatric and Personality Problems

Earlier studies found psychiatric disorders in more than 90% of suicides (Robins et al 1959; Dorpat and Ripley 1960; Barraclough et al 1974). Depressive disorders appeared to be the most common diagnoses, especially in the UK study of Barraclough and colleagues (1974) in which 70% of their suicides appeared to have suffered from depression. The lifetime risk of suicide in people with affective disorders is of the order of 15% (Guze and Robins 1970) and somewhat higher in those with manic-depressive illness (Goodwin and Jamison 1990). Substance abuse, especially of alcohol, was also common in the UK study, alcoholism being diagnosed in 15% of the suicides. Some suicides were suffering from schizophrenia, the lifetime risk in this condition being of the order of at least 10% (Miles, 1977). It is also known that many people who die by suicide have had personality difficulties (Ovenstone and Kreitman 1974). A word of caution is necessary regarding the study by Barraclough and colleagues since it only included people with a coroner's verdict of suicide. If people whose deaths were 'probable suicides' had also been included the prevalence of psychiatric disorder may have been somewhat lower. Also, recent studies from abroad of young suicides (Shafii et al 1988; Runenson 1989; Marttunen et al 1991; Marttunen et al 1993) have found a rather different picture, with substance abuse, personality disorders and adjustment reactions being frequent diagnoses in addition to depression. Thus the earlier findings might not be so relevant to many current suicides.

In spite of these caveats, improved detection and management of psychiatric disorders, particularly depression, must be important aspects of prevention. This is especially relevant in primary care and psychiatry.

Primary Care

An interesting study conducted on the Swedish island of Gotland has suggested that efforts to improve treatment of depression in primary care may be effective in suicide prevention. An intensive programme of education of nearly all of the 18 GPs on the island about the nature and treatment of depression and suicide risk was carried out in 1983 and 1984 (Rutz et al 1989a). In 1985 there was a significant fall in the number of suicides on the island, the rate of suicide in the rest of Sweden having remained unchanged (Rutz et al 1989b). While one must be cautious in interpreting the findings of the study, particularly in view of the relatively small size of the population of the island (56,000) and of the number of suicides, plus the fact that the suicide rate rose in the years after 1985 (Rutz et al 1992), it is nevertheless encouraging, particularly as the programme was also associated with an increase in prescribing of antidepressant drugs and a decline in psychiatric admissions for treatment of depressive illness. In Switzerland, Michel and Valach (1992) found that a single seminar plus written material on suicide appeared to be associated with improvement in GPs' attitudes and knowledge of suicide and suicide prevention.

The Defeat Depression Campaign organised by the Royal College of Psychiatrists and Royal College of General Practitioners aims to improve detection and treatment of depression in primary care (Paykel and Priest 1992). This should be supplemented by specific education about the management of suicide risk. Such a programme should be evaluated on a large scale in this country. However, such a focus for preventive efforts might be of less relevance for prevention of suicidal behaviour in young people, for while contact with GPs has been shown in the past to be frequent prior to both suicide and attempted suicide (Barraclough et al 1974; Hawton and Blackstock 1976) recent work by Chris Vassilas and David Gunnell described elsewhere in this volume suggests that relatively few young suicides have had contact with their GPs in the month prior to their deaths. Nevertheless, the Royal College of General Practitioners should give serious consideration to including experience in psychiatry as a compulsory part of the training of general practitioners. We know that a very large proportion of the patients who consult in general practice have emotional problems (Goldberg and Huxley, 1980). Improving their care would be an important advance and one that could also prevent some suicides.

Psychiatric Practice

Recent advances in the treatment of depression are very relevant for suicide prevention in both primary care and psychiatric practice. In addition to ensuring adequate and appropriate treatment of depression, using antidepressants (in full therapeutic doses), combinations of drugs (eg augmentation of tricyclic antidepressants with lithium carbonate) and psychosocial treatments where indicated, we now know that in order to reduce the risk of relapse to a minimum after recovery with antidepressant treatment *full* therapeutic dose of medication should be continued for several months (reviewed by Kupfer 1992). In the elderly, recent evidence suggests that it may be necessary to continue treatment for two years after recovery (Old Age Depression Interest Group 1993). The role of psychological treatments (eg cognitive behaviour therapy) requires further evaluation, especially with regard to helping patients who experience residual symptoms following depression and to reduce risk of relapse.

Prevention of episodes of depression in people with recurrent affective disorders is another important aspect of prevention of suicide. There is increasing evidence that occurrence of suicide may be reduced in patients maintained on lithium compared with those not on maintenance medication (Causemann and Müller-Oerlinghausen 1988; Coppen et al 1991), although it must be acknowledged that such studies are not entirely satisfactory since the evidence is usually not from placebo-controlled randomised trials. Thus, for example, there may be common factors associated with both absence of wish to pursue lithium therapy (or poor compliance with lithium) and suicide risk.

The risk of suicide is particularly high during the month following discharge from inpatient psychiatric care (Goldacre et al 1993). This emphasises the need for careful planning of aftercare, with daypatient care and community support where appropriate in addition to possible outpatient follow up.

Reduction in the high risk of suicide associated with substance abuse probably necessitates improved primary prevention, with educational and pricing policies perhaps being the main strategies. However, adequate treatment services for substance abusers must be available in all areas of the country. There is a particular need for good liaison between substance abuse services and general hospital services for attempted suicide patients. Alcohol and drug problems are common in this group of patients (Platt et al 1988) and substance abuse is a key risk factor for suicide following attempted suicide in the young (Hawton et al 1993).

In schizophrenia the risk of suicide is highest in young men. Unlike in depression, the risk is not especially high during episodes of acute illness but rather during remissions when insight into the effects of the illness and depression may lead to hopelessness and suicidal ideation (Drake et al 1984). In addition to use of prophylactic neuroleptic medication in patients at risk of relapse, long-term support by community psychiatric nurses must be a very important aspect of prevention in this group of patients. The recent third quinquennial national survey of the work of community psychiatric nurses estimates that as many as 80% of people with schizophrenia may not have a community psychiatric nurse, which is cause for alarm (White 1991). The review also demonstrated that there is an inverse relationship between the number of referrals to community psychiatric nurses that come from primary care teams as opposed to psychiatrists and the proportion of patients with chronic psychiatric illness on the nurses' caseloads. With the recent increases in both community psychiatric nurses and the proportions of their referrals which come direct from general practitioners, the working practices of community psychiatric nurses require further review.

Little information is available to help us in preventing suicide in people with personality disorders. Medication such as neuroleptics and lithium carbonate may have a limited role (Cowen 1990), as also may psychotherapy (Casey 1992). Long-term support by a member of a psychiatric team may also be helpful. It is to be hoped that current research on the probable link between certain personality characteristics (eg impulsivity and aggression) associated with suicide risk and behaviour and abnormalities of brain serotonin pathways (Mann et al 1989; Coccaro et al 1989) may in future lead to therapeutic innovations. This is an important area for further research.

Social and Physical Health Problems

It is widely recognised that certain social and health factors are associated with suicide risk. The primary prevention of such factors will be the most likely strategy to reduce suicide risk. However, their prevention will depend partly on government-determined social and economic strategies.

Unemployment and Financial Problems

The rate of suicide in the unemployed is considerably elevated compared with the employed (Platt 1984). However, the association between suicidal behaviour and unemployment is complex. The association could, for example, reflect the adverse effects that unemployment can have on mental health (Smith 1985) or might be a consequence of people with psychiatric disorders and other risk factors for suicidal behaviour being at increased risk of being unemployed. Furthermore, recent changes in unemployment rates in the young, which increased during the early 1980s, decreased in the late 1980s and then rose again, were not directly reflected in changes in the suicide rate (Charlton et al 1993) (although changes in the method of registration of unemployment, especially in young people, could provide an explanation for this apparent anomaly). It is nevertheless probable that the recent rise in young male suicides is in some part associated with overall rising rates of unemployment, although the degree of contribution of this factor is unknown. One of the obvious likely consequences of unemployment is poverty; this might be another linking factor between unemployment and suicide risk.

Family Breakdown and Divorce

Family breakdown may be relevant to recent changes in the suicide rate in the young, since it is recognised that family breakdown increases risk of subsequent emotional problems and that suicide risk is increased in the divorced (Charlton et al 1993). Thus the rapid increase in divorce rates in the 1960s, which would have affected the parents of many people who are now young adults, could have caused elevated rates of emotional problems and suicide in young people today, as could the current high rate of divorce among young people themselves. However, the different changes that have occurred in the suicide rates of young males and young females are hard to explain on this basis. One possibility is that marital breakdown may have different social consequences for the two sexes, at least for some people. It is recognised that marriage appears to be 'protective' for males in terms of psychiatric disorder but the reverse for females. There might also be greater support available within society for women who have suffered marital breakdown. Whatever the reason(s), prevention of unnecessary family breakdown must be relevant to suicide prevention in the young. Continuing and increasing support of the work of organisations such as Relate and conciliation services may be important in this regard.

Physical Illness

Suicide risk is elevated in chronic physical illness, particularly neurological, gastrointestinal, cardiovascular and malignant disorders (Sainsbury 1955; Dorpat and Ripley 1960; Whitlock 1986). In addition, there is a generally elevated rate of psychiatric disorder, especially depression, in people with physical illness (Mayou and Hawton 1986). Training of medical staff in the detection and management of such disorders may be relevant to suicide prevention. This should occur not only during clinical training of medical students but also during post-registration training. It appears that the risk of suicide is extremely high in people with AIDS and HIV infection (Marzuk et al 1988), although it is unlikely that AIDS has made a major contribution to the recent rise in the rate of suicide in young males in the United Kingdom (Charlton et al 1993). Primary prevention of the spread of HIV must be the main factor in prevention of this cause of suicide, although supportive networks, both lay and professional, are likely to be relevant in the prevention of suicide in those who are already infected.

High Risk Occupations

The proportion of deaths attributable to suicide or probable suicide is considerably elevated in certain occupational groups, especially veterinary surgeons, pharmacists, dentists, farmers and medical practitioners (Charlton et al 1993). There are no obvious explanations for this although access to lethal means of suicide, work pressures, and, for farmers at least, financial difficulties might be possible reasons. Therefore it is important to study a series of people in these categories who have died by suicide, using the method of psychological autopsy (Schneidman 1981), in order to examine possible causes so that preventive strategies can be suggested. It is also important that the supportive networks available for people with emotional and other problems within these professional groups be investigated.

Prison Suicides

Much attention has been paid to the recent increase in numbers of suicides in prisons, particularly in young male convicted prisoners and those held on remand (Dooley 1987). The key factor in prevention in this group is improved communication – between prisoners and prison staff and vice versa, between prisoners and their families and partners, and between prisoners and befrienders. This is addressed more fully elsewhere in this publication by Enda Dooley.

Availability of particular Means for Suicide

The coal gas story, in which reduction in the suicide rate by approximately one third occurred in the United Kingdom with the introduction of non-toxic North Sea gas (Kreitman 1976), is testimony to the fact that making a common method of suicide safe or unavailable does not mean that all would-be suicides automatically turn to another method (although clearly some will). The use of car exhausts, which is now one of the most common methods used especially in young men (Charlton et al 1992), must be an important target for suicide prevention. The introduction of efficient catalytic converters on cars could be an important element in suicide prevention (Clarke and Lester 1987), although simple modifications of exhaust outlets to make it impossible to insert a tube might also be effective.

While self-poisoning as a method for suicide has become somewhat less common in recent years (Charlton et al 1992), there has been an increased number of deaths from liver failure resulting from paracetamol poisoning (O'Grady et al 1991). Preparations of paracetamol containing methionine, which protects against liver damage, are available, but only on prescription. This means that they are of little current relevance to suicide prevention. Means should be found as soon as possible to make safer versions of paracetamol readily available. If this is going to be difficult to achieve then the amount of paracetamol available in a single container should be limited to a relatively safe maximum (eg 16–20 tablets).

The use of some of the newer antidepressants that are relatively safe in overdose compared with tricyclics has been widely advocated. On the other hand some clinicians have doubts about the relative efficacy of the newer antidepressants. Certainly the antidepressants which act specifically on the serotonin system do not appear to be *more* effective than the tricyclics and they are considerably more expensive (Song et al 1993). While clinicians tend to use safer antidepressants in people who are clearly at high risk of self poisoning, in reality it is unclear to what extent elimination of tricyclics would contribute to suicide prevention (Kelleher et al 1992).

Improving the safety of sites commonly used for suicide might also aid prevention. Thus erection of 'suicide barriers' on high bridges, as has happened on the Clifton Suspension Bridge in Bristol, should be considered.

Media Influences

Elsewhere in this publication, Stephen Platt has considered the possible role of media reporting and dramatization of suicide in encouraging further suicides. His detailed analysis of some of the research work in this field has highlighted the difficulty of assessing the contribution of this factor. However, while the methodology of most studies can be heavily criticised, the study that most stands up to scrutiny strongly supports such an effect (Schmidtke and Häfner 1988). Thus following the double broadcast in Germany of a serial in which the railway suicide of a 19 year-old man occurred, strong imitation effects were observable following the broadcasts, were most marked in young males, lasted longer in this group and corresponded to the audience viewing figures. Clinical experience, as Shaffer has discussed elsewhere in this volume, also lends support to a media effect on suicide, possibly most affecting the choice of method.

It is highly desirable that the dramatic reporting of suicides be replaced by simple factual reporting, that television producers should seek help from experts before including suicidal behaviour in programmes, and that such programmes be followed by adverts for helplines and other means of obtaining assistance. It is also desirable that a general code of practice about media portrayal and reporting of suicides be drawn up by a joint working group of media representatives and experts in the field.

Public Attitudes towards Suicide

Negative public attitudes towards psychiatric problems and their treatment probably inhibit many people who suffer psychiatric disorders from seeking help. Improved education of the public about the facts of psychiatric illnesses, including their amenability to treatment, may encourage more people with psychiatric disorders to seek help and thereby assist in suicide prevention. Education should highlight the risk of suicide. This might both further encourage help-seeking and reduce the burden experienced by family members and friends of people who have died by suicide (Wertheimer 1991). The media could make a very positive contribution to such educational measures.

Education in Schools

The importance and potential dangers of suicide prevention efforts through education strategies directed at school children have been examined by David Shaffer elsewhere in this volume. Educational programmes are most likely to be effective if they generally address methods of coping with difficulties and stresses in life rather than focus on suicidal behaviour *per se*. Evaluation of such a programme suggests that differing educational strategies may have to be used for females and males (Overholser et al 1990). Teachers should be helped to recognise signs of serious emotional disorder, particularly substance abuse, and of risk factors for suicidal behaviour, including spread of such behaviour in institutions.

Attempted Suicide

Attempted suicide by deliberate self-poisoning or self-injury is a continuing major health problem in the United Kingdom (Hawton and Catalan 1987), with at least an estimated 100,000 people being referred to general hospitals in England and Wales per year because of suicide attempts (Hawton and Fagg 1992a), up to 19,000 of these being teenagers (Hawton and Fagg 1992b). Rates of attempted suicide in the United Kingdom are among the highest in Europe (Platt et al 1988; Platt et al 1989). Suicide is closely linked to attempted suicide, approximately 1% of people who attempt suicide committing suicide within a year of an attempt and 3–5% within the following few years (Hawton and Fagg 1988). Furthermore, 40–50% of suicides have made previous attempts (Ovenstone and Kreitman 1974), and attempted suicide is the most robust predictor of completed suicide in people with psychiatric disorders (Hawton 1987).

In addition to any strategies for primary prevention of attempted suicide it is important that general hospital services for suicide attempters be of a high standard. However, in spite of official guidelines for the management of suicide attempters in general hospitals (Department of Health and Social Security 1984), it appears that the quality of general hospital services for these patients is highly variable. It is vital that these services be brought up to uniformly high standards. Important elements of a high quality service include multidisciplinary staff who are adequately trained and supervised, proper facilities where patients can be interviewed in privacy, availability of prompt assessment, a thorough assessment procedure, including interviews with relatives and other key individuals, and provision of aftercare from the same service whenever possible. In addition, district general hospitals should have information available on how primary suicide attempters come to the hospital, how many are fully assessed, and what aftercare is provided. They should probably also have information on compliance with aftercare and subsequent repetition of attempts, including suicides.

Local Working Groups on Suicide Prevention

It is important that working groups be established at district and regional level which can carry out or facilitate tasks relevant to suicide prevention. These might include overseeing local audit projects on suicide and attempted suicide, examining local risk factors for suicide and making recommendations about strategies for prevention, and supplying information to local purchasers of health care which will enable them to purchase services having specific relevance to suicide prevention. Such working groups should include team members from public health, psychiatry (both medical and nursing), general practice, social services, education and voluntary organisations (eg Samaritans).

Conclusions

A wide range of possible strategies for suicide prevention have been suggested. This reflects the multifactorial origins of suicide. It is highly desirable that efforts be made to determine the relative potential efficiency of different preventive strategies, in order to focus efforts most effectively. For example, reducing the availability of dangerous methods of suicide, improving the detection and treatment of depression and ensuring that sufferers from chronic or relapsing psychiatric disorders receive long-term support from psychiatric services might be the most cost-effective approaches. However, the need to elucidate the characteristics of young suicides, about whom we presently know so little, cannot be overemphasised. The effective approaches to prevention in this group are as yet unclear.

It is also important to be realistic and to recognise the limitations of suicide prevention. Suicide has existed throughout history (Alvarez 1974) and will never be totally eradicated. It is also important to acknowledge both the extent of risk of suicide in all psychiatric disorders, especially depression, schizophrenia, alcohol and drug abuse and major personality disorders of an aggressive or impulsive nature, and the difficulty in assessing this risk in the individual (Hawton 1987). The aim of preventive efforts should be the reduction of suicides to the lowest possible level. At the same time the fact that suicides will occur must be accepted. It is particularly important that those in the caring professions who are frequently doing their utmost to prevent suicide, often within services with meagre resources, are not subjected to automatic morale-sapping condemnation when a suicide occurs.

The Health of the Nation has presented us with an important challenge. It is to be hoped that it will lead to realistic attempts to improve the care of people with emotional and psychiatric problems and by this means to prevent suicide. It is essential that it be accepted that responsibility for such efforts lies not solely in one arena but that it requires determined attention from the Government, the Department of Health, health care providers, purchasers of health care, the media and education.

References

Barraclough B, Bunch J, Nelson B and Sainsbury P (1974). A hundred cases of suicide: clinical aspects. *British Journal of Psychiatry, 125,* 355–373.

Casey P R (1992). Personality disorders: do psychological treatments help? In *Practical Problems in Clinical Psychiatry* (eds K Hawton and P Cowen), pp 130–140. Oxford: Oxford University Press.

Causemann B and Müller-Oerlinghausen B (1988). Does lithium prevent suicide and suicide attempts? In *Lithium: Inorganic Pharmacology and Psychiatric Use* (ed N Y Birch), pp 23–24. Oxford: IRL Press.

Charlton J, Kelly S, Dunnell K, Evans B, Jenkins R and Wallis R (1992). Trends in suicide deaths in England and Wales. *Population Trends, 69,* 10–16.

Charlton J, Kelly S, Dunnell K, Evans B and Jenkins R (1993). Suicide deaths in England and Wales: trends factors associated with suicide deaths. *Population Trends, 70,* 34–42.

Clarke R V and Lester D (1987). Toxicity of car exhausts and opportunity for suicide: comparison between Britain and the United States. *Journal of Epidemiology and Community Health, 41,* 114-120.

Coccaro E F, Siever L J, Klar H M, Maurer G, Cochrane K, Cooper T B, Mohs R C and Davis K L (1989). Serotonergic studies in patients with affective and personality disorders: correlates with suicidal and impulsive aggresive behavior. *Archives of General Psychiatry, 46,* 587–599.

Coppen A, Standish-Barry H, Bailey J, Houston G, Silcocks P and Hermon C (1991). Does lithium reduce the mortality of recurrent mood disorders? *Journal of Affective Disorders, 23,* 1–7.

Cowen P J (1990). Personality disorders: are drugs useful? In *Dilemmas and Difficulties in the Management of Psychiatric Patients* (eds K Hawton and P Cowen), pp 105–116. Oxford: Oxford University Press.

Department of Health and Social Security (1984). *The Management of Deliberate Self-harm.* HN(84)25. Department of Health and Social Security, London.

Dooley E (1990). Prison Suicide in England and Wales, 1972–87. *British Journal of Psychiatry, 156,* 40–45.

Dorpat T L and Ripley H S (1960). A study of suicide in the Seattle area. *Comprehensive Psychiatry, 1,* 349–359.

Drake R E, Gates C, Cotton P G and Whitaker A (1984). Suicide among schizophrenics: who is at risk? *Journal of Nervous and Mental Disease, 172,* 613–617.

Goldacre M, Seagrott V and Hawton K (1993). Suicide after discharge from psychiatric inpatient care. *Lancet, 342,* 283–286.

Goldberg D and Huxley P (1980). *Mental Illness in the Community. The Pathways to Psychiatric Care.* London: Tavistock.

Goodwin F K and Jamison K R (1990). *Manic-depressive Illness*. Oxford University Press: New York.

Guze S B and Robins E (1970). Suicide among primary affective disorders. *British Journal of Psychiatry, 117,* 437–438.

Hawton K (1987). Assessment of suicide risk. *British Journal of Psychiatry, 150,* 145–153.

Hawton K and Blackstock E (1976). General practice aspects of self-poisoning and self-injury. *Psychological Medicine, 6,* 571–575.

Hawton K and Catalan J (1987). *Attempted Suicide: A Practical Guide to its Nature and Management (second edition)*. Oxford University Press: Oxford.

Hawton K and Fagg J (1988). Suicide and other causes of death following attempted suicide. *British Journal of Psychiatry, 152,* 359–366.

Hawton K and Fagg J (1992a). Trends in deliberate self-poisoning and self-injury in Oxford, 1976–1990. *British Medical Journal 304,* 1409–1411.

Hawton K and Fagg J (1992b). Deliberate self-poisoning and self-injury in adolescents: a study of characteristics and trends in Oxford, 1976–1989. *British Journal of Psychiatry, 161,* 816–823.

Hawton K, Platt S, Fagg J and Hawkins M (1993). Suicide following parasuicide in young people. *British Medical Journal, 306,* 1641–1644.

Kelleher M J, Daly M and Kelleher M J A (1992). The influence of antidepressants in overdose on the increased suicide rate in Ireland between 1971 and 1988. *British Journal of Psychiatry, 161,* 625–628.

Kreitman N (1976). The coal gas story: UK suicide rates 1960–1971. *British Journal of Preventive and Social Medicine, 30,* 86–93.

Kupfer D J (1992). Maintenance treatment in recurrent depression: current and future directions. *British Journal of Psychiatry, 161,* 309–316.

Mann J J, Arango V, Marzuk P M, Theccanat S and Reis D J (1989). Evidence for the 5-HT hypothesis of suicide – A review of post-mortem studies. *British Journal of Psychiatry, 155 (Suppl 8),* 7–14.

Marttunen M J, Aro H M and Lönnqvist J K (1993). Adolescence and suicide: a review of psychological autopsy studies. *European Child and Adolescent Psychiatry, 2,* 10–18.

Marttunen M J, Aro H M, Henriksson M M and Lönnqvist J K (1991). Mental disorders in adolescent suicide. *Archives of General Psychiatry, 48,* 834–839.

Marzuk P, Tierney H, Tardiff F, Gross E M, Morgan E B, Hsu M A, et al (1988). Increased risk of suicide in persons with AIDS. *Journal of the American Medical Association, 259,* 1333–1337.

Mayou R and Hawton K (1986). Psychiatric disorder in the general hospital. *British Journal of Psychiatry, 140,* 179–190.

Michel K and Valach L (1992). Suicide prevention: spreading the gospel to general practitioners. *British Journal of Psychiatry, 160,* 757–760.

Miles C P (1977). Conditions predisposing to suicide: a review. *Journal of Nervous and Mental Disease, 164,* 231–246.

O'Grady J G, Wendon J, Tan K C, Potter D, Cottam S, Cohen A T, Gimson A E S and Williams R (1991). Liver transplantation after paracetamol overdose. *British Medical Journal, 303,* 221–223.

Old Age Depression Interest Group (1993). How long should the elderly take antidepressants? A double-bind placebo-controlled study of continuation/prophylaxis therapy with dothiepin. *British Journal of Psychiatry, 162,* 175–182.

Ovenstone I M K and Kreitman N (1974). Two syndromes of suicide. *British Journal of Psychiatry, 124,* 336–345.

Overholser J, Evans S and Spirito A (1990). Sex differences and their relevance to primary prevention of adolescent suicide. *Death Studies, 14,* 391–402.

Paykel E S and Priest R (1992). Recognition and management of depression in general practice: consensus statement. *British Medical Journal, 305,* 1198–1202.

Platt S. (1984). Unemployment and suicidal behaviour – a review of the literature. *Social Science and Medicine, 19,* 93–115.

Platt S, Hawton K, Kreitman N, Fagg J and Foster J (1988). Recent clinical and epidemiological trends in parasuicide in Edinburgh and Oxford: A tale of two cities. *Psychological Medicine, 18,* 405–418.

Platt S et al (1992). Parasuicide in Europe: the WHO/EURO multicentre study on parasuicide. I. Introduction and preliminary analysis for 1989. *Acta Psychiatrica Scandinavica, 85,* 97–104.

Robins E, Murphy G E, Wilkinson R H, Gassner S and Kayes J (1959). Some clinical considerations in the prevention of suicide based on a study of 134 successful suicides. *American Journal of Public Health, 49,* 888–899.

Runenson B (1989). Mental disorder in youth suicide. *Acta Psychiatrica Scandinavica, 79,* 490–497.

Rutz W, Wålinder J et al (1989a). An educational program on depressive disorders for general practitioners on Gotland: background and evaluation. *Acta Psychiatrica Scandinavica, 79,* 19–26.

Rutz W, von Knorring L and Wålinder J (1989b). Frequency of suicide on Gotland after systematic postgraduate education of general practitioners. *Acta Psychiatrica Scandinavica, 80,* 151–154.

Rutz W, von Knorring L and Wålinder J (1992). Long-term effects of an educational program for general practitioners given by the Swedish Committee for the Prevention and Treatment of Depression. *Acta Psychiatrica Scandinavica, 85,* 83–88.

Sainsbury P (1955). *Suicide in London.* Maudsley Monograph No. 1. Chapman and Hall: London.

Schmidtke A and Häfner H (1988). The Werther effect after television films: new evidence for an old hypothesis. *Psychological Medicine, 18,* 665–676.

Schneidman E S (1982). The psychological autopsy. *Suicide and Life-threatening Behavior, 11,* 325–340.

Shaffii M, Steltz-Lenarsky J, McCue A, Beckner C and Whittinghill J R (1988). Comorbidity of mental disorders in the post-mortem diagnosis of completed suicide in children and adolescents. *Journal of Affective Disorders, 15,* 227–233.

Smith R (1985). Occupationless health. 'I couldn't stand it any more'. Suicide and unemployment. *British Medical Journal, 291,* 1563–1566.

Song F, Freemantle N, Sheldon T A, House A, Watson P, Long A and Mason J (1993). Selective serotonin reuptake inhibitors: a meta-analysis of efficacy and acceptability. *British Medical Journal, 306,* 683–687.

Wertheimer A (1991). *A Special Scar: The Experiences of People Bereaved by Suicide.* London: Routledge.

White E (1991). *The 3rd Quinquennial National Community Psychiatric Nursing Survey.* University of Manchester: Department of Nursing.

Whitlock F A (1986) Suicide and physical illness. In: *Suicide* (ed A Roy) pp 151–179. Williams and Wilkins: Baltimore.

5 Assessment of Risk
Gethin Morgan

The process whereby suicide risk is assessed is often taken for granted and rarely is it described in detail in clinical texts which tend to assume that the effective evaluation of risk necessarily follows once helper and suicidal individual meet together. But such is not the case. There are a number of hazards along the way. The purpose of this presentation is to look at these factors one by one in turn: and by systematically doing so, the hope is that our resulting awareness of them will increase the effectiveness of this very important clinical exercise.

Traditionally, at least in clinical psychiatry, the assessment of suicide risk has been equated with the process of matching the individual with a set of risk factors, both biomedical and socio-environmental, which have been shown to have a statistically positive correlation with increased suicide risk. The conventional risk factors have been derived from large cohorts of patients who have committed suicide.

Table 1   High Risk Factors for Suicide

Males > Females
Older Age Group
Divorced > Widowed > Single

Living alone
Socially isolated
Unemployed/Retired

Past Psychiatric History
Family History of Affective Illness
Previous Self Harm

Recent Event – Bereavement/Separation/Loss of Job
Poor Physical Health
Evidence of Depressive Illness
Abuse of Alcohol

Such an approach certainly has many limitations: it is more accurate over the long term, but it is very unspecific and insensitive over the short term, presenting the problem of high numbers of false positives and false negatives. It is precisely in the context of the immediate future that day-to-day clinical work takes place. Such factors will vary in relative weightings from one individual at risk to another and the golden rule must always be that the fundamental basis of risk assessment should be a full thorough clinical evaluation of each individual. The risk factors as illustrated in Table 1 are however useful as a check-list, for example to ensure caution when risk is considered insignificant in their presence. The clinician may therefore double-check the assessment of the individual against them.

The process of risk assessment

There is evidence that in practice, certainly with regards to psychiatric inpatients that detection of suicide risk poses many problems. In one series of 27 psychiatric inpatients who committed suicide either whilst in hospital or within three months of discharge, (Morgan and Priest, 1991) suicide risk had been discussed in 21, but only in 10 had precautions been taken to manage suicide risk (Table 2). Only 7 of the 27 suicides committed suicide actually on the ward, the remainder being able to leave the ward either without leave or with permission from the staff.

Table 2   Bristol Suicides: Ward Management (N = 27)

Suicide Risk Discussed	21
Precautions Taken	10

These figures mean that the clinical assessment of suicide failed in some cases to predict when suicide would occur. This might have meant faulty technique or perhaps it reflects the hazards of following through suicide risk which may vary in severity from time to time. There can indeed be sudden disastrous and unexpected relapse in persons who may seem to have improved up to that time. (Table 3)

Table 3   Bristol Suicides: Possible reasons why suicide was not prevented (N = 27)

Significant Clinical Improvement (problems remained unresolved in 12)	14
Alienation	15
Clinical Improvement +/– Alienation	**22**

The hazards of assessing suicide risk

The process of assessing an individual who is suspected of being at risk of suicide is very demanding indeed. We have to realise that a suicidal individual may not be just depressed, retarded and self-blaming as might be suggested from the finding that depressive illness is the psychiatric condition with the greatest risk of suicide. Psychiatric inpatients who proceed to suicide may show a variety of behaviours including that which is angry and challenging. Quite often they become alienated from those who are looking after them (Table 3) and this is particularly likely to occur when illness relapses recurrently: deliberate disability may then be suspected, as may excessive and unnecessary dependency on support from others (Table 4). The whole process is further complicated by the fact that the level of suicidal ideation may fluctuate very considerably from day to day, even within a single day. And so at times actively suicidal patients may reassure staff members when they are feeling somewhat improved for a short while (Morgan, 1979). It is probably only a very small proportion of suicidal

Table 4   Twelve Bristol Suicides

Suicide Intent Expressed Openly	12
Reassurance to Staff	6
Anger Towards Others	6
'Difficult' Behaviour	6
Staff Critical	8
Deliberate Disability Suspected	10
Depression With Self Blame	10
Loss of Support from Others	6

patients who set out to deceive, but undoubtedly a few do this when they have finally made up their minds to end their lives. Other suicides occur at times of misleading improvement when symptoms have ameliorated but the underlying cause has remained unchanged, and this is a particular hazard which should be negotiated before patients at risk are discharged from hospital.

Improving the efficiency of risk assessment procedures

Assessment of risk has to be carried out effectively in a variety of settings ranging from those in hospital such as A & E Departments, hospital wards, outpatient clinics, to various domiciliary community settings, prison and police stations. Attempts have been made to improve the predictive value of psychiatric diagnostic categories. Table 5 shows the delineation of high risk groups within conventional categories in an attempt to increase their efficiency in suicide prediction.

Table 5   Diagnostic Groups: Suicide Risk

Diagnosis		Risk Factors
Depression	:	Male, older, single/separated, socially isolated Previous DSH Persistent insomnia, self neglect, impaired memory, agitation
Schizophrenia	:	Male, younger Previous DSH and depressive episodes with anorexia/wt loss More serious illness, recurrent relapse
Alcohol/Drug Addiction	:	Adverse life events Previous DSH Depressed mood, serious physical complications

We also need to ask who carries out the assessment, how often is it done and how is it recorded. General practitioners have commented on the fact that in hospital it seems that the most junior trainee psychiatrists may be left to assess a particularly high-risk group, namely patients who have been admitted following episodes of deliberate self-harm.

Table 6   Sequence of Questions in Assessing Suicidal Risk

Hope that things will turn out well
Get pleasure out of life
Feel hopeful from day to day
Able to face each day
See point in it all
Ever despair about things
Feel that it is impossible to face next day
Feel life a burden
Wish it would all end
Wish self dead
Thoughts of ending life. If so, how persistently
Ever acted on them
Feel able to resist them
How likely to kill self
Ability to give reassurance about safety, e.g. until next appointment
Circumstances likely to make things worse
Willingness to turn for help if crisis occurs
Risk to others

Without doubt, entering upon the topic of suicidal ideation and impulses is in general a very challenging task. The individual at risk may not necessarily want to share these painful ideas with someone else, certainly not on the first occasion of meeting. It is necessary to lead into this painful topic very gradually. A possible list of sequence of questions is illustrated in Table 6. It is important to remember that these should not be presented as an inventory of direct leading questions: they should be posed as diadic opposites. Nevertheless some kind of lead often has to be taken in order to encourage the person to open up on these very painful ideas. It also must be remembered that once the ideas have been acknowledged there is still much to find out about them particularly how intense they are and the likelihood of the individual actually carrying them out. Circumstances which help are just as important as those which make things worse. We should also keep in mind the risk to others when there is severe depression with severe nihilistic ideas and total loss of hope.

It is unsafe to assume that anyone who talks about suicide is merely threatening and is therefore unlikely to carry it out. It is probably also true that more mistakes are made from not asking about suicide, sometimes for fear of implanting ideas of self-harm into the patients mind, than by careful sensitive questioning. Aggressive challenging interview technique may however be dangerous, especially in the case of individuals with poor impulse control. Excessive reassurance can also be harmful in depressed individuals who respond by feeling that the interviewer under-estimates the full extent of the despair.

The meaning of symptoms

It cannot be assumed that a complaint of having suicidal ideas and impulses is necessarily indicative of a risk that they will be carried out. The context is important: for example a depressive picture with self-blame would demand that they be taken very seriously. On the other hand someone with a personality disorder who may in the past have used a presenting complaint of having suicidal ideas as a way of controlling a situation or other people, may require a more challenging response. So much depends on the very careful history and mental state assessment. One recent study of patients who attended an A & E Department complaining of feeling suicidal (Hawley et al 1991) suggested that such presentation may primarily be a way of controlling situations or other people. However the utmost caution should be taken in the assessment of all such patients because even those who have sociopathic personalities with recurrent social crises can be at a significantly increased risk of suicide.

The use of suicide risk questionnaires

A great deal of research work has been carried out in attempting to devise inventories and formal standardised questionnaires to assist the process of assessing suicide risk. Such are the problems of specificity and sensitivity that scales of this kind can at the best be no more than a useful adjunct to routine clinical assessment. (Burk et al 1985)

References

Barraclough B M and Pallis D J (1975). Depression followed by suicide: A comparison of depressed suicides with living depressives. *Psychological Medicine, 5,* 55–61.

Burk F, Kurz A and Moller H-J (1985). Suicide Risk Scales: Do they help to predict suicidal behaviour? *European Archives of Psychiatry and Neurological Science, 235,* 153–157.

Drake R E, Gates C, Cotton P G and Whitaker A (1984). Suicide among schizophrenics. Who is at risk? *Journal of Nervous and Mental Diseases? 172,* 613–617.

Hawley C J, James D V, Birkett P L, Baldwin D S, de Ruiter M J and Priest R G (1991). Suicidal ideation as a Presenting Complaint: Associated Diagnoses and Characteristics in a Casualty Department. *British Journal of Psychiatry 159,* 232–238.

Morgan H G and Owen J (1990). *Persons at Risk of Suicide: Guidelines on Good Clinical Practice.* The Boots Company.

Morgan H G (1979). Death Wishes? *The Understanding and Management of Deliberate Self-Harm.* John Wiley, Chichester.

Morgan H G and Priest P (1991). Suicide and other Unexpected Deaths among Psychiatric Inpatients: The Bristol Confidential Inquiry. *British Journal of Psychiatry, 158,* 368–374.

Roy A (1986). Suicide in Schizophrenia. In: *Suicide* (Ed. A Roy). Williams and Wilkins, Baltimore.

Part 2

Perspectives on the Management of Suicidal Patients

6 Primary Care
Denis Pereira Gray OBE

The background

The size of the problem of suicide is shown by Department of Health (1990) statistics, which show a fall in standardised mortality ratio (SMR) for women from 100 in 1980 to 68 in 1988 but a rising SMR for men, from 100 to 110, particularly in younger men. The male/female ratio for suicide is now over 1.5:1.

Although it is often said that general practitioners see few suicides, in fact the rate is about 1 per 10,000 population, which means that bigger group practices will see one every year and most practices at least one every two years. The issue is not the number of suicides but the very much larger number of patients who are at risk, and the scale of this dreadful social tragedy. Family doctors have many patients still scarred 20 and 30 years after a suicide in the family.

The arithmetic of general practice

The arithmetic of general practice shows that, contrary to popular opinion that general practitioners have little time, they do spend a great deal of time with their patients: the challenge is to use it effectively.

General practitioners in the National Health Service have, on average, about 1900 patients and we know from the National Morbidity Survey (RCGP et al., 1990) that patients consult at the rate of 3.25 consultations each per year – at the lowest. The Department of Health (1991) in a national survey showed that the average consultation with general practitioners now lasts 8 minutes, which means that the average patient has 26 minutes a year with his/her general practitioner; thus a family of four, say 2 parents and 2 children, has an average of 104 minutes' contact each year. Given that the average duration of registration of an NHS patient with an NHS general practitioner is now 12 years, it follows that the average is 1240 minutes spent by members of that family with the doctor, or a total of over 20.8 hours.

This is the arithmetical background to British general practice and it explains why general practitioners really do get to know their patients as people.

Response to need

British general practice is also characterised by being heavily focused on medical and social need. It provides 7 consultations on average each year for patients over 75, 72% of all adult women see a general practitioner face-to-face each year, and there is increased contact with those who are most socially deprived and vulnerable (Crombie, 1984). The emotionally frail consult more often (Watts and Watts, 1952) and receive a longer period of time when they do (Westcott, 1977).

Three main groups

There are three main groups of patients who are potential risks for suicide. These are the depressives, the psychotics and those with personality disorders, especially those who have problems with alcohol consumption. This chapter concentrates only on depression, partly because it is numerically far and away the largest group and also because it may offer the greatest potential for preventing suicides.

The general practitioner approach

The academic literature poses two stark challenges to all working general practitioners: the problem of previous contact and the problem of underdiagnosis.

Previous contact

Research studies vary but it is generally agreed that about two-thirds of those who commit suicide have seen a general practitioner in the previous month and the working paper for the *Health of the Nation* on mental illness targets quotes a figure of 40% of completed suicides having seen a general practitioner within the previous week (DoH, 1992).

It is simply not known how many of those suicides could have been prevented, but it must be a very high priority to do planned, prospective general practitioner research on just that problem.

Underdiagnosis

The second problem of underdiagnosis was shown most clearly by Freeling and colleagues (1985), who suggested that London general practitioners at that time were underdiagnosing depression to the scale of about 50%. Other workers have confirmed this, although it is true that most of these studies have been undertaken by distinguished academics examining general practice where it is often under the most pressure, in the poorest premises, and with the least developed primary health care teams. It is time for more reports by those enthusiastic about this care.

In my own practice I identified during a recent 12-month period 114 patients from a list size of 1250, which amounts to 15% of all adults. This puts depression in the top three diseases in my practice population in terms of health needs' assessment. These patients have a striking female preponderance and in the middle-aged group as many as a quarter were diagnosed as depressed in a single year.

Notable characteristics of the patients, which fit previous studies were a high association with chronic disease of about 50%, 8% had cancer and 20% had a major marital problem.

A special challenge

It is of course the special challenge of being a generalist to work with both physical disease and psychological disease simultaneously; that is one of the most fascinating aspects of the job and it is also a particular challenge to unravel the complications of somatisation (Grol, 1988). In doing so general practitioners make a plea to the psychiatric community not to use the term "conspicuous morbidity", which jars on the family doctor's ears. The morbidity under discussion here is certainly not "conspicuous" in the ordinary sense of that word and it is often a considerable skill for the general practitioner to unravel it. It might indeed be almost better called the "hidden morbidity" of depression.

There seems to be a tendency to underestimate the suffering of patients who see general practitioners (Wright, 1988). In my small series of 114 patients in Exeter, 25% reported at times they felt hopeless, an additional 30% at times reported they felt life was not worth living, and an additional 20% had thoughts of suicide, although only about 5% had serious plans.

General practitioners would make another plea to psychiatrists not to refer to this group of patients as having "minor" or "neurotic" illness, as we never use the word neurotic in our discussions with patients because of its pejorative overtones. Certainly the quality of life which these patients lose is anything but minor. The implications of a fifth of these depressive patients having thoughts of suicide bears further thought, particularly in a smaller than average list. The practice patients are homogeneous so that there are over 100 patients in our average sized practice of 6,800 patients who have thoughts of suicide in any one year. It follows, since they consult at least four times a year, that there are as many as 400 consultations a year, or more than one a day, in which the doctors are assessing suicidal risk. Although it is always dangerous to extrapolate from small numbers, the implications of this finding are that there are probably as many as 1,500 patients with suicidal thoughts in a city like Exeter with a population of about 100,000.

Ten Targets

There are ten targets which could represent a plan of action for seeking to prevent suicide.

1. Recognising general practice

More needs to be done to recognise the contribution of general practice, where 95% of depression is detected and treated. Only about 5% of patients are referred to psychiatrists and it is necessary to place a much greater value on the work done in general practice than has been done in the past and also to seek to build up doctor skills in that setting.

2. Sensitivity to people and the doctor/patient relationship

General practitioners are pleased to acknowledge the contribution of Balint (1957) as a psychiatrist, who opened the door to the analysis of the doctor/patient relationship, and the profession will be eternally in his debt. Nor should we underestimate what general practitioners are already achieving. Eighty per cent of general practitioners reported that their general practitioner was "easy to talk to" and in the most strikingly favourable statistic about British general practice as many as 32% of a national random survey of general practitioners reported that their general practitioner was "something of a family friend" (Cartwright and Anderson, 1981). Jowell et al. (1990) in the annual *British Social Attitudes* showed that dissatisfaction rates now with general practitioners are running at about 12% compared with 15% for hospital admissions and 30% for hospital outpatients.

Risk factors

Much more can be done with risk factors but we must tailor them for effective use in general practice and refrain from using loose generalisations. For example, it is often said that the elderly are at risk for suicide; that is not very helpful for family doctors who may have 1000 patients aged over 65 in one medium-sized practice alone. Nor does saying "over the age of 75" help very much – many practices have over 500 such patients as well. Even saying "over-75s living alone" still means that there are over 150 patients.

Some risk factors are important markers. About two per cent of my Exeter patients have previously attempted suicide and that is a risk marker of considerable power.

What general practice is beginning to do is to identify and quantify risk factors through the new integrated computer systems to provide numeric triggers of patients needing special care.

4. Bridging research and clinical practice

Most of the definitions of what constitutes a case of depression in academic psychiatry are based on the scores the patients give to a whole variety of various research questionnaires. But most consultant psychiatrists in provincial practice and the vast majority of general practitioners in general practice do not use these instruments in their day to day work.

One of the major research priorities is therefore to find a way to build bridges between the research literature based on research questionnaires and the skills and working habits of good family doctors. It is known, for example, that the best family doctors can detect 90% of those known to have depression in ordinary consultations, without using research questionnaires. Those clinical skills must be captured – they are precious and they need to be taught more widely. In the meanwhile the work of Goldberg and colleagues (1988) is of particular importance in helping to provide for generalists a scientific basis of which questions are likely to be associated with particular psychiatric diagnoses.

5. Management

General practitioners and psychiatrists must unite in proclaiming the value of antidepressant medication. The public is very much against psychotropic drugs at present while at the same time the government is pressurising general practitioners to reduce their prescribing costs. General practitioners and psychiatrists need to stand together to support each other. If anything, it is likely that general practitioners should use more antidepressant medication rather than less and Hollyman and colleagues (1988) showed that simple tricyclic medication is effective in general practice.

6. Avoiding fashion

It is important to avoid fashions and to be appearing to dictate to each other how clinical practice should be undertaken. Of course new psychiatrists will want to use new drugs – all specialists like new techniques – but in 30 years as a family doctor, psychiatrists have recommended me to treat depressed patients with amphetamines, with benzodiazepines, and with *Drazine,* a drug which subsequently had to be withdrawn because of liver problems.

More recently the trend has been to prescribe SSRIs, but Song et al. (1993), in a large meta-analysis, has shown that the benefits even of these are "questionable". Psychiatrists need to be tolerant of general practitioners who often appear to be conservative in their prescribing habits, if only because the drug is only part of the treatment and general practitioners are committed to using the therapeutic relationship and altering environmental and social factors if they possibly can.

7. Practice organisation

There are many specific factors which may make a huge difference to quality of the care of depressives in general practice which are not always understood by those outside practice.

Personal lists (Pereira Gray, 1979) are of importance because Cartwright and Anderson (1981) showed two years later that patients were significantly more likely to consult for depression if they felt they knew their doctor well than if they did not. Similarly the issue of professional qualifications, which is of little interest outside general practice, is of importance because Cartwright and Anderson (1981) also showed that possession of the MRCGP made general practitioners more sensitive in that they considered much smaller proportions of their work trivial or inappropriate.

8. Teamwork

General practice is as committed to developing a multidisciplinary primary health care team as is psychiatry. The Department of General Practice in Exeter has a particular interest in this and both our MSc courses there are mutlidisciplinary. But in the prevention of suicide the educational top target must be the general practitioner and not, for example, the practice nurse, for four quite different reasons.

First, general practitioners see many more patients than practice nurses in general practice; in the elderly, for example, they cover 92% of the population compared with practice nurses, who see only 25% (Buxton and Pereira Gray, personal communication). Secondly, the general practitioner is needed to unravel somatisation (Wright, 1990). Thirdly the general practitioner is needed for most depressives to prescribe medication.

Lastly, in terms of duration of contact, practice nurses have a much shorter average duration of time in general practice because they move more than general practitioners, who tend to have more background knowledge of families over longer periods of time.

General practitioners therefore believe that the highest educational priority is educating general practitioners by peer teaching. General practitioners have always learned best from working models of good practice and however able or distinguished specialists may be, our experience (Pereira Gray, 1992) is that the quickest way to educate general practitioners is to give them a working model that they can copy from other general practitioners who are doing something well (Watts, 1976; Wright, 1993).

9. WHO triangle

The World Health Organisation's inverted triangle (Horder, 1983) is of strategic importance. It reminds general practitioners that their prime role is simply to support individuals and families in their homes. We have to respond to their wishes and to their needs and we have come to learn to

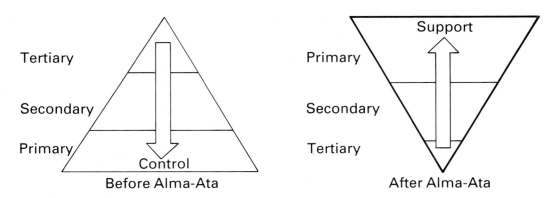

Figure 1. The relative roles of primary, secondary and tertiary care before and after the Alma-Ata Declaration. Reproduced with the permission of Professor H Vuori and the Editor of the *British Medical Journal* (Horder, 1983).

respect their autonomy and to work in partnership with them. Similarly the same triangle shows that the role of secondary care is to support primary care and to meet its wants and needs and not try to duplicate or control it.

Psychiatrists still have to learn how to respect the autonomy of primary care and how to work with general practitioners as equal partners. It is not an equal partnership yet.

10. Referral

Finally there is the issue of referral and the nature of shared care between general practitioners and psychiatrists. On the whole most general practitioners will contain the vast amount of emotional illness in the population, often including significant thoughts of suicide, without referral. When they do refer, however, they want support and they want it quickly. A response that an "urgent" appointment will be available in four weeks is common. If every British general practice can provide an urgent appointment in the surgery and even an urgent home visit on the day requested, how long will it be before secondary care provides general practitioners with the same service?

Conclusion

The *Health of the Nation* target for suicide should be endorsed and supported and it is important that the plan to reduce suicides by 15% is accepted as a serious commitment.

Research in one practice suggests that there are 100 patients in any year who have thoughts of suicide and it is a high clinical skill of general practitioners to bring those thoughts into the open, to counsel patients with them, and to support and treat them. The research priority must be to clarify these clinical skills and the natural history of depression and its management in the setting where they are mainly seen, namely general practice. It is then a second, urgent, educational priority to share the skills of good general practitioners who have found successful ways of helping these patients.

The long-term future has to be a new kind of partnership between psychiatry and general practice. It must be a partnership on equal terms. Finishing on the positive note: for the first time in British history, two medical Royal Colleges have agreed to collaborate in writing a book called *Psychiatry and General Practice* with editors from each College. This will be published as a mark of the emerging partnership early in 1994.

References

Balint M (1957) *The Doctor, His Patient and the Illness.* London, Pitman Medical.

Cartwright A and Anderson R (1981) *General Practice Revisited.* London, Tavistock Publications. Tables 14, 26, 30.

Crombie D L (1984) *Social Class and Health Status: Inequality or Difference. Occasional Paper 25.* London, Royal College of General Practitioners.

Department of Health (1990) *Health and Personal Social Services Statistics for England* . Table 1.5. London, HMSO.

Department of Health Statistical and Information Division (1991) *General Medical Practitioners Workload Survey 1989–90.* London, DoH.

Department of Health (1992) *Health of the Nation.* London, DoH.

Freeling P, Rao B M and Paykel ES (1985) Unrecognised depression in general practice. *British Medical Journal 290,* 1880–83.

Goldberg D et al. (1988) Defeating anxiety and depression in general medical settings. *British Medical Journal, 297,* 897–899.

Grol R (1988) *To Heal or to Harm. The Prevention of Somatic Fixation in General Practice.* London, Royal College of General Practitioners.

Hollyman J A, Freeling P, Paykel E S et al. (1988) Double blind placebo-controlled trial of amitriptyline among depressed patients in general practice. *Journal of the Royal College of General Practitioners 38,* 393–7.

Horder J (1983) The Alma-Ata Declaration. *British Medical Journal 286,* 191-4.

Jowell R, Witherspoon S, and Brook L (1990) *British Social Attitudes.* Aldershot, Gower.

Pereira Gray D J (1979) The key to personal care. *Journal of the Royal College of General Practitioners 29,* 666–78.

Pereira Gray D J (1992) *Forty years On – The Story of the First Forty Years of the Royal College of General Practitioners.* London, Atalink.

Royal College of General Practitioners, Office of Population Censuses and Surveys, Department of Health (1990) *Morbidity Statistics from General Practice.* London, HMSO.

Song F, Freemantle N, Sheldon T A et al. (1993) Selective serotonin reuptake inhibitors: meta-analysis of efficacy and acceptability. *British Medical Journal 306,* 683–7.

Watts C A H (1976) *Depressive Disorders in the Community,* Bristol, John Wright.

Watts C A H and Watts B (1952) *Psychiatry in General Practice.* London, J & A Churchill.

Westcott R (1977) The length of consultations in general practice. *Journal of the Royal College of General Practitioners 27,* 552–5.

Wright A F (1988) Psychological distress: outcome and consultation rates in one general practice. *Journal of the Royal College of General Practitioners 38,* 542–5.

Wright A F (1990) A study of the presentation of somatic symptoms in general practice by patients with psychiatric disturbance. *British Journal of General Practice 40,* 459–63.

Wright A F (1993) *Depression. Recognition and Management in General Practice.* London, Royal College of General Practitioners.

7 Secondary Care
Gethin Morgan, Rose Jones and Joy Wiltshire

A   In Hospital

Patients at risk of suicide may be encountered in the medical/surgical wards of the DGH, Accident and Emergency Departments, as well as in psychiatric inpatient units. Sound clinical care requires a written policy which is explicit, clearly understood by everybody, up-to-date and easily available.

Inherent in such a policy should be the belief that suicide prevention is worthwhile and feasible. It should not instil a sense of failure by suggesting that suicide can always be prevented. The main principle should be that suicide prevention is likely to follow from sound clinical assessment and management procedures, which are related to the basic principles of day-to-day practice rather than rare esoteric aspects of our clinical work. The care process follows a definite sequence.

Initial assessment and establishment of care plan

Clear procedures should be set out for the assessment of vulnerable patients as soon as they are admitted to a hospital ward: for example patients admitted following deliberate self-harm might be nursed in bed until full medical and psychiatric assessment has been carried out: and patients who are recognised as vulnerable likewise should remain in bed in pyjamas and not allowed items such as ties or braces and belts which might pose risk for them until such risk has been evaluated fully. All this may seem trivial and trite, but audit shows how desperately important it is. The admitting doctor should give a very clear indication to the nursing staff exactly what level of care is required during this admission period which is well known as a high risk time for suicide amongst inpatients. The essence of effective care is good communication.

Care Plan

Care should be based on active collaboration with the patient. The Victorian asylums were good at preventing suicide but not so good at curing people. The suicide caution card approach fell into disrepute because it gave the impression of treating the patient in an impersonal manner. As a reaction to it the open-door policy emerged, based on the premise that easy lines of communication (rather than rigid rules) and an increase in the knowledge and sensitivity of all persons who come in contact with a patient at risk, are the essentials of both therapy and prevention. Few would argue against this.

Yet it can also be said that such a philosophy is at times adopted in a *'laissez-faire'* manner: codes of practice may not be readily available or may never have been established in a psychiatric unit. Effective prevention of suicide in a hospital setting is likely to be compromised by such an approach.

An important component of any effective code of clinical practice should be the establishment of clear levels of supportive observation, matched with the degree of suicide risk which is monitored regularly. This process is

60

not equivalent to impersonal policing. It is closely analogous to care in intensive care medical wards, providing closer contact with members of staff and a working together against the terrible feelings of despair which may at times overwhelm persons with various forms of mental illness. In other words it should be an alliance between patient and staff, one which the patient welcomes and is not imposed.

There is no one mandatory way of establishing levels of supportive observation, but the principles are the same whatever the details. (Morgan and Owen 1991).

A problem arises when terms such as 'specialling' are used, words which do not have operationally specific meanings in themselves. Transfer from one unit to another may lead to dangerous ambiguity as a result.

Management problems

Table 1 Problems encountered in the Management of Suicide Risk in Hospital

Failure to gain admission

Danger times:

> Soon after admission
> Between 'Shifts' of Staff
> Leave: Patient or Staff
> Bank Holidays
> Discharge: May be Premature
> Follow-up Period

Physical hazards in hospital environment

Poor communication between staff

Lack of clear code of practice in care of suicidal

Failure to involve 'Key Others' in treatment process

Poor technique in assessing/monitoring risk

Terminal progressive alienation of patient

Problems specific to depressive illness

The hospital care of suicidal patients is beset with many problems (Table 1). These may be listed as follows:

Failure to gain admission to hospital

This is likely to become an increasing problem as bed numbers are reduced in favour of community care. It is imperative that if patients at risk are to remain in the community then a clear policy of managing suicide risk should be established and criteria which indicate admission need to be clear and unequivocal to everybody concerned.

Danger times

Any times of change in routine, such as staff change-over, extended holiday periods, the period soon after admission or after leaving hospital all signify increased hazard. Decisions to discharge a patient from hospital should not be based merely on symptomatic improvement. Unless situational/precipitating factors are dealt with effectively there is a risk of catastrophic relapse soon after the patient has returned to the community.

Faulty techniques

A clear explicit policy for the care of suicidal patients should be readily available in every inpatient facility and updated regularly. This should apply not only to levels of supportive observation, but also to the way in which risk is assessed, by whom and how frequently. The precise meaning and significance of expressed suicidal ideation can only be understood fully by placing it in the context of the overall mental state, the current situation and against the background provided by a full psychiatric history.

The various hazards in the assessment of suicide risk have already been discussed. It is particularly important to realise that many 'at risk' patients induce a fall sense of security in the staff that look after them: otherwise it is difficult to explain how so many suicides which occur in psychiatric inpatients take place in those who have been allowed to leave the ward or who have recently been discharged.

The process of terminal alienation between patient and staff is another ominous development. Failure to involve key other persons such as relatives, cohabitees and friends in the treatment process may mean that valuable potential sources of support may be ignored and indeed risk accentuated.

Clinical audit of suicide

This is an important component of good clinical practice whereby hazards and weaknesses in clinical procedures can be identified and corrected. The Health of the Nation indicates the need to develop multidisciplinary audit of unexpected deaths in psychiatric patients, including both suicides and open inquest verdicts. The most effective way to achieve this is to match coroners' data with those derived from hospital admission/discharge statistics. No audit of psychiatric services will be complete without including community mental health teams as well as inpatient units: it is in the clinical practice of community teams that new styles of multidisciplinary working together will need to be developed with imagination and sensitivity in order to co-ordinate the whole spectrum of distinctive clinical skills which should be available in such a team.

In the Community

Culverhay Community Mental Health Centre in Torbay was one of the first of its kind and opened in 1984 in preparation for the closure of a large psychiatric institution two years later. After the closure there was a growth of community teams throughout the district, but by 1989 there was growing concern in the community at the rising suicide rate and a suicide prevention conference was organised in November 1991. The aims of the conference were to increase knowledge about the management of people considered at risk of killing themselves and to provide the basis for a workable policy to reduce the risk of suicidal behaviour in the community. From the conference the Culverhay team developed a policy for assessment and to offer practical advice and clear guidelines on the management of a suicidal person.

The Culverhay Community Mental Health Centre has a multidisciplinary team of 12 WTE clinical staff including a consultant psychiatrist. It offers a walk-in facility available for people to self-refer and as a means of offering flexible treatment to those who are actually mentally ill. The Centre serves a population of 65,000 people: the main employment for the area is tourism, fishing and a large electronic factory. Because the area relies quite heavily on the tourist industry, unemployment is high in the winter months. The Centre averages about 50 referrals a month, mainly from GPs. In February 1993 there were 171 contacts through the duty crisis team. Of these 22 were at risk of a suicide attempt, two were considered to be at serious risk and one was admitted to hospital.

The Policy for suicide prevention at Culverhay was written by Rose Jones, principal clinical psychologist at the Centre. The first part deals with decision-making, first by assessment of the patient, following the guidelines described by Gethin Morgan; and, assuming the patients has been assessed as being at risk, then in collaboration with the patient about whether they are able to take responsibility for their own safety. Coming to an agreement with the patient that together we can ensure their safety may be the most difficult part of the crisis intervention. Maximising the patient's safety is something that needs to be continuously kept in mind throughout the crisis.

Having laid the foundations for working collaboratively with the patient and having gained their commitment to this approach, we can then begin to follow the suicide plan:

1   A critical aspect of helping people at risk of suicide is to form a relationship. To provide stability and continuity and to help the patient to feel it is safe to be honest about how desperate they may be feeling.

2   The patient needs to agree to daily contact: that either they will come to the CMHC or they can be visited at home by one of the team.

3   The patient needs to know how they can contact people and together we would make a list of names and numbers – their GP, Samaritans, a named friend who may be helpful.

4   Plan what the patient is going to be doing for the next 24 hours. This must be checked in a lot of detail: where they will be sleeping, who else will be around, whether there are going to be any gaps of time during which they might be more vulnerable. Perhaps any gaps of time when they might be alone, or when they might feel it's inappropriate or difficult to call somebody for help, such as the early hours of the morning. Strategies should be devised for coping with these gaps of time. Eg, the person may have plenty of people around in the evening and the morning, but if their partner works in the afternoon, and the kids are at school, so there might be a period of time – say between 2 and 4 when they are vulnerable. They need a plan to account for that piece of time – their appointment could be scheduled then, or they could arrange to go to a relative's house.

5   The next step is to begin some problem solving about difficulties that might have contributed to the current crisis. Are there any practical things the person can do themselves, or get help to do – such as arranging weekly payments on their debt if the major problem is financial. This buys some time so that the patient can start to get treatment and begin to work on their emotional difficulties, and to relieve some of the short term pressure.

6   It is important to include family and friends to support, encourage and to remain hopeful. Family and friends can also help with problem-solving, and it may be important to begin to open up communication channels between the patient and their family to overcome relationship difficulties.

7   The final part of the plan is to decide on some specific strategies for dealing with the urge to commit suicide. A "no-suicide" contract with the patient can be extremely useful as a tool to help deal with the urge to kill themselves. The contract is drawn up in the session with the mental health worker.

THE CONTRACT

The Client's Part:

1. I will attend all my appointments

2. If I get the urge to kill myself I will contact someone first and discuss it

3. If I start to feel more hopeless or depressed I will contact Culverhay

This contract cannot be changed without discussion by both parties

signed....................................
date..

The Therapist's Part:

1. I will ensure I (or another team member) am available for all appointments

2. The duty worker will see X each day (Mon–Fri)

3. X can telephone me as required (optional)

4. I will arrange admission to hospital if X no longer feels s/he can cope at home

This contract cannot be changed without discussion by both parties

signed....................................
date..

This is clearly not a legal document. Its main purpose is to facilitate communication and to give the patient something concrete to take away. Setting up the contract leaves the patient in no doubt that their concerns are being taken seriously. However it is important to know that if they start to feel worse or realise that they are not going to be able to cope, they can at any point ask for admission to hospital. The contract can be used as a final check of the patient's safety. If they are not able to sign the contract at the end of the session this is strong signal about the patient's ability to ensure their own safety and the plan may need to be reviewed. Finally the contract can be quite therapeutic at a later stage when the patient is feeling better and there can be a ritual tearing up of the contract.

After the patient has left the CMHC the mental health workers are left thinking about the intervention they have just made. Who needs to be informed of the patient's vulnerability: the GP, consultant psychiatrist, anyone the patient may need to contact. At this point the clinician should have access to peer supervision and support. A meeting with a suicidal patient can be very stressful and it is important that the clinic has a procedure so that the required steps are very clear. There also needs to be sufficient time and flexibility to allow the patient to make a plan which will maximise their feelings of self-respect and self-responsibility, while at the same time minimising the risks and ensuring the patient's safety as far as possible.

Advantages and limitations of Community Care	● A patient can use his/her coping skills to deal with stressors in a normal environment
	● Less stigmatisation
	● Less impact on self-esteem
	● Contact with family and friends is maintained
	● Patients maintain autonomy and responsibility
	● There is usually easier access to relevant family issues which can be addressed more directly.
Limitations of community care	● It may be more difficult to ensure safety as the service is a 9 – 5 Monday – Friday service. There has been considerable feedback from users of the service requesting a 24–hour accessible service which they feel would prevent hospitalisation.
	● It is more difficult to monitor physical conditions
	● It obviously involves carefully assessed risk-taking
	● Exposure to family tension or social problems may be counter-productive. For some, asylum may be the most therapeutic measure
	● Carers may be placed under undue strain which can also obviously be counter-productive.
The Management decision	1 When making the decision to manage a suicidal person at home then assessment, as we have already heard today, has to be carefully and thoroughly achieved. For example, it may be reassuring if the patient has suicidal ideas, but has not planned any definite action and is unlikely to be impulsive.
	2 An initial meeting may last for an hour, or two at the very most, and in that time the client and the worker need to build up a therapeutic alliance of some sort for a policy such as that at Culverhay to work.

3   Is there a commitment to a contract of treatment?

4   Good social support is a bonus, but does not exclude all those living alone.

5   History of impulsivity.

6   The patient needs to have alcohol and drug intake under control. Trying to undertake such a contract with someone who may be under the influence of alcohol or drugs is a big risk. Commitment is needed for individuals to take responsibility for themselves during the unsupported hours.

7   Other favourable points are that there have been no serious past attempts and also that there are no major stresses at home.

8   The patient's preference for his/or her mode of treatment is vitally important and we certainly do not advocate that community care is the only answer in every case. For some, admission to hospital may be the correct approach. But offering support at home, in our experience, can often be considered as a viable alternative to hospital admission.

9   Finally, it is important to take into account the individual's social situation, e.g housing and finances.

From the health care professional's point of view, adequate psychiatric training is essential and this has to incorporate skills in assessment and experience in dealing with the acutely mentally ill. This also has implications for post-professional training. For the team, supervision, advice and support is another very important feature as working with the suicidal can be very stressful and can raise anxiety in the professionals dealing with the suicidal person. Professionals need the opportunity to discuss the feelings evoked in them and to receive advice regarding the patient's management. If these are achieved adequately, the worker's confidence is greatly improved and this is an important factor in reassuring the patient.

It is very important with such a policy that there is sufficient time for regular and flexible treatment contacts: consistency is vitally important for the person to feel safe and secure within the home environment.

Finally, the professional must keep the team, including the G.P., carers, etc., informed of day to day changes, to ensure safety and consistency for all involved.

8 Local Authorities
Michael Kerfoot and Peter Huxley

Local Authority Social Services Departments have a clear role in the management of clients who deliberately harm themselves but, in general, have been slow to recognize and realize their potential in this area. Social workers can make a vital contribution to the psycho-social assessment of these clients, and to the planning and delivery of subsequent follow-up interventions. There is a difficulty in that this 'assessment and intervention' function is not unique to social work but overlaps with the roles of other professionals in medicine and nursing. In addition, there are organizational differences between social workers based in hospitals, and those in community settings in providing services to deliberate self-harm clients. Their priorities will be rather different as will be the demands from other parts of their workload. However, laid alongside the incomplete, vague, and unclear policy directives relating to social work with this client group, it is not surprising that Social Services Departments have tended to take a back seat.

It is also noteworthy that this client group are not generally regarded by any of the helping professions as being particularly responsive or rewarding to work with. Invariably their arrival in A and E Departments is ill-timed. In their crisis and confusion they can be hostile and abusive, withdrawn and sullenly uncooperative, or dependent and demanding. They are also difficult to engage in follow-up work once they leave the hospital. Of course this is not true of all deliberate self-harm clients but it is fairly true to the prevailing stereotype of such professional settings. Added to the reasons already outlined, this explains in part why professional social work has become peripheral to a client group which is in itself marginalized within the field of health and social care.

Although this does not present a very encouraging account of the social services perspective, it is one which is supported by findings from a recent study of social services responses to psychiatric emergencies, which was carried out by Peter Huxley and myself (Huxley and Kerfoot, 1992). For self-harm, the picture presented by the 82 authorities who responded is a poor one, and examples of good practice are the exception rather than the rule. There appear to be a few social work services available to deliberate self-harm clients but, in comparison to the London Boroughs and County Authorities, the Metropolitan Boroughs appear to have retained hospital social workers, and also have other social workers involved in work with deliberate self-harm. It is difficult to ascertain, however, whether retention of a hospital base for some social workers reflects clear policy or direction within an authority when there is so much restructuring of staff and services nationwide. The London Boroughs have fewer resources located in hospitals and rely much more on non-hospital based social workers to undertake deliberate self-harm assessments. The social services provided for deliberate self-harm clients are primarily 'daytime' services and do not extend outside of normal office hours. Out of hours, clients have to rely primarily upon the Emergency Duty Teams for intervention. Information on deliberate self-harm clients is rarely stored even though 75% of authorities say that they have either a wholly, or partly, computerized information system at their disposal.

We undertook visits to six local authorities (two counties, two metropolitan boroughs, and two London boroughs) and found that the picture presented was one of some uniformity and consistency in thinking about the problem of deliberate self-harm, but great diversity in actual practice. The major negative influences upon the development of social work services to this client group have been low staffing levels, a lack of an agreed policy between the various disciplines involved or, where a policy does exist, a failure to implement this with consistency.

In general, the input from social services departments for this client group was quite peripheral. In one sense this is not surprising when one considers the predominantly 'medical' nature of the emergency – the need for speedy and often unpleasant physical treatments, the clinical setting, the question of admission to hospital. However, it is surprising when considered alongside the volume of research-based literature supporting a psycho-social view of the behaviour (Kreitman, 1977; Morgan, 1979; Hawton and Catalan, 1987). People who deliberately harm themselves invariably do so in response to stresses within their personal relationships and social situation rather than because of mental illness. This would seem to call for professional input which reflects a social and interpersonal perspective on the behaviour as well as addressing any psychiatric concerns, but while this is recognized and acknowledged by field social workers, action is slow to follow.

Our survey of practice (which, based on six visits, can only be regarded as preliminary) identifies the initial assessment in A & E departments as the critical point for accessing social work services. A number of things can happen to a client at this point. They can be treated in the A & E department and then sent home or, the client may be detained in that department overnight for observation. If there is serious and continuing concern then the client may be admitted to a medical ward for more prolonged observation or investigation. The points of access for social work are (i) through the casualty officer who may refer to them, or (ii) through a duty psychiatrist who has been contacted by the casualty officer, or (iii) via a ward referral to the social worker covering that medical ward, where a client has been admitted. The point to be made is that each of these options requires someone other than the social worker to make a judgment, and to make a referral.

None of the authorities we visited provided direct cover to A & E departments. One metropolitan authority had a half-time post giving routine coverage to deliberate self-harm but the remainder have to rely upon a specific referral being made to them. A hospital based social work team in one of the London boroughs reckoned to receive about 50 deliberate self-harm referrals per year. In another London Borough there is at least one episode of deliberate self-harm seen every day in the A & E department, but few of these ever get to see a social worker. One of the metropolitan borough teams based in hospital is seeing about five cases per year and blames this on a combination of reduced numbers of social workers and erratic referral procedures. There was a very strong feeling on the part of most of the authorities that social work input was only requested when the patient presented awkward, threatening, or violent behaviour. Only one authority (a county) spoke with enthusiasm about its service to deliberate self-harm clients. In this instance the service was being provided from hospital by a well-qualified and resourceful nurse/therapist whose personality and drive had won her a good deal of support and co-operation from all quarters. Again, social work seemed peripheral to this service, only providing back-up when needed.

It is an inescapable conclusion that services such as these often require one individual to act as a catalyst, and to give the necessary impetus to the creation and development of the service. We know this from having created such a service for deliberate self-harm clients, within a hospital setting, where no such service existed before. Our keen, committed, and research-orientated approach, coupled with our enthusiasm, fired the goodwill and interest of others. This allowed a service to develop and gain stability, only to be thoughtlessly demolished some years later by restructuring and the relocation of social workers out of the hospital setting.

It was reassuring to find that, almost without exception, each of the local authorities we visited was concerned about its lack of service to deliberate self-harm clients. There seemed little doubt that staff believe a policy does exist although the extent to which this is a shared policy, or an agreed policy, is doubtful in view of the practices which have ensued. Certainly most of the authorities seen identified a marked disparity between policy and practice.

Previous research studies have shown that social workers can develop a clear role in services to suicidal clients (Newson-Smith and Hirsch, 1979) and can discharge this role effectively (Gibbons, Butler, Urwin, and Gibbons, 1978; Bateson, Oliver, and Goldberg, 1989). The management task need not be time consuming nor exhaustive in order to be effective, but the resources do need to be available and accessible. In many cases deliberate self-harm is a response to a particular crisis, often within the setting of more long-standing difficulties. In like manner, intervention techniques will utilize elements of the crisis in order to meet the problem. The crisis and immediate post-crisis periods are often the times when the most productive work can be achieved, but this does not negate the need in some cases for longer term psychotherapeutic interventions, if this is what the situation demands. For social work to fulfil this role would require a combination of hospital-based social work to cover the crisis period, and perhaps longer term input from a social worker in a community-based Mental Health Team. Sadly, the likelihood of either of these things happening has steadily decreased over the past decade.

It is the need for services such as these that causes us to view the advent of the new Community Care legislation with some dismay. My fear is that after April 1993 mental health social work may become synonymous solely with statutory work and, hence, unattractive to clinically oriented social workers who are used to a much more varied pattern of professional practice. The purchaser/assessor role which is envisaged for many currently employed in mental health teams is clearly a waste of expensively acquired social work intervention skills. There is already anecdotal evidence that the provision of 'assessment only' services is unrewarding, and that social workers quickly leave such posts.

Work with clients who deliberately harm themselves is often categorized under mental health social work and, like social workers in the mental health field generally, these workers will face competition for resources from other clients in the 'adult services' and 'community care' divisions of local authorities. These groups have a higher priority and already command most of the resources available. The hope of improving the local authority contribution to work with deliberate self-harm clients in such circumstances appears to be quite slim. This will not help the Department of Health achieve its Health of the Nation targets, because the social care essential to effective intervention is poorly planned and resourced, and is in the main conspicuous by its absence.

References

Bateson M, Oliver J P J, and Goldberg D P, (1989). A comparative study of the management of cases of deliberate self-harm in a District General Hospital. *British Journal of Social Work, 19,* 461–477.

Gibbons J, Butler J, Urwin P, and Gibbons J L, (1978). Evaluation of a social work service for self-poisoning patients. *British Journal of Psychiatry, 133,* 111–118.

Hawton K, and Catalan J, (1987). *Attempted Suicide: A Practical Guide to its Nature and Management (second edition).* Oxford. Oxford University Press.

Huxley P, and Kerfoot M, (1992). *Social Services Responses to Psychiatric Emergencies.* Interim and Final Reports to the Department of Health, London.

Kreitman N, (Ed.) (1977). *Parasuicide.* London, John Wiley and Sons.

Morgan H G, (1979). *Death Wishes? The Understanding and Management of Deliberate Self-Harm.* New York. John Wiley and Sons.

Newson Smith J, and Hirsch S R, (1979). A comparison of social workers and psychiatrists in evaluating parasuicide. *British Journal of Psychiatry, 134.* 335-342.

9 General Medical Services – Accident & Emergency Departments

Sonia Johnson and Graham Thornicroft

Introduction

In outlining strategies for suicide prevention in the general hospital casualty department, it is useful to consider the three groups of patients who make up the psychiatric workload of the casualty department. Firstly, deliberate self-poisoning or self-harm is one of the commonest reasons for attendance at the emergency department and is now much more frequent than thirty years ago. Hawton & Catalan (1987) describe a four-fold increase in casualty attendances following overdoses or deliberate self-harm in Oxford between 1963 and 1973, although a slight decrease in numbers has subsequently occurred.

Secondly, psychiatric morbidity is high among patients seen by casualty officers, even where their presenting complaints are ostensibly physical. For example, Bell et al (1990) found that 28 out of 120 daytime attenders with physical complaints at a central London casualty department reached 'caseness' on Goldberg's General Health Questionnaire, suggesting psychiatric morbidity, and a psychiatric diagnosis could be made for 24 of these 28 patients. Further studies by Muller et al (1967) and by Bassuk et al (1983) each survey casualty departments both in Britain and in the United States and report similar results. Indeed, Bartolucci and Drayer (1973), discussing emergency room psychiatric services in the United States, have argued that patients attend emergency rooms in crisis regardless of what other services are on offer, believing that emergency rooms provide a secure environment in which all problems will be resolved.

Thirdly the casualty department may also be the officially designated setting for the provision of psychiatric emergency services to patients with presenting problems of a more purely and overtly psychiatric type. The use of the casualty department as the main setting where patients referred for urgent psychiatric assessment are seen has become more frequent where services have moved from the psychiatric hospital into the community.

Psychiatric provision in casualty for each of these three groups varies greatly in extent, and the nature of services for each group may have important implications for suicide prevention. Those who have harmed or poisoned themselves are a clear focus for suicide prevention, and, in the last twenty years, substantial research programmes, particularly at the Barnes Unit in Oxford (Hawton and Catalan, 1987) and the Regional Poisoning Treatment Centre in Edinburgh (Kennedy 1972) have evaluated innovative services for assessment and intervention in this group of patients. This chapter will review this work. We shall argue, however, that the other elements of the casualty department's psychiatric services are also highly relevant to suicide prevention, particularly where it provides the main service for emergency assessment of patients with serious mental illness, a group at very high risk for completed suicide. There are far fewer studies of the requirements for a good emergency psychiatric service in the casualty department than of services specifically for those who have poisoned or harmed themselves.

71

In this chapter we shall describe the current central role of the casualty department in the provision of psychiatric emergency services in England and Wales, and discuss those difficulties in providing a good service in the casualty department which are identified in the literature on this subject and which have emerged from a survey we have conducted of the views of users of psychiatric emergency services throughout England and Wales.

Assessment and intervention in the casualty department in deliberate self harm and self-poisoning

It is well documented that the characteristics of those who do and who do not survive attempts to harm or poison themselves are distinct, and that many of the former group do not have a high level of suicidal intent. Whilst the incidence of parasuicide has risen, the incidence of completed suicide has fallen. However, whilst parasuicide and completed suicide should be viewed as to some degree distinct phenomena, parasuicide is a substantial risk factor for completed suicide, so that those who poison or harm themselves are a promising group for interventions aimed at suicide prevention. Hawton and Fagg (1988) studied suicide and other causes of death in a group of 1959 patients who attended the casualty department in Oxford between 1972 and 1975 following deliberate self harm or self poisoning. After a mean follow up of eight years, 2.8% had died through suicide or probable suicide, with around 1% of this group killing themselves during the year after the index attempt, 27 times the rate expected from statistics for the general population. Interestingly, death from other causes was also more frequent than the general population, with an overall death rate from natural causes 3.3 times as high as that expected from the ages of the group.

Several studies have aimed to identify helpful predictors of completed suicide after parasuicide. In Hawton and Fagg's study (1988), important risk factors for eventual suicide were advancing age (in females only), male sex, psychiatric disorder, long-term hypnotics, poor physical health, and repeated attempts. Particularly striking differences were found for incidences of detectable psychiatric disorder and of poor physical health at the index attempt. 80% of the group of eventual completed suicides had definite psychiatric disorder at the attempt time, compared with 49% of the rest of the sample, with 44% of completed suicides having had psychiatric disorder persisting for more than one year. 18% of the suicides and probable suicides were schizophrenic, as opposed to 3% of survivors. Appleby (1992) reviews work which examines in greater detail the clinical characteristics of completed suicides, and suggests that, amongst psychiatric patients in general, schizophrenia is the highest risk diagnosis, with young male schizophrenics with low mood, hopelessness and an awareness of the effects of illness being particularly at risk, whilst young male alcoholics with a short illness history, previous attempts, loss of close relationships and a history of parasuicide are at risk.

Whilst these demographic and clinical indicators have been found in a number of studies to have significant correlations with complete suicide, no single one is likely to be of very great value in clinical assessment in the casualty department, as each, taken alone, will give very large numbers of false positives and a substantial number of false negatives. Some researchers have sought to improve prediction by constructing instruments which combine a number of these indicators. Pallis et al (1982), used a discriminant function analysis of the clinical and demographic characteristics of 75 completed suicides and 146 attempts. Their results suggest that it is valuable to combine clinical information about symptoms and circumstances of the attempt with demographic information. Their combined scale, applied to a sample of 75 completed suicides and 146 attempted suicides assigned 91% of suicides and 83% of attempted suicides to the correct groups, although the retrospective form of analysis weakens the study. Clinical indicators emerging from their study as good discriminators include behavioural retardation, (more common in completed suicides), anger, fatigue, and having had a row in the previous 48 hours, (more common in the attempted suicide group). Pokorney (1983) reports a prospective study in which discrimination function analysis of a variety of clinical and demographic indicators was used to construct a scale which was applied to 4800 consecutive psychiatric admissions to a Veterans Administration Hospital. They found many items which had good correlations with subsequent suicides, but overall, the clinical usefulness of the scale was doubtful, as it produced many false positives and some missed cases.

Research into the predictors of completed suicide after parasuicide has produced interesting results, but assessment in the casualty department remains a clinical rather than a scientific task. A knowledge of these predictors of eventual suicide is indispensable in alerting the clinician as to which patients may be at high risk, but there is no single characteristic or combination of characteristics which does not give large numbers of false positives and considerable numbers of missed cases. Also, these studies largely concern long term risk, whereas the clinician in the casualty department is concerned primarily with short term risk and intervention. However, strategies for managing patients seen in the casualty department and considered to be at long term, rather than immediate risk, have been studied very little; this may be a promising area for future development of suicide prevention in the casualty department, and we will return to it below.

Assessment services

A central focus for evaluation of parasuicide has been the question of who should assess patients. The Hill Report (DHSS, 1964) advocated the establishment of poisoning treatment centres in district general hospitals to which all patients were to be referred, with assessment by a psychiatrist and a social worker. These official recommendations on psychiatric assessment for all patients were, however, widely disregarded in practice, and several studies have subsequently shown that psychiatric nurses, social workers and physicians, with training, can assess patients competently following attempted suicide. Newson-Smith and Hirsch (1979) compared the assessments of social workers and psychiatrists, and found good agreement between them, with social workers tending to be slightly more cautious that psychiatrists in their assessments of immediate suicide risk considering more frequently that admission was needed. This study also suggested that social workers made better assessments then psychiatrists of the interpersonal antecedents of parasuicide. Gardner et al (1978, 1979) compared physicians and general nurses given specific training in the assessment of parasuicide with psychiatrists, and found no significant differences in their assessments, suggesting that, with training, physicians are competent in deciding which patients need psychiatric assessment. However, limited time and negative attitudes among physicians to those who poison themselves may be an obstacle in practice to their efficacy in carrying out such assessments: Ramon et al (1975) found that such negative attitudes to patients who poison themselves are frequent among physicians, with those who are perceived as 'manipulative' rather than as suicidal being particularly stigmatised. Similarly Catalan et al (1980) compared the assessments by junior psychiatrists and by specifically trained psychiatric nurses, with the assessments being rated blind by consultant psychiatrists, and found no major differences in quality of assessment or in subsequent rate of repetition between the two groups. The evidence that professionals other than psychiatrists can carry out good assessment in the Casualty department is reflected in DHSS (1984) guidelines, superseding the Hill report.

An essential point about all these studies is that they emphasise that all professionals need special training to carry out these assessments in the casualty department, and such training is likely to be necessary for junior psychiatrists as well as for the other professionals who may be involved in assessment. The first task in assessment will be the identification of those who are at immediate risk of a further attempt and may require admission, but an adequate response will involve trying in all cases to understand the precipitants and meaning of the attempt for patients and family or friends. Hawton and Catalan (1987), describe the skills which need to be acquired to carry out such an assessment adequately. As well as history taking and mental state examination, they emphasise detailed reconstruction of the circumstances of overdose or self-harm, involvement in assessment of other family members, and careful assessment of psychological and social coping resources. An adequate training for these interventions will also involve acquiring a knowledge of all those local resources which may be helpful in the further management of the patient.

In considering future strategies for suicide prevention, it is important to ascertain how current practice in most centres relates to the findings and recommendations from model services and Government guidelines. The following table shows the findings from our survey of all District Health Authorities in England and Wales about which mental health professionals are involved in assessment of patients who present in Casualty having deliberately harmed or poisoned themselves (Johnson & Thornicroft, 1991):

Table 1   Professionals involved in psychiatric assessment of patients after deliberate self harm

Type of psychiatric professional	Sees all patients routinely	Sees some – available if referred	Rarely or never sees patients
Doctor	64 (37%)	108 (63%)	0
Nurse	12 (7%)	60 (35%)	99 (58%)
Social worker	15(9%)	88 (52%)	68 (39%)

In general, it appears that doctors remain the main professionals involved in this aspect of emergency work in most centres. However, nurses and social workers appear to be playing some part, and in a few centres they routinely review all patients who harm or poison themselves. In about half the Districts, some form of assessment by a psychiatric professional routinely occurs. In the remainder, initial screening will be the task of physicians or casualty officers, raising the question whether, in view of their high workload and negative attitudes, they are likely to be carrying out adequate assessments of all the important factors outlined above. Our study of current practices in psychiatric emergency work also raises some doubts as to how far the specific training for assessments emphasised in evaluations of model services is really likely to be generally available, as we found that 62% of district health authorities currently report that they have no specific in-service training for psychiatric emergency interventions.

Intervention

A number of reports have appeared over the past twenty years evaluating model services for intervention after parasuicide. However, their results are generally disappointing. Two central methodological problems bedevil this whole area of work. First, rates of completed suicide are very low compared with rates of parasuicide, so that numbers of patients larger than is usually feasible in a controlled clinical trial would have to be included to give rise to significant differences in suicide rate. Other parameters, such as repetition of parasuicide or effect on symptoms, are therefore used more often that suicide rate in evaluating the efficacy of interventions, which diminishes the helpfulness of these studies in considering strategies for the prevention of completed suicide. Second, what can ethically be withheld from patients who are at high risk of suicide? Those who are actively suicidal must be cared for intensively and cannot usually be included in intervention studies, and including a group for whom no intervention is provided after parasuicide may not now be considered ethical. One early study, which does not have randomised or matched control groups suggests that some psychiatric intervention, rather than no intervention, reduces both parasuicide and, possibly, suicide rates. Greer and Bagley (1971) compared a group who had, because of a failure of implementation of hospital policy, had no psychiatric assessment, with a group who had such an assessment and intervention, and found that the group without assessment had a higher rate of repeat attempts and a higher rate of suicide, though for the latter, numbers were very small and statistical significance was not reached. Kennedy (1972), in another early study without randomised control, described the work of the Regional Poisoning Treatment Centre in Edinburgh, where all patients are briefly admitted to the centre and promptly assessed by a psychiatrist, comparing the outcome of patients seen at this facility with the outcome for patients going to hospitals without such facilities and receiving generally very limited interventions, and find a decrease in further parasuicide in the group treated in the centre.

However, more recent work in which a substantial intervention is usually offered to control as well as experimental groups, has almost uniformly proved disappointing, with no significant differences between control and intervention groups being found (Hawton & Catalan, 1987, Moeller, 1989). For the ethical reasons described above, these studies have generally excluded those who require treatment for major mental illness or who are assessed as being at continuing high risk of suicide. Most of the British studies have used interventions which have been brief and problem-oriented, often recently with some cognitive component. Problems are defined, goals set, and steps needed to solve goals are outlined. Work aimed at prevention of further self-poisoning with this group has particularly emphasised open discussion of self-poisoning as a way of coping, presentation of hypothetical problems with discussion of alternative ways of coping with these problems in future, and open access to counselling services in future times of crisis. For example, Hawton et al (1981) have compared domiciliary intervention with flexible appointment times and open access to the therapist by telephone with weekly out-patient care, and found that, whilst domiciliary intervention gave better compliance and more opportunity for the inclusion in therapy of other family members, no significant difference in outcome was obtained. Gibbons et al (1978) studied the effects of a social work service with task-centred casework, and found some improvement in social problem resolution, but no difference in rates of repetition or in depressed mood. Moeller (1989) describes a study carried out in Germany, which differs from most of the British studies in using a psychodynamically based intervention, and finds that the results for the experimental group are significantly worse that those for the control group.

Some of this work does indicate that some groups may benefit more than others from experimental services of these types. Hawton et al (1987) compared a brief period of counselling in out-patients with referral for care back to general practitioners with advice on further management which might include referral by the GP on to other agencies. Again, no overall benefit was found, but for women and for patients with relationship problems the out-patient counselling did produce improvement, in terms of the proportion of psychosocial problems which seemed to have been resolved and of symptoms, a result which suggests that it may be promising to look separately at the best forms of intervention for different groups of patients, rather than trying to find a generic form of service which fits the needs of all. This is supported by Chowdhury et al (1973) who found that their experimental aftercare service with domiciliary visits and 24 hour phone contact was of significant benefit to women.

Thus resources for research and the development of innovative services have been concentrated on those parasuicide patients who do not have major mental illness and do not appear to be at immediate high risk of suicide, and, whilst many good studies have been designed and imaginative services developed, the knowledge gained from this work so far is very limited. At present it appears likely that some form of intervention for this group of patients is preferable to no intervention, but that there are no great differences in efficacy between the various interventions designed, although the question of whether particular sub-groups of patients benefit more from certain interventions remains a promising one for further exploration. It may be that, in terms of suicide prevention, the wrong group of patients is being focused on. These studies by definition exclude those at immediate high risk and also exclude those who suffer from major mental illnesses, and research on predictors of completed suicide demonstrate that major mental illness, particularly schizophrenia, is a major risk factor for schizophrenia and major depression (Thornicroft & Sartorius, 1993).

In considering the role of A & E department in suicide prevention, a new emphasis may therefore be timely on the role of the casualty department as a place of assessment and intervention for the severely mentally ill in emergency rooms. Severely mentally ill patients may present in the casualty department not only after attempted suicide, but also at any time when an acute deterioration in their mental state has occurred or when their usual support network has broken down, and at these times, they are likely to be at higher risk of suicide, and the efficacy of the casualty department in assessing and managing will be important to suicide prevention.

Casualty department as main site for emergency psychiatric assessment

In contrast with the extensive literature evaluating services for assessment and intervention in parasuicide in those without major mental illness, there has been little systematic investigation of the effectiveness of casualty departments in providing emergency psychiatric services in general. The 1960s saw some enthusiasm in the United States for the establishment of multidisciplinary crisis intervention teams based in the casualty department (Frankel et al, 1966, Spitz et al 1976, Blane et al, 1967), but otherwise casualty department services have been neglected in favour of more innovative forms of model service. Yet there is good evidence that on both sides of the Atlantic, the casualty department continues to be a major site for the emergency management of the severely mentally ill, in whom effective suicide prevention is likely to involve the provision of an effective and accessible service at times when their mental state deteriorates or their support network breaks down and they are at particularly high risk of suicide.

The emergency room's increasing use as the primary site for emergency psychiatric intervention in the USA has been repeatedly described (Hopkin, 1985, Goldfinger and Lipton, 1985, and Wellin et al, 1987). This trend may in part be related to the increasing adoption in American services of more biological models, and the accompanying tendency to seek greater integration with general medical services at a time when there seems to have been a decline in faith in the crisis intervention model. As Solomon and Gordon (1987) point out, the move to the general hospital emergency room as the primary site for the delivery of psychiatric emergency services has also been advanced by the tendency of community mental health centres to contract the local general hospital to operate the emergency part of their services, and, in the 1980s, by a general diminution in community mental health care.

The A & E department appears also still to be a central part of emergency psychiatric services in England and Wales. Our nationwide survey of psychiatric emergency provision carried out in 1991 (Johnson & Thornicroft, 1991), showed that 66% of Districts make use of the casualty department for emergency assessment of patients referred by general practitioners to the psychiatric services at night, whilst 50% use it during the day. It is striking also that during the day, many Districts are beginning to offer alternative places of assessment away from the main hospital, such as community mental health centres and day hospitals, a substantial minority use some multidisciplinary assessments, with community psychiatric nurses or social workers carrying out assessments jointly with doctors, and crisis intervention teams are available in some Districts, yet at night, almost all these community based and multidisciplinary services vanish, leaving a single duty SHO or registrar to operate an emergency service based in the casualty department, often with concurrent responsibilities to the psychiatric wards. For example, assessment services based outside hospital during office hours were reported as existing in 63% of Districts, but only one District had such a service outside office hours, whilst 26 Districts have crisis intervention teams, but only 5 of these teams operate outside office hours. Thus the casualty department service remains central to emergency provision.

From our survey, this appeared at times to be unsatisfactory to providers and to users and relatives. In a survey of the opinions of MIND and National Schizophrenia Fellowship groups about a variety of aspects of emergency service provision, casualty department services were rated as one of the poorest forms of emergency provision, with only 25% of groups rating their local service as adequate or good.

Whilst some emergency assessments are now beginning to take place in settings outside hospital, this appears to supplement rather than to replace hospital based activity. A striking feature of this work is the widespread use of A & E departments for assessments. This frequent use of the casualty department may be a by-product of its convenience after the move to the district general hospital. This appears to have taken place completely in about a third of Districts and partially in about a further third, and also a consequence of the concentration of resources on community mental health centres and sector teams, rather than on centralised services such as psychiatric emergency clinics. However, there is still some room for doubt as to the efficacy of the community mental health centre in managing the severely and acutely mentally ill, and hospital facilities are still in general use for this purpose. The adequacy of facilities for emergency assessment in hospital therefore remains an important issue for suicide prevention, particularly at night-time, when it may be uneconomical and impractical to continue to provide services on a sectorised basis (Johnson & Thornicroft, 1991).

So what are the requirements for an adequate casualty department service for the management of psychiatric emergencies, particularly in the severely mentally ill? From our own study, and from the limited literature discussing casualty department services, we suggest the following will be important:

- **Adequate supervision and specific training for staff in the Casualty department:** Our survey indicates that casualty department emergency services are likely to be staffed by a single SHO or registrar, and that specific training for emergency interventions is infrequently available. Discussing American services, Spitz (1976) emphasises that medical staff working in A & E departments are often very junior and have relatively little supervision. He describes the antagonism towards patients often found in general staff in the casualty department and the punitive attitudes towards psychiatric patients which tend to evolve. He emphasises the need for training for all staff in methods of assessment and in resources available for emergency management of psychiatric patients. Ellison et al (1989), in a review of the American literature on psychiatry in the emergency room discuss several studies which suggest that junior psychiatric staff in the emergency room are often demoralised and see this placement as a 'rip-off', in which large demands for service provision are made, with poor training and supervision. Working in an environment where many aggressive and distressed patients are seen, rapid decisions have to be made and contacts with patients are intensive but soon interrupted will create a need for good support and supervision. Poorly trained and poorly supervised junior staff are unlikely to be highly effective in assessing potentially suicidal patients.

- **Multidisciplinary teamwork:** Katschnig, Konieczna and Cooper (1991) discuss the very varied skills needed to manage the different forms of psychiatric emergency, which include acute severe deteriorations in mental state in previously well people, requiring primarily medical interventions, and crises caused by minor social stresses or breakdowns in support networks in those who are severely mentally ill, where a more psychosocial strategy will be needed. The various skills needed are unlikely always to be available from a single professional, so that an ideal casualty service should have professionals of different disciplines available.

- **Adequate setting for assessment and waiting periods:** In our survey, a frequent complaint about Casualty services was that physical facilities were not adequate. Good assessment and intervention will be impeded by a lack of quiet interview rooms free from interruptions and of secure facilities.

- **Accessibility:** Our study indicates that self referral facilities are available in only a minority of hospital services (32%), so that patients trying to refer themselves to psychiatric services will first have to be seen by casualty officers in most centres. There is some discrepancy between the priority allocated to the development of such facilities by voluntary sector groups, and that allocated in planning by Districts. It is striking that, whilst accessibility was the aspect of services most frequently perceived as a strength by the health authority respondents and was very infrequently mentioned by them as problematic, lack of self referral facilities and of clearly defined routes to care was the problem which appeared most frequently to concern voluntary groups. Some consultant respondents explicitly commented that they did not consider the absence of self referral facilities to be a weakness, and the presence of self referral facilities does have some obvious inherent problems for mental health professionals. In particular, it means that they are afforded no protection from the 'chronic crisis patients' described as often evoking disillusionment and hostility in mental health professionals. However, there does seem to be a marked consumer demand for easier access to services. Where self referral is not possible, training of casualty officers in emergency psychiatric assessments and screening for suicide risk becomes particularly important.

- **Effective screening for physical disorder will be important,** as those who go on to complete suicide have been shown to have an elevated rate of poor physical health (Hawton and Fagg, 1988, Appleby, 1992).

- **Good facilities for following up severely mentally ill seen in the casualty department:** Any substantial improvement in the success of casualty departments in suicide prevention is likely to rest on the development of assertive strategies for following up severely mentally ill patients seen in the casualty departments. At present, the main focus for assessment is the making of a decision about short term risk and whether the patient may safely be discharged. Solomon and Gordon (1986/7) describe the 'revolving door' which often develops, with a failure to engage patients in any long term care or rehabilitation. If a referral for out-patient care of some form is made, strenuous efforts are not often made to determine whether this has been taken up. Hillard et al (1983) have carried out a study of suicide in psychiatric emergency room attenders, with a mean follow up period of 3.7 years. They found that 22 of 5284 attenders had committed suicide within the state in this period, seven times the expected rate for the general population. The risk factors identified were male sex, depression, schizophrenia and multiple visits. None committed suicide immediately after their visit, but several did so without receiving any further care and without following through a referral made from the emergency room. For seriously mentally ill patients seen in the casualty department, the suicide risk will be a long-term one, and having the facility in the casualty department to arrange long term community follow up will be the most effective strategy for suicide prevention, particularly as patients using the casualty department may well not be registered with a general practitioner (Bell et al 1991).

Summary

Research work on suicide prevention in the casualty department has up to now focused principally on assessment of patients who have attempted suicide and interventions for those in this group who do not appear to have severe mental illness or to be at high immediate risk of suicide. Whilst some follow up service after parasuicide is probably more effective than none at all, none of the experimental services developed has been shown to have any very clear benefit in reducing further attempted or completed suicide, although it may be promising to explore further whether particular services have benefits for particular sub-groups of those who attempt suicide. However, a major problem in reducing suicide for services of this type is that they do not target the severely mentally ill patients most at risk of suicide. A promising direction for further research and planning may be to consider how effectively the casualty department provides emergency assessment and short and long term interventions for these patients. There may be scope for improving the efficacy of the casualty department in suicide prevention by improving staff training and supervision, multidisciplinary teamwork, accessibility of psychiatrists via the casualty department and arrangements for following up patients with psychiatric disorder discharged from the casualty department.

References

Appleby L (1992). Suicide in Psychiatric Patients: Risk and Prevention. *British Journal of Psychiatry 161*, 749–758.

Bartolucci G and Drayer C S (1973). An overview of crisis intervention in the emergency rooms of general hospitals. *American Journal of Psychiatry, 130*, 953–959.

Bassuk E L (1985). Psychiatric emergency services: can they cope as last resort facilities? *New Directions for Mental Health Services, 28*, 11–20.

Bassuk E L and Gerson S (1980). Chronic crisis patients: a discrete clinical group. *American Journal of Psychiatry, 137*, 1513–1517.

Bassuk E L, Winter R and Apsler R (1983). Cross cultural comparison of British and American psychiatric emergencies. *American Journal of Psychiatry, 140*, 180–184.

Catalan J, Marsack P, Hawton K E, Whitwell D, Fagg J and Bancroft J H J (1980). Comparison of doctors and nurses in the assessment of deliberate self-poisoning patients. *Psychological Medicine, 10*, 483–491.

Chowdhury N, Hicks R C and Kreitman N (1973). Evaluation of an aftercare service for parasuicide (attempted suicide) patients. *Social Psychiatry, 36*, 67–81.

Department of Health and Social Security (1984) The Management of deliberate self harm HN(84)25, HMSO London.

Ellison J M, Hughes D H and White K A (1989). An emergency psychiatry update. *Hospital and Community Psychiatry, 40,* 250–260.

Gerson, S. and Bassuk, E. (1980). Psychiatric emergencies: an overview. *American Journal of Psychiatry, 137,* 1–10.

Gibbons J S, Butler J, Urwin P and Gibbons J L (1978). Evaluation of a social work service for self-poisoning patients. *British Journal of Psychiatry, 133,* 111–118.

Greer S and Bagley C (1971). Effect of Psychiatric Intervention in Attempted Suicide. *British Journal of Psychiatry, 1,* 310–312.

Hawton K, Bancroft J, Catalan J, Kingston B, Stedeford A and Welch N (1981). Domicilary and out-patient treatment of self-poisoning patients by medical and non-medical staff. *Psychological Medicine, 11,* 169–177.

Hawton K and Catalan J (1987). *Attempted Suicide: A Practical Guide to its Management.* Second edition. Oxford: OUP.

Hawton K and Fagg J (1988). Suicide, and Other Causes of Death, Following Attempted Suicide. *British Journal of Psychiatry, 152,* 359–366.

Hawton K, McKeown S, Day A, Martin P, O'Connor M and Yule J (1987). Evaluation of out-patient counselling compared with General Practitioner care following overdoses. *Psychological Medicine 17,* 751–61.

Hillard J R, Ramm D, Zung W W K and Holland J M (1983). Suicide in a Psychiatric Emergency Room Population. *American Journal of Psychiatry, 140,* 459–462.

Hopkin J T (1985). Psychiatry and medicine in the emergency room. *New Directions for Mental Health Services, 28,* 47–53.

Johnson S and Thornicroft G (1991). Psychiatric Emergency Services in England and Wales. Report of study commissioned by the Department of Health.

Katschnig H and Cooper J (1991). Psychiatric emergency and crisis intervention services. In *Community Psychiatry: The Principles* (eds Bennett, D. H. and Freeman, H. L.) Edinburgh, Churchill Livingstone.

Katschnig H and Konieczna T (1990). Innovative approaches to delivery of emergency services in Europe. In *Mental Health Care Delivery* (eds I. Marks I and R. Scott) Cambridge, Cambridge University Press.

Kennedy P (1972). Efficacy of a regional poisoning treatment centre in preventing further suicidal behaviour. *British Medical Journal, 1972 iv,* 255–257.

Moeller H J (1989). Efficacy of different strategies of aftercare for patients who have attempted suicide. *Journal of the Royal Society of Medicine, 82,* 643–647.

Newson-Smith J G B, and Hirsch, S. R., (1979). A comparison of social workers and psychiatrists in evaluating parasuicide. *British Journal of Psychiatry, 134.* 335-342.

Pallis D J, Barraclough B M, Levey A B, Jenkins J S and Sainsbury P (1982). Estimating suicide risk among attempted suicides: 1. The development of new clinical scales. *British Journal of Psychiatry, 141,* 37–44.

Pokorney A D, (1983). Prediction of suicide in psychiatric patients. *Archives of General Psychiatry, 40,* 249–257.

Ramon S, Bancroft J H J, Skrimstone, A M (1975). Attitudes to self-poisoning among physicians and nurses in a general hospital. *British Journal of Psychiatry, 127,* 257–264.

Scherl E K and Schmetzer A D (1989). CMHC emergency services in the 1980s. *Community Mental Health Journal, 25,* 267–275.

Solomon P and Gordon B, (1986/7). The psychiatric emergency room and follow up services in the community, *Psychiatric Quarterly 58* 119–127.

Spitz L (1976). The evolution of a psychiatric emergency service in a medical emergency room setting. *Comprehensive Psychiatry, 1,* 99–113.

Thornicroft G and Sartorius N (1993). The course and outcome of depression in different cultures: 10 Year Follow-Up of the WHO Collaborative Study on the Assessment of Depressive Disorders *Psychological Medicine.* 1993 23, 1023–1032.

Wellin E, Slesinger D P and Hollister C D (1987). Psychiatric emergency services: evolution, adaptation and proliferation, *Social Sciences and Medicine, 24,* 475–482.

10 The Challenge of Suicide Prevention in a Local Service

Geraldine Strathdee, Ann Watts and Douglas Beaton

Introduction

This paper is written from the perspective of clinicians involved in the development of a sector community mental health service. Our response to the Health of the Nation initiative has been to set up an operational policy group to make its implementation a reality within our clinical setting. Underpinning our efforts are the cogent comments of psychiatric and public health colleagues (Appelby, 1992; Renvoize & Clayden, 1990).

Table 1

'Protective factors are under-researched but are likely to lie in the nature of psychiatric care'.

Appelby 1992

'the suicide rate might provide an objective, albeit indirect, measure of how well the local health services are meeting the needs of the mentally ill in the district, as well as suggesting a need to re-examine current organisation and resource allocation.'

Renvoize & Clayden 1990

The literature on suicide risk factors and epidemiology is fulsome, but while there appears to be a generally held view that reduction in the lethality of the commonly used methods of suicide, increased recognition and the earlier detection of the suicidal patient, including those at potential risk, the appropriate monitoring and treatment of the suicidal patient is paramount, as is public education on the subject (Pfeiffer, 1986), few of these strategies have been subjected to evaluation. Based on the hypothesis therefore, that the development of appropriately targeted, high quality services will reduce the suicide rate, our local sector service has developed a preliminary strategy which specifically addresses suicide prevention.

The local service contex

Our sector population of 47,000 is in the South Peckham, Nunhead and Forest Hill areas of South London. The service model is the decentralisation of both acute and continuing care and rehabilitation services into two sector-based teams. These are PACT (Psychiatric Assertive Outreach and Continuing Care team) and PACE (Psychiatric Acute and Crisis Intervention team). Although the two teams have their base in a community mental health centre jointly commissioned with social services, the strategy of service development is the progressive integration with the sector's ten core primary health care practices, social work team, two neighbourhood housing offices and other voluntary community agencies including the churches, user and ethnic groups.

The Health of the Nation handbook indicates that for a mental health team sector of 50,000–100,000, between 6–12 suicides will occur annually, of whom 2–5 will be among the known patients. Within our primary care colleagues, every general practice of a list size of 6000 can expect one suicide per annum.

A Five Part Plan

Table 2   Working towards suicide prevention in a local service: a five part plan

1   Identification & Assessment

2   Adequate, Accessible & Acceptable Services

3   Healthy Alliances

4   Training Strategy

5   Audit

Table 2 outlines the five components of the sector plan which form a framework for practical action. Firstly, the necessary information infra-structure and assessment procedures to provide comprehensive knowledge on individuals at risk are outlined. Secondly, the need to develop services which are most likely to directly affect the suicide rate are proposed. Thirdly, the content, range and target audiences of training strategies are defined. Fourthly, a strategy to create the healthy alliances among community agencies essential to the development of safer community care is delineated, and finally a plan of audit to review issues relating to attempted and completed suicides is proposed.

1   Information Infra-Structure and Suicide Prevention

Fundamental to the development of strategies for prevention of suicide is the identification and assessment of vulnerable individuals at risk of suicide. A number of excellent reviews of the epidemiology of suicide have been presented (Pritchard, 1992; Appelby, 1992) and these are summarised below and in Table 3. The remainder of this section provides a brief summary of methods of identification of vulnerable individuals, the development of case-registers and methods of assessment.

Table 3   Suicide risk factors

Socio-demographic factors

Male
Older-Young
Unemployed
Single/widowed/divorced

Clinical status

History of mental illness	
schizophrenia	10%
affective disorder	15%
personality disorder	15%
alcohol dependence	15%

Past suicide attempts

Recent suicide attempt

Service predictors

Onset of an acute phase
In-patient admission
1 week-3 months after discharge
Recent GP contact
Discharge against medical advice
Negative staff attitudes

Method/Other predictors

66% females take paracetamol overdoses
33% males car exhausts
Spring/early summer

Socio-demographic status	The suicide rate in men is twice that among women, and in both sexes the rate rises with age (Sainsbury, 1986; Kreitman, 1988). In recent years, suicide rates among men have risen in the UK, especially young men (Burton et al, 1990). Pritchard (1992) concludes that as there has been no increase in mental health disorders, (the most common aetiology for suicide), logic compels him to share Platt's (1984) view that unemployment is a significant factor.
Clinical status	Depression is the most common mental health disorder associated with suicide (Barraclough & Hughes, 1987; Arto et al. 1988; Wilkinson, 1982). The Health of the Nation handbook delineates the order of risk for the three other groups which carry high mortality rates.

affective disorder	15%
personality disorder	15%
alcohol dependence	15%
schizophrenia	10%

	Previous deliberate self-harm or suicidal behaviour is a constant predictor of future attempts. Weissman (1974) reports a suicide rate of 1% per annum following suicide attempts. Paerregarrd (1975) found that after 10 years, 11% of 484 attempted suicides had died by suicide, the period of risk being highest immediately after the index attempt.
Service Status	Most people who take their own lives have had contact with their doctor within weeks or even days of their death. In a study of 47 completed suicides, 16 failed suicides and 24 attempted suicides of people who jumped from a high bridge over 15 years, Cantor et al. (1989) found that one-third of all incidents occurred while the individuals were in-patients and another one-third as outpatients. Murphy (1975) likewise found that 91% of deaths by overdose and 71% of suicides by other means, had been under the care of a physician in the previous 6 months. The author's apposite conclusion was that the detection of pathology was more successful than the subsequent interventions. Patients who discharge themselves against medical advice are also at particular risk. Kreitman & Foster (1991) prescribe the use of tripartite risk scales which predict risk based on a mechanism for scoring the variables of risk described above.
The Development of a Case-register of Vulnerable Individuals	Merely identifying patients at risk is not enough. Research has demonstrated that only just over half the patients with severe mental health disorders remain in contact with the specialist services (Pantellis et al. 1988; Lee & Murray, 1988). A significant proportion of the others have the primary care team as their sole contact (Jones et al 1986; Horder, 1990; Kendrick, 1992). The ready availability of on-site personal computers has enabled the establishment of case-registers of vulnerable people in local services but it is essential to follow this with a systematic and continuing strategy to improve assist clinical care.

Table 4   The information infra-structure and suicide prevention

Identification of vulnerable individuals
Development of a case-register
Effective minimum data-set
Problem-orientated records
Assessment of suicide risk
Routine use of standardised assessments

In our sector, after seeking advice on the ethical aspects from MIND (Sayce, 1992), we have worked in close collaboration with GPs, social services, neighbourhood housing offices and police and churches to identify individuals with severe mental health disorders who are no longer in contact with the mental health team. They are then, through the agency with whom they have most contact and the best relationship, offered contact with our service and given information on a local mental health resources.

The need to develop clinical information systems which assist clinical decision-making at the individual level and rational needs-led service delivery and planning, particularly to vulnerable patient groups is increasingly recognised (Taylor, 1992; Strathdee & Thornicroft, 1992). One of the main problems for clinicians is the lack of accessible, accurate information contained in the notes. Traditionally, the focus has been on gathering information with which to make a diagnosis (Turk et al. 1988). Within the past year, the Royal College of Psychiatrists has, through the work of the research unit, created minimum data-sets linked to the establishment of clinical information systems (Lelliott et al. 1993).

Assessment of suicide risk

The frequency with which suicidal patients have had contact with their doctors in the period preceding their deaths testifies to the difficulties in assessment and prediction of suicidal risk. Several studies (Goh et al, 1989; Barraclough et al, 1974; Ovenstone & Kreitman, 1974) indicate that while patients may have indirectly communicated hopelessness or suicidal thoughts, clinicians may not act to determine and prevent intent. In a recent paper Rice et al. (1991) found a surprisingly small sample of clinician's using standardised assessment tools. The reasons are multiple: many instruments are designed for research rather than clinical work, require expensive training, do not inform clinical decision-making, are time-consuming to administer, and cannot be used as part of routine clinical practice. In their excellent and practical text *Guidelines on Good Clinical Practice,* Morgan & Owen (1990) produce exemplary clear assessment procedures, linked to individual care plans.

2   Adequate, Accessible and Acceptable Services

If, as Appelby (1992) suggests, it is the nature of psychiatric care which is likely to exert a protective influence, then it is vital that we review the adequacy, accessibility and acceptability of current services. In relation to suicide prevention, three questions arise. Firstly, which services components are most likely to target the severely mentally ill, most vulnerable to suicide risk? Secondly, which of these have clearly identified, evaluated models which can be implemented in district services? Thirdly, what form must these services take to be accessible and acceptable to service users? In this section we focus on the needs to examine provision in the five key areas of in-patient units, crisis intervention, case management and assertive outreach, primary care liaison, and special risk groups.

Table 5   *Adequate, Accessible & Acceptable Services*

Safe Hospital Services

Crisis Services

     24 hour, 7 day crisis outreach
     Continuity of care
     Experienced professionals
     Community crisis beds
     Respite beds
     Psychoeducational interventions in relapse prevention

Case Management & Assertive Outreach Services

     Integral to all district services
     Focus on Care Programme approach vulnerable groups
     Individuals at risk of admission

Primary Care Liaison

     Joint case-registers of severely ill
     Joint good practice protocols
     Primary care based outpatient clinics
     Joint audit

Special Targeting of High risk groups

     The elderly living alone
     Individuals with Co-morbidity
     Prison diversion

There is universal agreement among professional and user groups (MIND, 1983, Royal College of Psychiatrists, 1990) of the principles which should underpin community services. They should be: local, accessible, comprehensive, flexible, accountable, meet special needs, focus on strengths, empower and develop skills, consumer-orientated, normalised and incorporate natural supports. The extent to which our services operationalise these principles, either at the level of *individual* care plans or in relation to the *total* service is unknown. It is perhaps a rather untried and untested hypothesis in the days of a cash-limited health service, that, were services to be of a higher quality, less stigmatising and therefore more acceptable to patients, they would have a powerful influence on outcome. It may seem a ludicrous idea, but no more than the equally untried and untested recent push to develop a community treatment order.

In-patient Units and Suicide prevention

As indicated above, patients are often most at risk of suicide in the acute stages of their illness. Crammer (1984) and Kahne (1968) noted the importance of ward milieu, suggesting that rates of suicides were likely to be influenced by the physical design of the ward, the staff training, numbers and morale of staff and the turnover of patients and staff. Thus the busy acute general ward may fail to provide the safe environment needed. Table 6 defines some of the elements of in-patient care which need to be specifically targeted to work towards achieving a safer service.

Table 6   Safety and In-patient Units

Ward Environment

> Physical site and safety
> Activity level of the ward
> Length of stay
> Degree of dependency

Supervision Policies

> Clarity of definition and procedure
> Adequate removal of dangerous items

Staff Attitudes

> Staff-patient relationship
> Staff training

Communication

> Staff relationships
> Multi-disciplinary teamwork

Staff levels and Resources

> Staff turnover
> Staff morale
> Safety management versus budget management

Discharge planning

Maudsley In-patient Working Party, Childs & Tibbles, 1993.

Ward environment is affected by the activity levels and rate of turnover of patients. With increasingly high bed occupancy rates (Audit Commission, 1992), the length of stay is reduced, often at a time of high risk. Increasingly, only the most distressed and disturbed patients are admitted and their high level of dependency requires adequate staff for safe supervision levels. Clarity in the procedures for supervision is paramount. The potential for confusion in interpretation of what constitutes 'close', 'maximum', 'intensive supervision' requires detailed local explanation and consensus. Childs & Tibbles (1993) allude to the conflicting roles of ward managers, who have responsibility to balance need and work within a budget. Poor staff communication, sometimes as a result of conflict in staff relationships or failure of clear multi-disciplinary decision-making have been blamed for poor morale and subsequent failure to attain the safety standards necessary. With concerns over the possible added risks of community care policies, resulting in faster discharge of patients at vulnerable times in their illnesses (Morgan, 1990) the need for good communication, not just in the in-patient phase, but in discharge planning is paramount.

Crisis Intervention Services

The provision of acceptable and effective crisis intervention is regarded by service users (Rogers et al., 1993) and general practitioners (Strathdee, 1990) alike as a crucial component of an effective mental health service. Table 5 summarises some of the important elements: rapid response to the crisis, home-based assessment available, involvement of *experienced* mental health professionals 24 hours, 7 days per week and ease of involvement of social services. Increasingly, the availability of community placements as an alternative to the highly aroused, charged atmosphere of many acute wards today are being sought. Examples of the crisis houses (Bond, 1989, Turkington et al. 1991), family placements (Marx et al 1973) and respite facilities (Geiser et al, 1988) of the USA have been slow to develop in the

UK. In the previous chapter Thornicroft (1993) demonstrated that current service provision falls well short of these ideals with crisis care being delivered by experienced mental health professionals only between working hours, with casualty departments retaining an important role in crisis care.

Case Management & Assertive Outreach

The effectiveness of systems of case management in meeting the complex health and social needs of individuals with severe mental disorders has been one of the most successful themes of community care (NIMH, 1987; Thornicroft, 1991). British implementations (Muijens et al, 1990; Ogynett, 1992) demonstrate improved outcomes in parameters including patient satisfaction, social and clinical status and decrease in loss of contact with services. However, the majority of these studies lack detailed description of the specific therapeutic approaches and the nature of specific training in suicide prevention.

As indicated above, the proportion of patients who refuse or drop out of specialist care can be as high as 45%. In this group, hospital based specialists have been slow to recognise the need for outreach services. Critics fear that a community approach will inexorably lead to a focus on the 'walking well' rather than the severely ill. The evidence, however, is that where services have explicitly stated, priority target groups, assertive community care is more likelihood to meet the needs of the severely ill. Examples include; the traditional crisis intervention services, the domiciliary consultation (Sutherby et al. 1993); crisis intervention teams (Low & Pullen, 1988; Boardman et al, 1987); primary care liaison clinics (Tyrer et al 1988): primary care clinics for the homeless and mentally ill offenders (Joseph, 1990).

Primary Care Liaison

Only a minority of those individuals with mental health disorders are referred on to the specialist services by their general practitioners. The reduction in hospital based services has increased the role of the primary care team in the management of the acutely ill and those with severe difficulties at risk of suicide. General practice is no stranger to the need to care for those with long-term disorders and Wood (1990) describes the successful strategies used to improve the quality of care of those with asthma and diabetes. These include computerised, practice-based and district-wide registers linked to a recall and management system which allows self-audit; provision of essential facilities such as diabetic advice; chiropody and rapid access to laboratory and other facilities; educational packages for GPs in the care of diabetes; active involvement of practice nurses; training packages for patients linked to a national self-help group. Modifications of similar service delivery, educational and audit strategies are currently being piloted in mental health (Kendrick, 1992; Busciewicz & Strathdee, 1993). Additional local initiatives include outpatient clinics for the seriously ill in the practices; jointly developed (mental health team and primary care team) good practice protocols in the management of crisis; needs assessment in the consultation for those with severe illness; eating disorders and alcohol withdrawal; joint practice based registers of the seriously ill in the 15 main practices with which we liaise and systematic audit of agreed good practice (Strathdee & Phelan, 1993).

Special Targeting of High Risk Groups

Among the groups at high risk of suicide are the elderly in socially isolated circumstances, patients with concomitant drug and alcohol disorders and those at risk of imprisonment. It is beyond the scope of this paper to review useful strategies in each of the areas, but the rigorous approach recommended for one of these groups suggests a useful approach. A series of strategies proposed for DHAs and primary care services which have a high proportion of elderly living alone; are regular visiting by health visitors & district nurses of the elderly living alone, especially after bereavement; the encouragement of a more rational and conservative drug prescribing policy; better education of health professionals to the greater recognition of the potentially suicidal person and the prompt treatment of mental illness in the elderly; and the careful monitoring of elderly patients living alone following discharge from general and psychiatric hospitals.

3   Creating Healthy Alliances

The Health of the Nation urges us to develop healthy alliances in order to achieve our targets of suicide prevention and Table 7 identifies some of the lead agencies for such involvement.

Table 7   Healthy Alliances

Users and Carers
Primary Health Care Teams
Social Services
Neighbourhood Housing Offices

Community Groups
Voluntary Sector
Churches
Police
General Medical Services
Community Pharmacists

This concept lies at the heart of community care and is based on a number of fundamental and logical precepts. Firstly, the range of influences on the mental health of individuals has been described above and it is obvious that no single agency can hope to meet their number and complexity. Secondly, it is becoming increasingly recognised that 'community' care does not merely refer to a location but to the need for schools, businesses, churches, police and other locality services to work together to develop a sense of identity and establish a network of agencies working in partnership. Thirdly, while the conventional hospital based services may be the pathway into care (Goldberg & Huxley, 1992) for many patients, they often have a poor record in engaging special needs groups, particularly those from the ethnic minorities. Working with and through community groups may be the way to engage such individuals. Finally, recent community care legislation operationalises in law the procedures of joint assessment and intervention required to implement community care (Thornicroft et al. 1993).

Working towards healthy alliances

How then should these healthy alliances be created? Table 8 suggests a range of service planning and delivery initiatives, training and audit strategies which have been implemented in Southwark.

Table 8   The Components of a Healthy Alliance

Service Provision

Formal/Informal Liaison Sessions
Flexible, rapid response to crisis
Information Packages
Discharge Planning
Communication practices
Care Programme Approach
Support Systems/Groups

Service Planning

Active JCCPGs
Examination of the local pathways into care
Services Directory of local resources
Jointly Commissioned facilities
Good Practice Protocols

Training & Audit

Joint & Inter-agency audit

Two areas deserve special mention. Principal among those with whom we need to achieve collaborative working are our patients and their families. It is an interesting reflection of current psychiatric practice that although we work in *collaboration* with our patients, words such as *compliance* still occur in our literature, suggesting that patients obey, conform, submit. Is this really a therapeutic approach worthy of the 1990s? Several studies of the outcomes of psycho-educational interventions where patients are helped to understand and gain control over their illnesses indicate that this approach results in an improved outcome (Churchill, 1985; Greenberg et al, 1988; Gibbs et al, 1989). Communication practices between clinicians and their patients and between each other have formed the subject of much criticism (McIver, 1991). Lack of communication is often the product of lack of understanding of each others strengths, skills and weaknesses. Joint and mutual training is a powerful antidote as demonstrated in the Southwark area, where joint training initiatives between health, social services, the police and housing departments resulted in improved outcomes of knowledge, interest and understanding of each others working practices (Phelan & Strathdee, 1993).

4   Training and Education

The need for involvement of professionals, users, carers and community agencies in training has been stressed above. Training needs to encompass not only the skills of assessment and management, but also the influence of attitude on outcomes. The relationship between staff hostility and repetition of parasuicide attempts is well rehearsed. Patel (1975) showed that 44% of junior doctors and 40% of nurses were unsympathetic towards patients who take overdoses. Ramon (1980) found that hostility was more common where the attempts were thought to be manipulative. Pierce (1986) found that patients had a more favourable view of staff than staff had of themselves. A number of studies have indicated that GPs may not ask patients at risk about suicide plans or about previous suicide attempts (Murphy, 1975). Richman & Rosenbaum, (1970) noted that suicide arouses anxiety in doctors, perhaps because they lack the skills to deal with suicidal patients. In a Swiss study, Michel & Valach (1992) describe a model for the training of GPs. which we have adopted for our own staff induction pack.

Table 9   Staff Induction Pack 1993

Health of the Nation Targets
Basic Epidemiology
Suicide risk factors
Clear guidelines for suicide assessment
Role of the staff in recognising and treating suicide risk
Practical issues in management & Rx of suicidal patients

Strathdee, Beaton, Watts & Ward, 1993.

Similarly, carer and family attitudes as well as their clinical knowledge are important factors in suicide prevention (Kreitman, 1986; Murphy, 1986; Domino & Swain, 1986). Pierce (1986) found a significant association between repetition of an act of deliberate self-harm and the perception of an unsympathetic attitude within the family. One third of his sample of 100 patients believed that their family was unsympathetic to their action.

5   Audit

The death or near death of a patient is a sad and traumatic event for fellow patients and staff, as well as relatives and carers. It is important to learn constructive lessons from these tragedies. Table 10 presents a checklist of specific questions to be answered in the event of a completed suicide.

Table 10   A System of Audit & Review of Suicide

Identification of vulnerability and Assessment

Was the vulnerability/risk identified
Was this clearly recorded in the notes/a suicide risk register/or a data base
Was the information on vulnerability factors easily available & accessible in notes
Were risk and intent clearly identified
Was this communicated to all who needed to know (immediate care staff, on call staff, emergency services, GP & family

---

The management plan

Did it address immediate issues of safety and supervision
Provide clear guidelines for all professionals
Include active treatment of mental health disorder/medium term interventions
Recommendations for safe drug prescribing
Address social problems & needs
Plans for continuing assessment
Clearly define responsibilities of mental health staff, GP, carer and user

---

Communication & Interpreters

Were communications rapid & appropriate to urgency (telephone or face to face, fax, letter)
Was there access to an interpreter if required

Discharge Planning & Continuing Care

Were all necessary professionals and carers at the discharge meeting
Were facilities for outreach available
Was there 24 hour, 7 day provision for emergencies

Counselling for Relatives, Patients & Staff

Is there a policy for support and counselling fellow patients/staff/ wards
Practical steps clearly defined cf. property, contact nos. of those who need to be informed
Is bereavement counselling available for the relatives or help in obtaining it
Procedures for attending the identification of the body and the coroners' court clear with support from senior staff

---

This draws on the work developed by the Maudsley audit team and the internal audit of our sector (PACT and PACE) teams. As a performance indicator, suicide rate may be subject to annual fluctuations from year to year as has been demonstrated by the North Devon studies (Nicholson, 1992). However, as Renvoize & Clayden (1990) advocate, this may be overcome by focusing on the number of deaths occurring within the past three years, or by adopting quality control techniques such as cusum surveillance.

References

Appelby L, (1992). Suicide in psychiatric Patients: Risk & Prevention. *British Journal of Psychiatry, 161,* 749–758.

Arto M, Demeter E, Rihmer Z et al. (1988). Retrospective psychiatric assessment of 200 suicides in Budapest. *Acta Psychiatrica Scandinavica, 77,* 454–456.

Audit Commission (1992). *Lying in wait: The use of medical beds in acute hospitals.* HMSO.

Barraclough B, Bunch J, Nelson B et al (1974). A hundred cases of suicide. *British Journal of Psychiatry, 125,* 355–373.

Barraclough B and Hughes J, (1987). *Suicide: Clinical and epidemiological Studies.* Beckenham: Croom Helm.

Birchwood M, Smith J, Macmillan F, Hogg B, Prasad R, Harvey C and Bering S (1989). Predicting relapse in schizophrenia: the development and implementation of an early signs monitoring system using patients and families as observers, a preliminary investigation. *Psychological Medicine, 18,* 649–656.

Boardman J (1987). *The mental health advice centre in Lewisham. Service usage: Trends from 1978–1984. Research Report No. 3.* The National Unit for Psychiatric Research and Development, Lewisham.

Bond G, Witheridge T, Wasmer D, Dincin J et al (1989). A comparison of two crisis housing alternatives to psychiatric hospitalisation. *Hospital & Community Psychiatry, 40,* 177–183.

Burton P, Low A and Briggs A (1990). Increasing suicide among young men in England & Wales. *British Medical Journal, 300,* 1695–1697.

Buszewicz M and Strathdee G (1993). *The establishment and use of case-registers for patients with chronic psychotic illnesses in general practices.* Unpublished Research Report.

Cantor C, Hill M and McLaughlan E (1989). Suicide and Related behaviour from river bridges A Clinical perspective. *British Journal of Psychiatry, 155,* 829–835.

Childs R and Tibbles P (1993). The report of the Maudsley Suicide Working Party. *Maudsley Report.*

Churchill D N (1985). Compliance – how to measure it. *Modern Medicine Canada, 40,* 1068–1070.

Crammer J (1984). The special characteristics of in hospital inpatients. *British Journal of Psychiatry, 145,* 460–476.

Domino G and Swain B (1986). Recognition of suicide lethality and attitudes towards suicide in mental health professionals. *Omega, 16,* 301–308.

Falloon I R H, Shanahan W, Laporta M and Krekorian H A R (1990). Integrated family, general practice and mental health care in the management of schizophrenia. *Journal of the Royal Society of Medicine, 83,* 225–228.

Geiser R, Hoche L and King K (1988). Respite care for mentally ill patients and their families. *Hospital & Community Psychiatry, 39,* 291–295.

Gibbs S, George C and Walters J (1989). The benefits of prescription information leaflets (1). *British Journal of Clinical Pharmacology, 27,* 723–739.

Goh S, Salmons P and Whittington R (1989). Hospital suicides: are there preventable factors? *British Journal of Psychiatry, 154,* 247–249.

Goldberg D and Huxley P (1992). *Common mental disorders.* A bio-social model. Routledge.

Greenberg L, Fine S, Larson K et al (1988). An inter-disciplinary psychoeducational programme for schizophrenic patients and their families in an acute care setting. *Hospital and Community Psychiatry, 39,* 277–282.

Health of the Nation Handbook. (1993). Department of Health.

Horder E (1990). *Medical care in three psychiatric hostels.* Hampstead and Bloomsbury District Health Authority. Hampstead and South Barnet GP Forum and the Hampstead Department of Community Medicine.

House of Commons Health Select Committee: Community Supervision Orders, HMSO 1993.

Jones K, Robinson M and Golightly P (1986). Long-term psychiatric patients in the community. *British Journal of Psychiatry, 149,* 537–540.

Joseph P, Bridgewater J A, Ramsden S S and El Kabir D J (1990). A psychiatric clinic for the single homeless in a primary care setting in inner London. *Psychiatric Bulletin, 14,* 270–1.

Kahne M (1968). Suicides in Mental hospitals: a study of the effects of personnel & staff turnover. *Journal of Health and Social Behaviour, 9,* 255–266.

Kendrick A (1992). The shift to Community Mental Health Care: the impact on general practitioners. In Jenkins R, Field V and Young R (eds). *The Primary Care of Schizophrenia.* HMSO.

Kreitman N (1986). The clinical assessment and management of the suicidal Patient. *In Suicide* (ed A Roy). Baltimore: Williams & Wilkins.

Kreitman N (1988). Suicide, age & marital status. *Psychological Medicine, 18,* 121–128.

Kreitman and Foster (1991). The construction and selection of predictive scales with special reference to parasuicide. *British Journal of Psychiatry, 159,* 185–192.

Lee A S and Murray R M (1988). The long-term of outcome Maudsley depressives. *British Journal of Psychiatry, 153,* 741–751.

Lelliott P, Wing J et al. *Information in psychiatry: a black hole.* Proceedings of a conference.

Low C B and Pullen I (1988). Psychiatric clinics in different settings: a case register study. *British Journal of Psychiatry, 153,* 243–245.

Marx A, Test M and Stein L (1973). Extrahospital management of severe mental illness: feasibility and effects of social functioning. *Archives of General Psychiatry, 29,* 505–511.

Michel K and Valach L (1992). Suicide prevention: spreading the gospel to general practitioners. *British Journal of Psychiatry, 160,* 757–760.

McIver S (1991). *Obtaining the views of users of mental health services.* King's Fund Centre.

MIND (1983). *Common Concern.* London: MIND Publications.

Morgan H and Owen J (1990). Persons at risk of suicide. *Guidelines on good clinical practice.* Boots.

Morgan H (1992). Suicide prevention. Hazards on the fast lane to community care. *British Journal of Psychiatry, 160,* 149–153.

Muijens M, Marks I, Connolly J and Audini B (1992). Home-based care and standard hospital treatment for patients with severe mental illness: a randomised controlled trial. *British Journal of Psychiatry, 160,* 379–384.

Murphy G (1975). The physician's responsibility for suicide. 1, an error of commission; 2. Errors of omission. *Annals of Internal Medicine, 82,* 301–309.

Murphy G (1986). The physician's role in suicide prevention. *In Suicide* (ed A Roy). Baltimore: Williams & Wilkins.

National Institute of Mental Health (1987). *Towards a Model for a Comprehensive Community-based Mental Health System.* Washington DC: NIMH.

Nicholson S (1992). Suicide in North Devon: epidemic or problem of classification? *Health trends, 24,* 95–96.

Ogynett S (1992). Case management in mental health. London: Chapman & Hall.

Ovenstone I and Kreitman N (1974). Two syndromes of suicide. *British Journal of Psychiatry, 124,* 336–345.

Rice K and Donnelly P (1991). Use of rating scales by consultant psychiatrists. *Psychiatric Bulletin, 15,* 114.

Royal College of Psychiatrists (1990). *Caring for a Community: 1. The Model Mental Health Service.* London: Royal College of Psychiatrists.

Paerregaard G (1975). Suicide among attempted suicides: a 10 year follow-up. *Suicide, 5,* 140–144.

Pantellis C, Taylor J, Campbell P (1988). The South Camden schizophrenia survey. *Psychiatric Bulletin, 12,* 98–101.

Patel A (1975). Attitudes towards self poisoning. *British Medical Journal, 2,* 426–430.

Pfeiffer C (1986). Suicide prevention: current efficacy and future promise. *Annals New York Academy of Science, 487,* 341–350.

Phelan M and Strathdee (1993). Community care in practice: a training course for hostel and housing workers. *Psychiatric Bulletin,* (in press).

Pierce D (1986). Deliberate self-harm: How do patients view their treatment? *British Journal of Psychiatry, 149,* 624–626.

Platt S (1984). Unemployment and suicidal behaviour: a review of the literature. *Social Science & Medicine, 19,* 93–115.

Pritchard C (1992). Is there a link between suicide in young men and unemployment? A comparison of the UK with other European Community Countries. *British Journal of Psychiatry, 160,* 750–756.

Renvoize E and Clayden D (1990). Can the suicide rate be used as a performance indicator in mental illness? *Health Trends, 22,* 16–20.

Ramon S (1980). Attitudes of doctors and nurses to self poisoning patients. *Social Science and Medicine, 14,* 317–324.

Richman J and Rosenbaum M (1970). The family doctor and the suicidal family. *Psychiatry in Medicine, 1,* 27–35.

Rogers A, Pilgrim D and Lacey R (1993). Experiencing psychiatry: users' views of services. *MIND*.

Sainsbury P (1986). The epidemology of suicide. *Suicide* (ed. A Roy) pp 17–40. New York: Williams and Wilkins.

Sayce L (1992). *The use of case registers in psychiatry*. A MIND occasional paper: MIND publications.

Strathdee G (1990). The Delivery of Psychiatric Care. *Journal of the Royal Society of Medicine, 83,* 222–225.

Strathdee G and Thornicroft G (1992). Community sectors for needs-led mental health services. In Thornicroft G, Brewin C and Wing J. *Measuring Mental Health Needs.* Gaskell.

Strathdee G and Phelan M (1993). The Maudsley Practical Handbook Series. *A Series of Good Practice Protocols in the Management of common mental health disorders in the community.* Boots.

Thornicroft G, Ward P and James S (1993). Care management and mental health *British Medical Journal, 306,* 768–771.

Sutherby K, Srinath S and Strathdee G (1991). The Domiciliary Consultation Service: outdated anachronism or essential part of community psychiatric outreach? *Health Trends, 24,* 103–106.

Taylor J (1992). Linking psychiatric case registers to decision support systems. *Psychiatric Bulletin, 16,* 275–278.

Thornicroft G (1991). The concept of case management for long-term mental illness. *International Review of Psychiatry, 3,* 125–132.

Thornicroft G, Ward P and James S (1993). Care management and mental health. Countdown to community care series. *British Medical Journal, 306,* 422–426.

Turk J, Loza N, Kazinski J et al (1988). The Bethlem Royal & Maudsley Hospital Item Sheets – the development and reliability of an instrument for routine collection of summary clinical data. *Psychiatric Bulletin, 12,* 422–426.

Turkington D, Kingdon D and Malcolm K (1991). The use of an unstaffed flat for crisis intervention and rehabilitation. *Psychiatric Bulletin, 15,* 13–15.

Tyrer P (1985). The 'hive' system: a model for a psychiatric service. *British Journal of Psychiatry, 146,* 571–575.

Wiessman M (1974). The epidemiology of suicide attempts. *Archives of General Psychiatry, 39,* 737–746.

Wilkinson D G (1982). The Suicide rate in schizophrenia. *British Journal of psychiatry, 140,* 130–141.

Wood J (1990). A review of diabetic initiatives. *Health Trends, 22,* 39–43.

11 The Samaritans
Simon Armson

As Chief Executive of The Samaritans, I represent a movement that has given 40 years and 10 million hours of listening to those who are at the point of suicide, or whose overwhelming feelings of despair place them at serious risk of taking their own life. Last year alone, a contact was made over $2\frac{1}{2}$ million times at our 200 branches – a call every 12 seconds.

What is vital, I believe, if we are to see the incidence of suicide fall, is for there to be a partnership between all of those concerned about the care of the suicidal. There are here today, representatives of so many professions, disciplines, organisations, departments. We each provide a strand of support: each strand on its own may be fine and delicate but, when woven together, these individual strands form a strong and secure safety net with which to catch those who step off the edge of their life.

We all share common objectives. First, there is the direct provision of a service to those who are at risk of dying by suicide and secondly, there is the desire to cause a wider awareness of those feelings which may make people suicidal and the most appropriate approaches to support such people. I believe that The Samaritans has a great deal of expertise and experience to contribute towards these two objectives.

Maybe from the outset we need to acknowledge that, based on our own experience, many of those at the highest risk of suicide never come into contact in any way with any of the statutory services designed to help them. They may distrust the official services, steer clear of professionals and avoid anyone with a label to do with 'mental health' – psychiatrists, psychologists, therapists. Unfortunately, the public's perception of the professionals is not always as accurate as the members of the professions might wish it to be.

Many therefore who need support at a time of crisis turn to the voluntary organisations – to MIND, to Saneline, to ChildLine, for example, and, in particular, to us, to The Samaritans. It is good to see the role of voluntary organisations acknowledged in the Health of the Nation White Paper.

A reduction in the suicide rate is unlikely, therefore, if the sole focus of attention is directed at the established "official" services. In fact, if you look at a few of the high risk groups this point becomes plain, and it may be argued that, while I'm extremely glad of this chance to address you, the balance of these 2 days is tilted askew.

If I may offer just one example: it is estimated that only half of those suffering from a major depression receive treatment of any form. Of these, 90% are treated by their GP and only 10% are referred to further psychiatric support.

Even the most sensitive, aware and supportive General Practitioner has limited time to offer a depressed patient, and it's a rare member of the psychiatric services who is on call and available 24 hours a day, every day to anyone who wants to self refer. And yet one frequently quoted study

(Barraclough et al, 1974) found that of those who took their own life, 70% suffered some form of depression.

Table 1: Major Depression

50% of sufferers receive treatment
Of these, 90% are treated by G.P.s
10% are referred to further psychiatric support
70% of suicides suffered depression

It is perhaps important to make mention here of the debate over "mental illness" versus "mental health" and the risk involved in making the assumption that *all* those who are at risk of suicide are, *by definition*, mentally ill. This may not be the time or place to pursue these arguments, but they should at least be acknowledged.

Who *do* those at risk turn to if they positively choose to avoid "the men and women in white coats"? It is to those who are perceived to be different from a professional. So, to return to the balance of these 2 days and the 1/33 of the time that I have to represent the experience of the voluntary sector, you may appreciate the temptation I have to overrun!

I would like to be sure that everyone is fully aware of the work of The Samaritans, so forgive me if I take some time to describe the movement.

As I said at the beginning, we are approaching our 40th birthday. Our Founder picked up the phone for the first time on November 2nd 1953. We actually, though, have another equally significant anniversary which falls 4 months later. Our wise Founder discovered after a few weeks of frantic, single-handed activity, that unexpectedly and it seemed inexplicably, the numbers of those waiting to see the "expert" dwindled. He discovered that the people in crisis were talking instead to those kindly, ordinary people who had come along to help by making cups of tea or putting up shelves. And what's more, after sharing their feelings with these gentle, caring folk, the callers were going away with the burden lightened – with the valve opened on the pressure cooker of their feelings. They didn't need the "expert" after all.

So The Samaritans could be said to have truly started when Chad Varah recognised, (I would say 'discovered' or even 'invented') *befriending*, and handed the movement over to the tea-makers and shelf fitters. He realised the power of what he came to call the "listening therapy" – the great fourth therapy to add to psychiatry, psychotherapy and counselling.

T.S. Eliot has a line which captures it beautifully:–

"the luxury of an intimate disclosure to a stranger".

I don't want you to think that Samaritan volunteers are simply tea-makers; anything but. Our volunteers may be ordinary people, chosen for their qualities rather than their qualifications, but they are extraordinary ordinary people. They are carefully selected – and many people fail to be selected – for their ability to listen, actively and supportively; for their ability to communicate warmth; for seeing 'people' not problems; for caring about 'feelings' not facts; for being able just to sit there rather than wanting to so something; for being able to resist any temptation – or not even feeling it – to advise, to judge, to solve problems, to promote one idea or philosophy; they are chosen for their tolerance, their humility, their patience; and for their willingness to stand alongside someone who is teetering on the edge of the precipice of their life and to hold their hand. Also, for their willingness to be hurt by the pain of those who call them, and for their ability to be wounded but not to bleed. This selection process never stops. At any time a volunteer can be asked to leave if the quality of their befriending has slipped.

We train or prepare our prospective volunteers rigorously within national guidelines that are widely respected outside our movement. This preparation never stops either. It is a requirement of membership to attend regular ongoing training.

The ability to remain a Samaritan, despite the harrowing and emotionally draining nature of befriending, comes from our strong and secure structures of support. Samaritan volunteers work within principles and practices that govern the way we respond to callers, and include our promise of complete confidentiality, and our respect for the right of those who contact us to make their own decisions, even if that decision is to die.

We are not, therefore, a suicide prevention agency such as may be conjured up by visions of call tracing, screaming alarms, blue lights flashing through the night and pills or knives being wrestled from hands. What we know, though, is that we have been for many, many people, poised between choosing life and choosing death, the crucial factor and support that led them to come down on the side of life. In this way, we have indeed prevented many suicides.

Suicide is, of course, a universal concern and The Samaritans is also a member of Befrienders International, the worldwide organisation of those groups dedicated to developing volunteer action to prevent suicide. There are a further 100 affiliated centres in 25 other countries.

In the United Kingdom and Republic of Ireland, over 22,400 Samaritan volunteers in nearly 200 branches and groups, answer two and half million calls for help every year: half a million of these being from callers who contact us for the first time.

In terms of accumulated experience, let us take a volunteer of 15 years' standing. Typically, he or she will respond to about 200 contacts a year, of which about 100 will be from those considering or at active risk of taking their own lives. That adds up to contact with about 1,500 suicidal people in one volunteer's time as a Samaritan – even more if they are a member of a very busy branch.

This is a lot of experience and a lot of expertise and it explains why, while we may be happy to avoid the label "professional", we are equally quick to avoid the label "amateur".

People often ask me, journalists mainly, why is the suicide rate rising for such and such a group? Why are more young people taking their own lives? What is the effect of employment, recession etc. on the suicide rate? And I have to say that I don't really have the answers.

As Samaritans we see ourselves more in the role of firemen than forensic scientists. We can tell you that there is a big fire going on out there and that we will do our level best to try and put it out. We can't always tell you what started the fire – although in certain instances, overwhelming circumstantial evidence (the equivalent of a can of petrol and a box of matches), may make us fairly certain that we know at least one of the contributory causes. We also know that suicide is a complex, multi-faceted act. Any suicide has been made up of difficulties, pressures, pains, disappointments, sorrows, that combine to drag the individual down into the dark.

So that is The Samaritans in a nutshell. Does Samaritan befriending work? Well, I'd love to stand here now and claim great things. In truth, I have no real proof. We are – as you will appreciate – dealing with areas hard, if not impossible, to quantify. Even with one single individual call we're never truly certain of the outcome.

You will be aware, as we are, of the studies undertaken to assess or to try to assess the effect on the suicide rate of those centres and groups established to support the suicidal. I won't rehearse now the findings of Bagley, of Barraclough, Jennings and Moss, of Hawton and Lester and Brewer. Findings have been, admittedly, inconclusive and, to be frank, we find the whole issue as difficult as anyone else. This does not alter our knowledge that befriending does save lives.

Some research has concentrated on the comparative effect of removing the means of suicide – the coal gas/natural gas discussion, for example. Stengel, 1973, wrote: "it is often thought that if a common poison or some other method of suicide were made unavailable, the suicide rate would markedly decline. This is far from certain."

This, of course, has relevance to the whole discussion of tackling the problem of reducing the suicide rate by concentrating on removing one or two *means*. We have to look deeper to look into people's most profound motivations and sadness, to come close and touch their pain rather than so hemming them in with restrictions that they concentrate on searching for the bolt hole through which to hurtle to eternity.

Dr. Jean-Pierre Soubrier, 1978, whilst considering the effect of restriction of available means, concluded: "*But*, these precautions will be most successful if they are designed not merely to prevent the body from being fatally injured, but also to enable the soul to be comforted and understood and the unconscious mind to blossom. In that regard, befriending is a better method....."

Proof, therefore, remains elusive, the sort of proof that commands scientific respect. I used earlier the example of the petrol can at the scene of a fire being circumstantial evidence. May I offer some circumstantial evidence of my own? In doing so I realise that there may be those present who may feel that my evidence does not pass the more rigorous tests of academic research.

In the ten years from 1981 to 1991, recorded verdicts of suicide in Great Britain fell from 4,941 to 4,418: an 11% drop. In the same ten years, overall calls to The Samaritans increased by 49%. The same percentage of increase (49%) was seen in those who contacted us for the first time.

Looking now at the statistics for women. Recorded verdicts of suicide have fallen in the same ten years by 45%. Unfortunately, we don't have figures for the number of female Samaritan callers in 1981, but in the *four* years between 1987 and 1991, calls from women increased by 10%, an additional 128,000 calls.

If I could quote P. M. Darragh 1991: "It is interesting to reflect that intervention "helps-lines" such as those operated by The Samaritans are most frequently used by young women, now one of the groups with the lowest rates of completed suicide".

In the same period we see a 39% drop in recorded verdicts of suicide of those aged over 55. In one year, 1990 to 1991, there is a 9% drop. In the *same* year, first time calls from the over *60's* (note that there is a 5 year discrepancy here) increased by 34%: 10,800 more calls from people in this age group.

And finally we have seen an appalling rise in the rate of suicide among the young – the under 25's – this now seems to be beginning to go over the top of the curve. There was a 31% rise in recorded verdicts from 1981 to 1991 *but* a *drop* from 1990 to 1991. In this same year, first time calls to The Samaritans from the under 25's increased by 21%: 23,500 more calls from people in this age group. It is certainly no coincidence that these two age groups have been the focus of a major part of our work to reach out to those in high risk groups.

Returning to my question of how *do* you assess the effectiveness of the listening therapy – and it is something we regularly discuss and strive to address – may I ask you to consider briefly the difficulties. A contact with a caller may be anonymous, the caller may only ring once and you may never know the outcome of the crisis.

Yet, after 40 years of experience, we have gained the confidence to say we *know* that it works. We know this from stories told to us later: from those rare times when people *do* ring back: from those of our volunteers who turn up in preparation classes and say "I called you a few years ago and I know befriending saved my life. I'd like to become a volunteer." And we sometimes even receive Christmas cards:

> "Happy Christmas from someone whose life you saved in August. Thank you for being there."

So what contribution can The Samaritans make to helping to ensure that the suicide reduction targets in "Health of the Nation" are met? Or rather, what contribution can we make in ensuring that fewer people choose to take their own lives regardless of "targets"? Maybe I should start by making our position entirely clear. We are extremely keen to bring our experience and expertise into the partnership for the future. However, in doing so, we *will* remain totally committed to our own principles and we will never compromise these. We cannot and we *will* not agree to act as a "buck-stops-here" for everyone affected by the rationalisations of mental health policies. Our commitment to the suicidal is unwavering, which means we will not be able to offer support to those who are *not* suicidal, yet are unsupported by other services.

Also, Samaritan befriending does not always comfortably fit the boxes required of the "contract culture". While our branches rely on a degree of financial support from their local authorities; in doing so, they will not alter our fundamental practices – for example, on disclosure of confidential information – in order to meet official requirements. I think it is important that these points are understood.

What do we know helps to prevent suicide? As Samaritans, we know what helps suicidal people choose life. We know what tips that balance. It is having someone who has the time to listen – really listen – to all the confusions and ambivalence and despair and emptiness. And not only the time to listen, but the ability to be able really to hear and to create the emotional space for the safe expression of those huge jagged feelings.

It is offering complete and utter confidentiality and it is being as non-judgemental and as non-directive as can be reasonably expected (totally so for ourselves, different disciplines may have differing requirements). It is using what we call the 4 great "A"s. It is offering the *appropriate* support. It is being *acceptable* to those in crisis. It is being easily *accessible*. And it is being *available* when needed: not for just a few minutes

Wanted: Someone to operate this life support machine.

A Registered

The Samaritans

CALL US FOR INFORMATION. OUR NUMBER IS IN THE PHONEBOOK

a week – an hour's session with the "experts" – but being there every day, every night.

The Samaritans do not, of course, have a monopoly on caring for the suicidal, but our long and deep experience of supporting those in crisis gives us the confidence to continue to participate, wherever we can, in any efforts to reduce the numbers of people taking their own lives and to seek all opportunities to do so. The opportunity to form a partnership with health and social care professionals is a vital one.

To this partnership, we can bring our offer of emotional support, that is complementary to other therapies and treatment, 24 hours a day, every day of the year. We can offer information gathered in our branches and centrally to assist in research into suicide. We can offer experience and expertise in training staff and professionals at all levels in listening skills, suicide awareness, and ways of supporting those at risk.

Our own focus for the future is two-fold. First, in terms of continuing to deliver our service, and, secondly, in contributing to a wider public understanding.

The Samaritans' vision is that fewer people will take their own lives because:–

> Samaritan befriending is always available at any hour of the day or night for all those passing through personal crises and at risk of dying by suicide.

and because:–

> Samaritans provide society with a better understanding of suicide, suicidal behaviour and the value of expressing feelings that may lead to suicide.

We will continue to pursue this two-fold vision not because of a notion and a target dreamed up by a government, but because we have been committed for the last 40 years to reducing the suicide rate. We have much to contribute from this long experience in life support and from 10 million hours of listening to those considering suicide.

References

Bagley C, (1968). The evaluation of a suicide prevention scheme by an ecological method. *Social Science and Medicine,* 2 1–4.

Barraclough B M, Bunch J, Nelson B, Sainsbury P, (1974). A hundred cases of suicide: clinical aspects. *British Journal of Psychiatry,* 125, 355–373.

Barraclough B M, Jennings C and Moss J R, (1977). Suicide prevention by The Samaritans. *Lancet,* i, 237–239.

Darragh P M (1991). Epidemiology of Suicides in Northern Ireland 1984-1989. *Irish Journal of Medical Science* Vol 160 no. 11 354–356.

Lester D (1991). Do suicide prevention centres prevent suicide? *Homeostasis, 33,* No. 4.

Soubrier J P (1978) *Answers to Suicide.* London. Constable. p 158–159.

Stengel E (1973). *Suicide and Attempted Suicide.* London. Penguin Books p 42.

12 Prisons
Enda Dooley

Introduction

Death in prison, especially self-inflicted death, has caused major concern in recent years. Official concern has resulted in a number of government reports (Home Office 1984; 1986; 1990) dealing with this subject. Public and official concern has been exacerbated by the dramatic increase in prison suicides during the last few years. The increase in the rate of prison suicide has far outstripped the rise in the average daily population (ADP) which has occurred during the 1980's Table 1 illustrates graphically the rise in self-inflicted deaths compared to the rise in the Average Daily Population (ADP). After reaching a peak of 50 deaths in 1990 in both 1991 and 1992 41 people killed themselves while in prison in England and Wales. Possible reasons for this levelling off are discussed later.

Table 1

YEAR	ADP ('000)	SUICIDES	SUICIDES 10^5 ADP
1983	43.5	27	62.1
1984	43.3	27	62.4
1985	46.2	29	62.8
1986	46.7	21	45.0
1987	48.4	46	95.0
1988	49.9	37	74.1
1989	48.6	48	98.8
1990	46.9	50	106.6
1991	46.8	41	87.6
1992	45.9	41	89.3

In view of this concern and the lack of descriptive data regarding the characteristics of inmates who kill themselves the author reviewed all unnatural deaths occurring among those in prison custody in England and Wales during the years 1972 to 1987 inclusive. In addition to studying those deaths which received a coroner's verdict of suicide (Dooley 1990a) other unnatural death verdicts were also surveyed (Dooley 1990b). This resulted from discussion with prison medical officers and Home Office staff who felt that a number of deaths which were self-inflicted in prison were, for various reasons, not being recorded as suicides by coroners. The characteristics of these "consciously self-inflicted deaths" were compared to the suicides (Dooley 1990b). It is worth noting that H.M. Chief Inspector of Prisons in a report on prison suicide (Home Office 1990) has recognised this somewhat arbitary distinction and spoken of "self-inflicted deaths" rather than "suicides". A comprehensive discussion of this particular aspect of the problem is contained in a recent text on the subject of prison suicides (Liebling 1992). This paper summarises the findings of this research and, in the light of the recent report by the Chief Inspector of Prisons, comments on the implications for minimisation or prevention of death in prison.

Unnatural Death in Prison 1972–87

During the sixteen years 1972–87 inclusive a total of 442 verdicts of unnatural death were brought in by coroners on individuals dying in prison in England and Wales. Of these, 300 were classified as suicide and the remaining 142 received other verdicts indicating that death was not due to natural causes.

Prison Suicide

As mentioned above a total of 300 prison deaths during the period in question were considered to be suicides. It was possible to trace the records in 295 cases.

Five (1.7%) of the suicides were female. While this is less than the proportion of females in the prison population (c. 3%) the difference is not significant.

The mean age at death was 32.9 years and this is significantly older than the prison population mean age of 26–27 years. Thirty-one (10.3%) were under 21 years of age when they died. In terms of ethnic background the suicide group did not differ significantly from the overall prison population (based on 1987 figures). There was no evidence that suicide in prison was more common in ethnic minorities.

A significant excess of suicides occurred during the months of July-September compared to the rest of the year. It has been suggested that this may be related to either longer delays before appearing in court during the summer months, or even to the fact that this delay in combination with hot weather may make living in prison even more intolerable. The numbers on any particular day of the week did not differ significantly. Almost 50% occurred at night (i.e. between midnight and 8 a.m.) with the rest scattered evenly throughout the day.

The previous finding that suicide was much more common during the **early stages** of imprisonment was supported by this study. Over a quarter killed themselves within a month of initial reception and over 50% within three months. It should be noted, however, that almost a quarter had been in prison over a year when they killed themselves. Almost 50% of these suicides were on remand at the time of death. This was very significantly in excess of the average remand population over the period of the study which was 11% of the ADP.

In looking at those suicides who were sentenced at the time of death those serving longer sentences (over 4 years) were significantly over-represented. Over 25% of the sentenced suicides were serving a life sentence compared to a prison average of 4.4% over the period of the study. Significantly more of the sentenced suicide group had been convicted of violent or sexual offences compared to the sentenced prison population.

Some form of asphyxiation, usually hanging, was the method of death in over 90% of these deaths with small numbers dying from overdoses and other means. Almost a third had a previous psychiatric history. In addition, approximately 25% had a history of alcohol and/or drug abuse. 43% had self-injured at some time in the past and 22% had done so during the period of custody that preceded death. It was notable that previous methods of self-injury mirrored those used in the community (i.e. overdoses or wrist-cutting).

In only 16% of cases was the risk of suicide noted prior to death. While this is a concern (given the nature of custody with observation, access to staff, etc.), it should be borne in mind that motivation or desire to self-injure is not constant and may develop rapidly in a prison situation in response to various stressors and circumstances.

An attempt was made from the records and comments available tentatively to establish a motive for the suicidal act. In some cases a suicide note made clear the motivation. At the other extreme in 10% of cases there was, in spite of investigation at the time, subsequent inquest, etc. no apparent motive for the suicide.

Where a motive was attributable 40% of cases were considered due to an inability to cope with imprisonment (sentence length, regime, victimisation, etc.).

A further 15% were considered to have killed themselves due to outside pressures (family, legal, etc.).

Guilt for the offence was considered the most likely motive in 13% of cases (60% of this group had been charged or convicted of homicide and 16% had killed their spouse. 30% had committed offences with a sexual component).

In 22% of cases it was considered that suicide occurred in the context of mental disorder and that this was a direct cause of death.

Unnatural Deaths

During the period under study 142 deaths in prison received unnatural verdicts other than suicide. On further review it was considered that in 52 of these cases death had been "consciously self-inflicted" (CSI). While in many cases the method and circumstances of these 52 deaths were identical to deaths recorded as suicide elsewhere it may be that the onus on the coroner to establish proof of intent before bringing in a suicide verdict led to an open or misadventure verdict.

These 52 deaths were compared to the 295 suicide verdicts described above and were found to be similar in most respects. A number of significant differences did emerge, however, which merit comment. Significantly more of the CSI group were female, were single, died by methods other than hanging (especially fire), and had self-injured previously during the period of custody in which death occurred. Fewer were on remand compared to the suicide group. The finding among the suicide group that death occurred most commonly at night was reversed. Over 80% occurred during the day-time or evening (especially 8 a.m. to 5 p.m.). In addition, significantly more of the CSI Group had been prescribed major Tranquillisers during the month prior to death.

What conclusion may be drawn from this comparison? It would appear that in the prison context coroners are less likely to bring a suicide verdict where it can be implied that the victim hoped for intervention (deaths occurring during the daytime using less immediate methods). In addition, it would appear that a history of previous self-injury, recent psychiatric treatment, or psychotic illness may also have influenced the coroner in doubting the genuine intent or capacity to form intent. The excess of females in this group (bearing in mind that self-injury is more common in females both in prison and in the community) may also have caused coroners to doubt the genuine intent of female deaths.

Lessons for Future Prevention

The most recent report by H.M. Chief Inspector of Prisons on prison suicide (Home Office 1990) has outlined the preventive strategies employed to date by the Prison Department. These were outlined in Circular Instruction 20/1989 (and CI 52/90) dealing with Suicide Prevention. This involves identifying inmates who may be suicidal, helping them, reducing opportunities for further self-injury, and ensuring education and communication between staff. Action required by various staff following the completion of a Reception Screening form (F1996) or a Referral Form (F1997) are outlined in some detail.

There are, however, a number of difficulties with this type of risk monitoring. Suicide risk, especially in prison, is not a constant factor in most cases. It depends on a number of stressors both within and without the prison. some of these may be acute and some chronic. Using screening methods based on known risk factors will produce far more "at risk" cases than will ever attempt to commit suicide. This in turn, has the problem of diminishing the impact on staff of such risk screening. In addition, screening on observation or information will miss those cases who give very little or no indication of their intention.

While it will never be possible to prevent all prison suicides (no more than it would be possible in the community) the minimisation of prison suicide should be possible given that the current rate is approximately 5–6 times the rate for young men aged 15–34 years in the general population (Mc Clure 1987). Successful minimisation will require an examination of the effects and stresses of imprisonment together with steps to minimize these. The process of imprisonment, especially remand, is not only accompanied by loss of liberty but also loss of control over various facets of one's existence. The prison regime exacerbates this helplessness by removing any vestiges of dignity (overcrowding, slopping out, etc.) and denying the individual any responsibility for himself. The prisoner does what he is told and little else. Frequent changes of staff and location exacerbate these feelings. At a time of significant overcrowding and huge turnover (especially in remand prisons) changes in staff working patterns, particularly since 1987–88, have led to a situation in some cases where the level of staffing (and hence support and communication opportunities) has decreased.

The ability of individuals to cope with rapidly changing stresses varies. Prisons contain large numbers of people with various intellectual, educational, and psychological vulnerabilities. What is known is that when subjected to sufficient stress eventually coping ability is overwhelmed and the organism breaks down. The form of breakdown and degree of overt manifestation may vary. Eventually the stage of *helplessness* passes on to one of *hopelessness* where suicide may be seen as the only means to resolve an intolerable situation.

In a somewhat similar way the rapid increase in the prison population in the late 1980's, along with other factors outlined above, may have overwhelmed the coping ability of the Prison system as an organisation. Death in prison may have been one manifestation of this organisational breakdown. As the population has decreased somewhat over the last few years the organisation has followed in its ability to again function relatively efficiently. This thesis would appear to be supported by the drop in the number of suicides in 1991 and 1992 following the peak reached in 1990 which has lagged behind the drop in the overall prison population.

Various strategies regarding the altering of prison regimes and the need for culture change have been recommended (Home Office 1990; Smith 1991). What is apparent is that methods reliant on observation, e.g. close supervision, video monitoring, etc., are only viable in the short term, acute situation. Isolation from contact with others is only likely to exacerbate feelings of hopelessness. Experience has indicated that to tackle this sense of helplessness and ensuing hopelessness there is a need to improve dramatically communication, both internally between staff and inmates, and externally between inmates and the outside world (families, legal advisers, etc.). Internal communication requires adequate staff (regardless of discipline) to be available to inmates on a regular basis and adequate training for staff to enable them to pick up the subtle clues which may indicate the need for further intervention. Communication with the outside could be facilitated by extending the access to telephones by prisoners (with appropriate controls) and by more liberal visiting and access procedures.

References

Dooley E (1990a). Prison Suicide in England and Wales, 1972–87. *British Journal of Psychiatry*, 156, 40–45.

Dooley E (1990b) Unnatural Deaths in Prison. *British Journal of Criminology*, 30, 229–234.

Home Office (1984). *Suicide in Prison. A Report by H.M. Chief Inspector of Prisons.* London: Home Office.

Home Office (1986). *Report of the Working Group on Suicide Prevention.* London: Home Office.

Home Office (1990). *Report of a Review by H.M. Chief Inspector of Prisons for England and Wales of Suicide and Self-Harm in Prison Service Establishments in England and Wales.* London: Home Office.

Lester D (1987). Suicide and Homicide in USA Prisons, *Psychological Reports*, 61, 126.

Liebling A (1992). *Suicides in Prison.* Routledge: London.

McClure G M G (1987). Suicide in England and Wales, 1975–1984. *British Journal of Psychiatry*, 150, 309–314.

Smith R (1991). "Taken from this place and hanged by the neck..." *British Medical Journal*, 302, 64–65.

13a Recent Studies of Contacts with Services Prior to Suicide – Bristol
Christopher Vassilas

Introduction

Concern has been expressed recently in the UK over the increase in suicide rates in young adults (McClure, 1984; Lowry *et al*, 1990; Burton et al, 1990; Dunnel, 1991). The Health of the Nation (1992) has now set targets for health authorities to reduce the rates of suicide in the district for which they are responsible. Before this can be done up to date information is required on suicides and their presentation to health care professionals. Previous studies (Seager & Flood, 1965; Ovenstone & Kreitman, 1974; Barraclough *et al,* 1974; Chynoweth *et al,* 1980) have shown that a substantial proportion of suicides consult their general practitioners during the month prior to their death. As part of a wider study in Avon which examined suicides with and without psychiatric contact we looked at the contacts in the year preceeding suicide. It was hypothesised that those with no previous history of psychiatric contact and younger suicides would have fewer contacts with their general practitioner than those with a previous psychiatric history and older suicides.

Method

The County of Avon comprises the cities of Bristol and Bath, the town of Weston-Super-Mare and the surrounding countryside, the total population is 952,900.

For the 20 month period from March 1990 to October 1991 the coroner's records for the county of Avon were examined. A note was made where a verdict of suicide, open or accidental death was returned by the coroner. Summaries of all open verdicts and verdicts of death by accident or misadventure, where the death was due to the same causes as those of suicide (King, 1983), were presented to a panel of 3 consultant psychiatrists. For suicides where death was delayed following the act leading to death consultation times were calculated according to the time of act not the time of death. If a majority of the panel felt the verdict was suicide then the death was included in the study. The general practitioner responsible for the deceased was identified with the co-operation of the Avon Family Health Services Authority. General practitioners were then interviewed with a simple questionnaire concerning the patient and a search was made for the psychiatric records of all suicides. Where necessary the general hospital records were also examined. Psychiatric contact was said to have taken place when a subject had seen a psychiatrist either as an outpatient or as a psychiatric inpatient.

For each of the subjects general practitioners also provided the following data concerning an age sex matched control: dates of consultation, reason for consultation and the prescription of any medication.

Results

A total of 83 suicides were identified and 91 open deaths and deaths by misadventure. Eleven deaths (6%) occurred in non Avon residents. Sixty one of the open and accidental deaths (67%) were judged by the panel of psychiatrists as being suicides. Of the 144 subjects considered in the study two subjects had recently immigrated from abroad and were not registered with a general practitioner and two subjects were convicted prisoners. One patient had destroyed his general practice records. In the case of one patient the general practitioner refused to discuss the clinical details other than to indicate that there had been no contact in the previous year with the patient but no information on a control was obtained. In one case included in the study the general practice records had been lost but information was available through direct discussion with the general practitioner. One hundred and thirty nine subjects (96%) were thus included.

Of the 107 males and 32 females in the sample, 51 (37%) were aged under 35. 18 out of the 51 suicides under 35 years of age and 49 of the 88 who were aged 35 and over had ever had psychiatric contact (chi-square = 5.37523;df = 1;p<0.05).

Table 1 below compares the number of patients who consulted their general practitioner for any reason in the time stipulated, prior to their death. For all time periods those who were over 35 years in age were significantly more likely to have consulted their general practitioners than those under 35 years old.

Table 1 Comparison of numbers of suicides (and percentages) consulting their general practitioners before death comparing those under 35 years of age to those 35 and over.

Time prior to death	Patients under 35 years old (n = 51) consulting	Patients over 35 years old (n = 88) consulting	Chi-square df = 1
1 week	2(4)	23(26)	9.35**
4 weeks	10(20)	42(48)	10.9***
13 weeks	21(41)	58(66)	8.05**
26 weeks	28(55)	66(75)	5.07*
1 year	32(63)	67(78)	3.99*

*P<0.05;**P<0.01;
***P<0.001

Table 2 below shows that those with a history of psychiatric contact are significantly more likely to have consulted with their general practitioner for all time periods considered compared to those suicides who have no history of psychiatric contact, a similar pattern to that seen in the comparison of under 35 years and over 35 years old.

Suicides under 35 years of age were found to be more likely to have consulted their general practitioner in a given time period than did matched controls (table 3). This contrasts with those suicides over 35 years old who for each given time period were significantly more likely to have consulted their general practitioner (table 4).

The number of consultations for physical or psychological reasons in the one month before death were enumerated separately. Tables 5 and 6 show no excess of consultations for those suicides under 35 years of age when compared to controls for either psychological or physical reasons. For the suicides over 35 years of age there was only a significant difference for psychological reasons.

110

When contact with any doctor in the four weeks before death is considered then the total number of patients with a contact rises to 64 (46%).

Table 2 Comparison of numbers of suicides (and percentages) consulting their general practitioners before death comparing those with a history of psychiatric contact to those without.

Time prior to death	Patients with a history of psychiatric contact (n = 67) consulting	Patients with not history of psychiatric contact (n = 72) consulting	Chi-square df = 1
1 week	21(31)	4(6)	13.74***
4 weeks	34(51)	18(25)	15.64***
13 weeks	50(75)	29(40)	16.69***
26 weeks	58(87)	36(50)	16.60***
1 year	60(90)	41(57)	18.58***

***P<0.001

Table 3 Numbers of suicides under 35 years old consulting their general practitioner compared to matched control patients from the same practice.

Time prior to death	Consultations by matched pairs (n = 51)				Odds Ratio
	Suicide alone	Control alone	Neither	Both	
1 week	2	1	48	0	[1] NS
4 weeks	10	6	36	0	[0.45] NS
13 weeks	16	6	24	5	[0.053] NS
26 weeks	18	10	13	10	[0.19] NS
1 year	16	12	7	16	[0.57] NS

Binomial distribution used to calculate significance values as numbers too small for McNemar's chi-square.

Table 4 Number of suicides 35 years old and over consulting their general practitioner compared to matched control patients from the same practice.

Time prior to death	Consultations by matched pairs (n = 87)				Odds ratio (95% CI)	McNemars Chi square [Binomial if values too small]
	Suicide alone	Control alone	Neither	Both		
1 week	22	2	62	1	11 (2.7 to 95.9)	[***]
4 weeks	30	7	38	12	2.67 (1.27 to 6.25)	13.08**
13 weeks	32	12	17	26	2.67 (1.34 to 5.68)	8.2**
26 weeks	27	10	11	39	2.7 (1.27 to 6.25)	6.9**
1 year	22	13	6	47		1.83 NS

McNemar's chi-square; df = 1;**P<0.01;***P<0.001

Table 5 Number of consultations for suicides aged under 35 years old and those 35 and over with their general practitioner for psychological reasons compared to matched controls from the same practice.

Matched Pairs	Mean number of consultations in the 4 weeks before death (SD)	Mean of the difference (95% Confidence Interval)	Wilcoxon signed rank test
Age < 35 v	0.24 (0.76)	0 (−36 to	Z = 1 NS
Control		0.36)	
(n = 51)	0.24 (0.95)		
Age > 35 v	0.98 (1.5)	0.77 (0.42 to	Z = 4.19
Control		1.12)	P = <0.001
(n = 87)	0.16 (0.76)		

Table 6 Numbers of consultations for suicides aged under 35 years old and those 35 and over with their general practitioner for physical reasons compared to matched controls from the same practice.

Matched Pairs	Mean number of consultations in the 4 weeks before death (SD)	Mean of the difference (95% Confidence Interval)	Wilcoxon signed rank test
Age < 35 v	0.29 (0.94)	0.20 (−0.1 to 0.48)	Z = 1.1
Control (n = 51)	0.10 (0.30)		NS
Age > 35 v	0.40 (0.9)	0.16	Z = 1.35
Control (n = 87)	0.24 (0.61)	(−0.04 to 0.36)	NS

Discussion

As expected the proportion of suicides under 35 years of age in the present study (37%) is far higher than in a study conducted in Bristol 30 years ago (Seager & Flood, 1965) when 11% of the sample were under 40 years old; Barraclough *et al* (1974) found 29% of suicides in Wessex were below 45 years of age and in Ovenstone's (1973) Edinburgh sample 19% of suicides were under 35 years of age. In the present study 88% of those under 35 years old were male and it is among young males that suicide rates have increased progressively in recent years. The proportion of the overall study sample with a psychiatric history on the other hand is similar to the older studies (about 50%). In the present series as a whole those suicides with a psychiatric history were twice more likely than others to consult their general practitioners.

The proportion of suicides (36%) in contact with their general practitioners in the four weeks prior to death is on the low side in comparison with older studies (39% to 69%). Looking closely at subgroups it can be seen that only a small proportion of those under 35 years of age had contacted their general practitioners. Although the present study did not use the full method of 'psychological autopsy' many of the suicides in young males appeared to be of an impulsive nature, a finding confirmed elsewhere (Hoberman & Garfinkel, 1988). Clearly educational campaigns aimed at general practitioners such as the one used in Sweden with such apparent efficacy (Rutz *et al*, 1992) are important. For those with no psychiatric contact and who are under 35 years of age other strategies must be found. Perhaps one way forward lies in the campaign against depression jointly launched by the Royal College of General Practitioners and the Royal College of Psychiatrists (Paykel & Priest, 1992). One of the aims of which is to reduce the stigma which is still attached to mental illness. Hawton (1992) has recently called for a full study of a series of suicides utilising the laborious and time-consuming 'psychological autopsy' method last used in the United Kingdom nearly 20 years ago (Barraclough, 1974) in an attempt to highlight the factors associated with suicide in this group.

References

Barraclough B, Bunch J, Nelson B, Sainsbury P. A hundred cases of suicide: clinical aspects. *British Journal of Psychiatry* 1974; 125: 355–73

Burton P, Lowry A, Briggs A. Increasing deaths among young men in England and Wales. *British Medical Journal* 1990; 300: 1695–6.

Chynoweth R, Tonge J L, Armstrong J. Suicide in Brisbane-a retrospective psycosocial study. *Australian and New Zealand Journal of Psychiatry* 1980; 14: 37–45.

Dunnel K. Deaths among 15–44 year olds. *Population Trends* 1991; 64: 38–43.

Hawton K. By their own hand. *BMJ* 1992; 304: 1000.

Hoberman H M and Garfinkel B D. Completed suicide in youth. *Canadian Journal of Psychiatry* 1988; 33: 494–502.

King E. Identifying out-patients and ex-patients who have died suddenly. *Bulletin of the Royal College of Psychiatrists* 1983; 7: 4–7.

Lowry A, Burton P, Briggs A. Increasing suicide rates in young adults. *British Medical Journal* 1990; 300: 64.

McClure GMG. Trends in suicide rate for England and Wales 1975–80. *British Journal of Psychiatry* 1984; 144: 119–126.

Ovenstone IMK. A psychiatric approach to the diagnosis of suicide, and its effect upon the Edinburgh statistics. *British Journal of Psychiatry*, 1973; 123: 15–21.

Ovenstone IMK, Kreitman N. Two syndromes of suicide. *British Journal of Psychiatry* 1974; 124: 336–45.

Paykel ES, Priest RG. Recognition and management of depression in general practice: consensus statement. *British Medical Journal* 1992; 305: 1198–202.

Rutz W, Von Knorring L, Walinder J. Long term effect of an educational program for general practitioners given by the Swedish Committee for the Prevention and Treatment of Depression. *Acta Psychiatrica Scandinavica* 1992; 85: 83–8.

13b   Recent Studies of Contacts with Services Prior to Suicide – Somerset

David Gunnell

Introduction

Local information on trends in suicide rates, the characteristics of those committing suicide and their patterns of contact with health services are of value when planning appropriate health promotion programmes for mental health. Of equal importance this information may be used both in professional educational programmes and as a baseline against which to evaluate the success of any such programmes. This study was undertaken by Somerset Health Authority's Public Health Medicine Department. The aims of the study were to examine trends in suicide and parasuicide in the district, to review in detail the characteristics and consultation patterns of those committing suicide between August 1990 and July 1992 and to seek explanations for Somerset's slightly raised standardised mortality ratio (SMR) for suicide. The findings from the study are currently being used in discussion with local health professionals to inform local decision making and target setting in response to the Government Health of the Nation White Paper (HMSO 1992).

Methods

Adelstein and Mardon recommend that for statistical purposes and to obtain a true picture of the rate of suicide it is necessary to add open verdicts (ICD E980–989) and accidental poisonings (ICD E850–859) to the officially classified suicide figures (ICD E950–959) (Adelstein and Mardon 1975). For the purposes of this study deaths from accidental poisoning were excluded, there having been only 19 such deaths in the last sixteen years in Somerset.

Trends in rates of suicide in males and females at different ages were calculated using VS3 returns from the Office of Population Censuses and Surveys (OPCS). More detailed analysis of all suicides among Somerset residents in the 24 month period August 1990–July 1992 was undertaken by inspection of coroner's records for those deaths which occurred within their jurisdiction and by examination of the deceased's GP held medical records. Information obtained from the inquest and medical record inspection was recorded on a structured enquiry form and analysed using d base 3+ and Epi-Info. Suicides occurring in the time period were identified from death certificates for Somerset residents returned routinely to the Health Authority by registrars of births and deaths. As a group of age and sex matched controls was not available against whom to compare consultation patterns, data from the general household survey 1989 (HMSO 1989) was used as a proxy for this. Unemployment figures for the South Western Region as a whole were used as a continuous unadjusted series of unemployment figures does not exist for the County of Somerset.

Results

Population Based Data

The mean annual number of suicides in Somerset for the years 1981–1991 was 49 (range 37–65 per year, ICD E850 to E859, E980 to E989). The age distribution of those committing suicide between 1981 and 1991 is given in Figure 1. Peak numbers of suicides occur for men in the 35–44 age group and for women aged between 55 and 74 years. The five year standardised mortality ratio for Somerset (1987–1991) was 110 for males and 85 for females. After a slight decline in the early 1980's, there has been a sharp increase in the rate of suicide amongst males aged 15–44 since 1986 (p < 0.001, Figure 2).

Figure 1   Suicide: Age Distribution

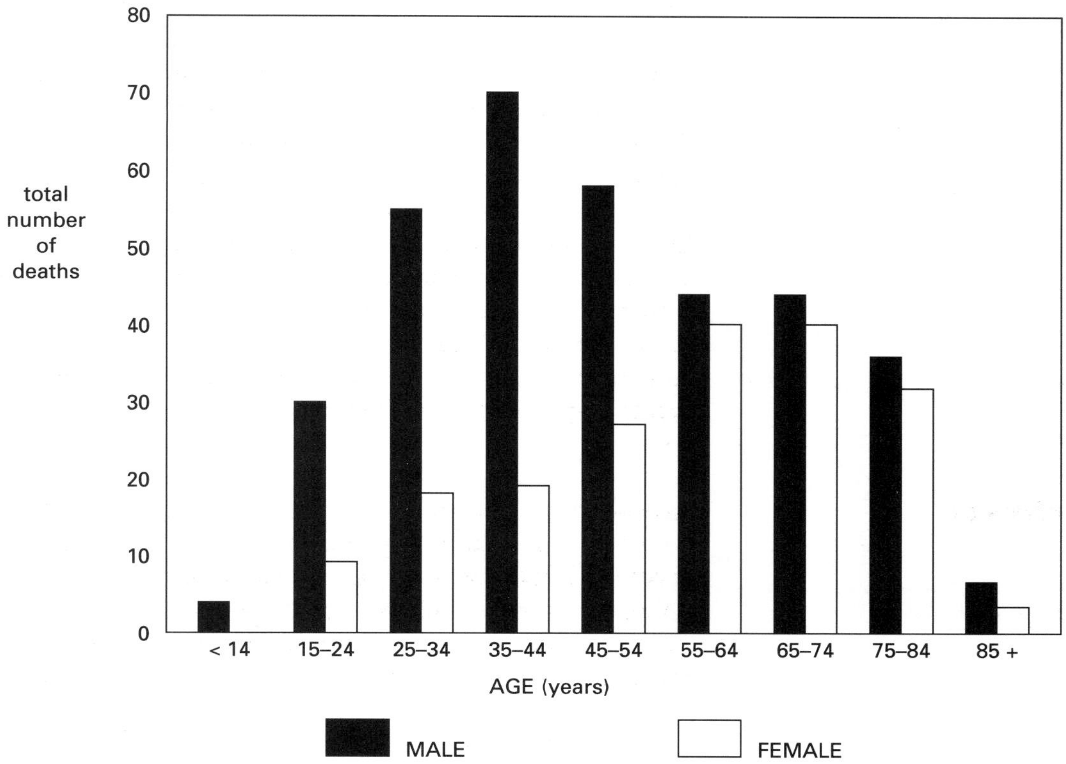

Somerset Health District 1981–91.

Unemployment may be seen as a time lagged indicator of economic recession. The correlation between South Western Regional male unemployment figures and rates of suicide amongst those of working age (ie those aged 15–65) in the year prior to the unemployment figures was assessed (Figure 3). During this time period unemployment rates rose and fell. The correlation found at local level was 0.63 (95% confidence intervals 0.41–0.85) Figure 3.

Case Note Study

Details on 101 suicides occurring between August 1990 and July 1992 were obtained from death certificate returns to the Health Authority. 85 of these were given verdicts of suicide and 16 open verdicts by Coroner's Courts. It was not possible to ascertain the completeness of the 1992 data although it is known by reference to Coroner's records that none of the suicides occurring in Somerset was missed, although some occurring elsewhere may have

Figure 2   15–44 year old male suicide
Somerset: 1980–91

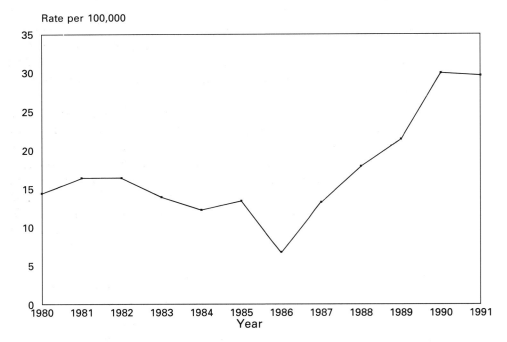

Chi sq. test for trend post 1986 p < 0.001.

Figure 3   Suicide & Unemployment
Somerset: 1976–92

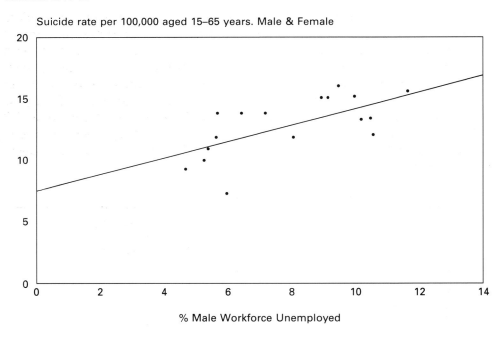

S.W. Region Unemployment, 1 yr. time lag.

r=0.63
95% CI 0.41 to 0.85

been. Reference to OPCS mortality data suggests details of four Somerset residents committing suicide in 1990/1991 were not retreived. GP held medical records were available for 86 (85% of these deaths). Eight of those dying by suicide were not registered with Somerset GPs and their medical records were thus still held at the Family Health Services Authority in their previous district of residence. Inquest reports were available for 77 (76%) of deaths. 14 deaths occurred outside the district and 10 Coroner's reports were not found for local deaths.

In the 24 month study period there were 82 male suicides and 19 female suicides. The mean age of male suicide was 43 (range 18–87) and that for females 52 (range 21–90) years. 49% of those committing suicide were males aged less than 45 years. Table 1 summarises findings from the records relating to previous parasuicide, history of alcohol dependence and psychotropic medication. These figures are broken down for both the whole sample, where the information was available, and for males aged 15–44. Of those under recent psychiatric care (within 1 yr) 12 of 24 (50%) were taking antidepressant medication.

Table 1   Findings from review of Case Notes and Coroners Records

	All ages	15–44 yr male
History of previous parasuicide	34 (37% n=93)	16 (37% n=43)
History of alcohol dependence	18 (25% n=72)	7 (24% n=34)
Psychotropic drug prescribed*	32 (34% n=94)	9 (20% n=45)
Antidepressant prescribed **	19 (20% n=94)	2 (4% n=45)

*   c f Barraclough B et al. A Hundred Cases of Suicide: Clinical Aspects. Br. J. Psych 1974: 125: 355–73. 80% of this sample were taking prescribed psycotropic medication.

**   Of those under recent (within 1 yr) or current psychiatric care 12 of 24 (50%) were taking antidepressants.

Previous and current (last twelve months) contact with psychiatric services was also examined. Information on psychiatric history was available for 92 of those committing suicide. 44 (48%) had never had contact with psychiatric services, 24 (26%) had had past contact and 24 (26%) were either in current contact with psychiatric services or had been in contact in the twelve months prior to their suicide. Comparable figures for 15–44 year old males were 29 (67%) with no contact, 7 (16%) had past contact and 7 (16%) were in current contact. 95% of women committing suicide but only 42% of males committing suicides had a history of past or present psychiatric contact.

Table 2   Time since last contact with health care professional

	All ages* (n=92) cumulative %	15–44 yr males (n=42) cumulative %
(1) Same day	5.4%	2.4%
(2) Within 1 week	25.0%	14.3%
(3) Within 1 month	41.3%	38.1%
(4) Within 3 months	59.8%	59.5%
(5) Within 6 months	72.8%	76.2%
(6) Within 1 year	85.9%	88.1%

*   c f Barraclough B.   :   48% 1 week   p < 0.05
    Br. J. Psych 1974;   69% 1 month   p < 0.001
    125: 355–73.   83% 3 months p < 0.0002
                          93% 1 year   NS

Table 2 summarises the time since last contact with a health care professional (either general practitioner, psychiatrist or member of psychiatric team). Overall approximately 40% of those committing suicide consult or are seen within one month of their death and 60% within three months of death. Comparison is made with figures of the work of Barraclough et al, and significant differences are found between the proportion of the sample consulting at one week (p<0.05) one month (p<0.001) and three months (p<0.0002) (Barraclough et al 1974). Of those seeing their GP within one week of death 79% of consultations were recorded as being of a psychiatric nature.

The number of women committing suicide was too small to enable comparison of consultation patterns with the general household survey data. For men, Mantel-Haenszel summary odds ratio for consultation within two weeks of death was 1.94 (95% confidence intervals 1.01 to 3.71 p=0.05). Thus, in this sample, men committing suicide were significantly more likely to consult their general practitioner in the two weeks prior to death when compared to the general population figures for men.

Detailed information on events leading up to and possibly provoking death were available on 83 of those committing suicide. In 21 (26%) cases matrimonial or relationship difficulties were apparent and in 14 (17%) severe financial difficulties were stated. Other significant events were present in 14 (17%) and no precipitant was identified in 32 (40%) of those committing suicide. 60% of those with a psychiatric history had no clear precipitant, as opposed to 17% of those with no such history.

Discussion

Charlton et al have described changes in the rate of suicide for different age groups of men and women (Charlton et al 1992). Most conspicuously, rates of suicide are increasing in men in the 15–44 year old age group and these changes are also apparent in the Somerset population. 49% of those committing suicide in the two year study period between 1990 and 1992 were men aged less than 45. Using the simple methodology as described, information was obtained on 95% of Somerset residents committing suicide in the two year period examined. Of those 101 suicides, 8 were not registered with a local GP and 14 committed suicide outside the district. 48% of those committing suicide had had no contact with psychiatric services, 26% were in current contact and 26% had had some contact in the past. These figures are similar to those found by Barraclough et al and more recently Morgan (Morgan 1992). Young males were less likely to be in current contact with psychiatric services although this difference was not statistically significant. A previous suicide attempt is a recognised predictor of future successful suicide, with 35–50% of suicides giving such a history (Kreitman 1989). 39% of those committing suicide in Somerset had a history of previous parasuicide.

Barraclough et al found in their study of 100 suicides occurring between 1966 and 1968 that 48% of those committing suicide had had some contact with health services in the week before death, 69% in the month before death and 83% in the three months before death. In this series, significantly smaller proportions of those committing suicide had been in recent contact with a health care professional. This reduced level of consultation may be related to the different age structure of those committing suicide in the 1990s and in particular the increased proportion of young adult males who are known to consult less often. The differences may also reflect changed perceptions of the usefulness of services available or decreased access to primary care. Alternatively these differences may be artefactual and relate to differences in study design: this study included unselectively all those given open and suicide verdicts and was district of residence based rather than district of death based. However, only 16% of suicides examined were given open verdicts and local coroners estimate 75% of these were probably suicides. If these reduced rates of consultation are not artefact it is a surprising finding at a time when GPs have smaller list sizes and psychiatric illness is seen as less stigmatising. Using figures for age adjusted male consultation rates from the general household survey it was still apparent that those committing suicide were more likely to have consulted their GP in the two weeks prior to death (odds ratio 1.94 p=0.05).

Another difference between this series and that reported by Barraclough is the prevalence of psychotropic drug prescription amongst suicide vicitms. 66% of this sample were taking no psychotropic medication. In Barraclough's series, 80% of patients were taking such medication. The two samples were however similar with respect to the proportion of patients taking antidepressant medication: 19 (20%) of our sample were taking these drugs, similar to the 21% reported by Barraclough.

Young adult males were examined separately as they represent a group in which suicide rates are increasing. A greater proportion (80%) were taking no psychotropic medication. Only 5 (14%) had been in contact with health care professionals in the week before death and a greater proportion (67%) had had no contact with psychiatric services. No difference was found, however, in the proportion of young adult males with a history of parasuicide or alcohol abuse.

Whilst the above findings are of help when planning and targetting health promotion programmes and assessing the effectiveness of these, it is important also to remember the limited impact direct health service action may have on a problem with so many and complex psychological determinants. This is especially so for young men for whom different strategies are probably required. Monitoring interventions and trends will present difficulties due to the relatively small number of suicides occurring at district level (Todd 1992).

A database of basic information on all suicides to Somerset residents is being set up to monitor trends and evaluate changes in the pattern of local suicide. Such a database would be of greater value if data from a number of neighbouring districts, pursuing similar strategies, were pooled. This would overcome problems associated with interpreting data on the small number of suicides that occur at district level.

The increased proportion of young adult men committing suicide highlights the need both to target initiatives at this group and to seek explanations for the increasing rate of suicide in this age group. The finding that most of those (75%) who commit suicide are not in current contact with psychiatric services demonstrates the need for collaboration with agencies outside the health service and a need to publicise sources of help available to people at times of crisis. The low proportion of subjects taking antidepressants (often at inappropriately low doseages) highlights the need for local and national educational initiatives for primary health care workers.

References

Adelstein A, Mardon C. Suicides 1961–71. *Population Trends 1975, 2,* 13–18.

Barraclough B, Bunch J, Nelson B, Sainsbury P. A Hundred Cases of Suicide; Clinical Aspects. *British Journal of Psychiatry 1974, 125,* 355–73.

Charlton J, Kelly S, Dunnell K, Evans B, Jenkins R, Wallis R. Trends in Suicide Deaths in England and Wales. *Population Trends 1992, 69,* 10–16.

General Household Survey 1989; Office of Population Censuses and Surveys.

The Health of the Nation, A Strategy for Health in England. London HMSO 1992.

Kreitman N. Can Suicide and Parasuicide be Prevented? *Journal of Royal Society of Medicine 1989, 82,* 648–652.

Morgan H G. Suicide Prevention; Hazards in the Fast Lane of Community Care. *British Journal of Psychiatry 1992, 160,* 149–153.

Todd C J. Reduction in the Incidence of Suicide; A Health Gain Objective for the NHS. *Journal of Psychopharmacology* 6(2) Supplement 1992; 318–324.

Part 3

Aftermath of Suicide

14 The Relative's Response
Gethin Morgan

It is appropriate here to consider the needs of a wide range of survivors after a suicide has occurred. Not only relatives may suffer greatly but close friends, colleagues and health care professionals may also be profoundly distressed. Other persons who became involved in the event itself, for example policemen and train-drivers are also at risk. The circle of people who may experience distress, and perhaps need help, is often larger than we might suppose: a teenage suicide may have ramifications in many others not only in children but also teachers at school. Some relationships may have remained hidden, for example when persons who committed suicide were homosexual and had developed very private relationships which the other partners cannot subsequently acknowledge. To obtain help under such circumstances can then be difficult.

The reaction to suicide

The reaction to loss following a suicide is fundamentally the same as any grief reaction. Super-added factors can however complicate the process and make it more difficult to resolve. The event of suicide itself, the manner of death, and all the inevitable procedures which follow can of course be extremely distressing for relatives, cohabitees and others such as health care professionals who are obliged to participate in them. Society's judgemental attitude to suicide and indeed to survivors may not help, and the media can appear insensitive to their distress. The deliberate nature of a suicidal death inevitably leads to an agonising self questioning in survivors who tend to see themselves as inadequate, often feeling guilty and a focus of criticism. Suicide may appear to be not only a judgement on life itself, but also on others who had been closely associated with the person who chose that form of death. Survivors may also experience intense anger when they feel that the suicide could have been prevented, for example when the person had been under medical care and clinical management is construed as having been inadequate. Such a reaction is more likely to occur when relatives feel they have not been consulted or otherwise involved appropriately in the process of care as it took place.

Meeting the needs of survivors

There is no single formula here. Those who offer help must be sensitive to the wishes of each individual survivor: inappropriate help, or that which is pressed too vigorously can be as distressing as providing none at all.

Immediate: Simple practical help may be what is more needed at first, for example giving lifts or doing the shopping. As family members gather together, the opportunity arises for open sharing of distress and the communication of painful facts. But even then survivors may prefer to suffer alone.

The role of professionals such as the police and coroners is significant at an early stage: it involves definite skills, particularly concerning how to impart bad news. Some are extremely good at this, but the task is so difficult that appropriate training should be available for everyone faced with the unenviable task of helping survivors in this way.

The basic process of helping the bereaved applies throughout. Giving time to, and listening in a constructive way, in itself can be of enormous value. If this is acknowledged then those who set out to help survivors will as a result feel enabled and confident in what they can do without necessarily referring on for more specialist advice.

Longer term needs: The process whereby grief is resolved may take many months and following suicide many complicating factors can make recovery a very slow matter. Any adequate network of care should reach out in a sensitive way so that all who want help feel able to come forward to declare their need and then obtain the type of assistance they feel they can accept. This means that a whole range of helping styles should be made available. Some survivors may want one-to-one support with some kind of health care professional. Others may prefer group forms of help such as that provided by voluntary agencies which include CRUSE or the Compassionate Friends. Whatever help is provided the basic process of promoting expression of distress, sharing and listening will apply at all stages.

References

This section is indebted to the book by Alison Wertheimer, *A Special Scar: The Experience of People Bereaved by Suicide*, published by Tavistock/ Routledge, 1991. This contains a useful bibliography of references.

15 The Media Response
Stephen Platt

Introduction

Does any of the mass media (television, movies, newspapers) have the power to affect how people behave? The debate about the relationship between media violence and real-life aggressive behaviour has been vigorously pursued over the past few decades, and appears to have been won by those who argue that a casual link does indeed exist (Huesmann and Malamuth, 1986a). But what of the power of the media to affect **self-directed** violence, ie suicide (fatal deliberate self-harm) and parasuicide (non-fatal deliberate self-harm)? This topic has only recently become fashionable among politicians and policy makers although modern scientific research dates back at least twenty years.

In 1897, in his famous book *Suicide*, Durkheim (1952) noted that there is no behaviour more contagious than suicide but also argued that imitation has no influence upon the suicide rate. This is because those who kill themselves in the course of a contagious epidemic are psychologically vulnerable individuals who would have died by their own hand eventually anyway. They have merely "brought forward" the timing of their deaths. The contagiousness of suicide, the tendency for such deaths to cluster together in time and space, has been documented innumerable times in both community and institutional settings (Hawton, 1978; Robbins & Conroy, 1983; Rubinstein, 1983; Walsh & Rosen, 1985), and is beyond doubt. Two important questions remain, however: firstly, whether the **mass media** play an important role in the processes of imitation and contagion; and, secondly, whether the link between mass media portrayal of self-violence and real-life suicide is **causal**.

The most serious and sustained attempt to answer these questions has undoubtedly been made by an American sociologist, David Phillips. In a series of papers, he has investigated the impact of publicised non-fictional suicide stories on suicide (Phillips, 1974; Bollen & Phillips, 1982; Phillips & Bollen, 1985; Phillips & Carstensen, 1986), the impact of publicised non-fictional suicide stories on motor vehicle accidents with a suicidal component (Phillips, 1977; Phillips 1979; Bollen & Phillips, 1981), the impact of murder-suicide stories on non-commercial aeroplane crashes (Phillips, 1978; Phillips, 1980), and the impact of fictional television suicide stories on suicide (Phillips, 1982a). (For reviews of these studies by the author himself, see Phillips, 1982b; Phillips, 1985; Phillips, 1986a; Phillips, 1986b.) This review briefly examines four of his papers (devoted to overt rather than covert suicide) as a starting point for consideration of the major methodological and theoretical issues which are to be found in this important area of research. The review will conclude by making recommendations for future developments.

"The Werther effect"

In three studies (Phillips, 1974; Bollen & Phillips, 1982; Phillips & Carstensen, 1986) the increase in suicide following the mass media reporting of non-fictional suicide was investigated. For his seminal study Phillips (1974) scoured the front page of the New York Times over the years 1946–68 and managed to find a total of 33 suicides reported there. (It is of interest to note that the majority of these turned out to be villains rather than heroes – in trouble with the law, Nazi officials, Ku Klux Klan leaders, underworld figures.) In order to examine their effect, he compared the totals of suicide deaths (all ages, both sexes) in the United States in the week after the reported suicide and the same week during control years before and after the year in which the mass media suicide was reported. This quasi-experimental control period supposedly controlled for seasonal effects and linear trends.

Phillips argued that the following three predictions should hold if suicide stories trigger imitative deaths: firstly, the number of observed suicides following a suicide story should be greater that the number of expected suicides (based on the control periods); secondly, the more publicity devoted to a suicide story, the larger should be the rise in suicides; and, thirdly, the effect should be greater in New York than elsewhere. Since all three predictions were supported by the data, and alternative explanations (the coroner effect, prior conditions and bereavement) could be ruled out, Phillips concluded that these newspaper stories about suicide had indeed triggered real-life imitative suicides. This phenomenon he termed "The Werther Effect", after the hero of Goethe's book whose suicide seemingly sparked off an alarming epidemic of copycat behaviour throughout Europe by similarly melancholic and lovelorn young men.

Subsequently, attention turned to the impact of television. Bollen and Phillips (1982) examined daily United State suicides (both sexes, all ages) for the years 1972–1976. Seven stories about specific individual suicides carried on at least two of the network evening news programmes were identified and two methods were used to control for extraneous variables: quasi-experimental analysis (as in the original study) and regression analysis. It was found that suicides increased significantly after these stories were broadcast, with peaks at 0/1 and 6/7 days and the excess disappearing after about 10 days. Phillips and Carstensen (1986) restricted their attention to suicide among persons aged 10–19 years over the period 1973–79. On this occasion 38 televised suicide stories were identified, covering both specific individuals and more general features on the topic, and regression analysis was the only technique used to control for extraneous variables. There were two major findings: firstly, the observed number of suicides during the first week of the broadcast was significantly greater than the number expected; and, secondly, the greater the publicity devoted to a story, the greater the subsequent increase in suicide ('dose-response' effect).

Phillips's work: methodological issues

Four major methodological weaknesses have been identified in these studies. The first is mis-specification of the statistical model. Phillips quite rightly draws attention to techniques available for controlling the influence of extraneous variables, but he nowhere discusses the substantive question: **which** variables are to be controlled for? He only includes days of the week, month, year and public holidays. What of other sociological variables which are known to be associated with the suicide rate, such as economic conditions or social integration? Their exclusion may lead to an exaggerated estimate of the importance of the mass media factor. That this is so has been shown in several studies. Horton and Stack (1984) explored the relationship between the number of seconds coverage of suicide stories on the 6 o'clock news, an index of suggestion-imitation, and the monthly suicide rate. After controlling for average duration of unemployment (a measure of the economic theory of suicide) and the divorce rate (an index of the marital integration theory of suicide), the imitation-suggestion index was unrelated to the suicide rate. Wasserman (1984) re-examined the findings from Phillips' 1974 study, extending the time period to 1977. Using the quasi-experimental technique, Wasserman replicated Phillips' finding that there was a greater than expected increase in suicide following news stories about suicide. However, when he went on to undertake a regression analysis in which controls for duration of unemployment, war and seasonal effects were introduced, the coefficient for front-page stories was not significant. In other words, there was no overall relationship between news coverage and the subsequent suicide rate after controlling for unemployment and seasonal trends (war was shown to have no effect on suicide). Later work by Stack on the impact of real-life suicide stories involving divorce/marital problems (Stack, 1990a) and noncelebrity suicides (Stack, 1990b) demonstrated that unemployment is more closely associated with changes in the suicide rate than any story variable.

This issue of model misspecification is important when we consider a second key methodological problem, that of the ecological fallacy, which is the assumption that statistical relationships between individuals can automatically be inferred from relationships between aggregated data. This problem was first noted in sociology by Robinson (1950) over 40 years ago, but was identified nearly 30 years earlier in psychology. Selvin (1958) gives an example from Durkheim, who argues that since the rate of suicide in departments of France varies according to the proportion of persons with independent means, then the rate of suicide among individuals of independent means will be higher than the suicide rate among persons without independent means. But the ecological association is consistent with either of the two extreme hypotheses: **none** of the people who commit suicide have independent means, or **all** of them have independent means. The **ecological** association between characteristics of departments reveals nothing about the **individual** association between a person's wealth and whether or not he/she commits suicide. Phillips makes the implicit assumption that the rate of suicide among those who watched the programmes/read the newspaper must, at the very least, be higher than the rate among non-viewers/non-watchers. But is it safe to make such an assumption? Selvin (1958) argues that events such as suicide are so rare that no inferences about individual-level relationships can be made from aggregate mortality data. Stack (1980) refers to the availability of certain techniques for assessing the presence of cross-level bias. One concerns model mis-specification: missing out key explanatory variables from the model can result in the ecological fallacy. We have already seen that Phillips is guilty of such an omission. The other technique is statistical, but Hammond (1973) points out that while the tests available can prove the presence of cross-level bias, they cannot definitely prove its absense. Both Hammond and Irwin and Lichtman (1976) go on to make the point that the problem of inferring individual behaviour from aggregate data can most profitably be interpreted as one of theory rather than method. As we shall see, the poverty of theory in Phillips' work makes any individual-level inferences most dangerous.

A third methodological problem concerns the type and number of stories used in the studies, i.e. the independent variable. In his 1974 study, Phillips uses newspaper stories, in the 1982 study television news items about specific suicides, and in the 1986 study specific and general news items. He argues that the discovery of significant findings across three studies using different indicators for the independent variable can only strengthen our confidence in the non-spuriousness of the findings. Unfortunately, this is not the case. For instance, if we compare the 1982 and 1986 papers, we find that there were only seven suicides listed in the former paper for the years 1972–76, whereas there were 16 covering one fewer year (1973–76) in the latter paper (and that excludes the general suicide stories). Only five suicides are common to both studies. Of these, two produce concordant findings in the two studies, while three produce conflicting results. Whether this is due to the use of different analyses (quasi-experimental *versus* regression) or different age groups (all ages *versus* teenager only) or both, is unclear. But it certainly shows that the difficulty of compiling an exhaustive list of stories is not confined to the investigation of fictional suicide.

Another example of the dramatic differences resulting from a different choice of stories is provided by Kessler *et al* (1989) replication of the Phillips and Carstensen study. They extended the years covered to 1984 and the number of broadcasts to 87, more than double the original 38. Overall, during the whole time span 1973–84 there was no reliable mass media effect among adults, although some evidence of a dose-response relationship appeared among teenagers in the period to 1980. This replication demonstrates clearly the consequences of varying the number of years and the number of broadcasts in the analysis.

The fourth methodological issue relates to the specification of the dependent variable. It is reasonably clear from social learning theory (Bandura, 1973) that people are especially likely to model the behaviour of those with whom they share certain characteristics. This implies that imitative violence should be greatest among those who most closely resemble the media model. But Phillips does not disaggregate his data by the characteristics of the media model, or of the potential imitators (general public). The only concession to theory is in his 1986 study where he looks for effect among teenagers, on the grounds that teenage suicides have been thought to occur in clusters, which are themselves caused by imitation. This is a rather half-hearted attempt at disaggregation and misses entirely the more important issue of **method specific imitations**, and the relationship between method, gender and age in imitation.

The impact of fictional representations of suicidal behaviours

Thus far we have considered only Phillip's research on non-fictional media coverage. What of the impact of fictional portrayals of suicidal behaviour? Phillips (1982a) examined the impact of 13 soap opera "suicide stories" (of which all but two were in fact parasuicides) broadcast on American television during 1977. After correcting for effects of public holidays, non-fictional suicide stories and temporal suicide trends, suicides (particularly female) were found to increase after soap opera stories. Motor-vehicle deaths (particularly those occurring in single vehicle crashes) and non-fatal accidents also increased significantly. But in a subsequent paper, Kessler and Stipp (1984) corrected errors made by Phillips in dating the soap opera suicide stories, enlarged the sample and used a more precise time-series regression approach. Their analysis failed to provide evidence linking soap opera suicide stories to subsequent real-life suicide deaths. Phillips (1986a) himself has publicly accepted that his study "failed".

With one exception, the more general evidence concerning the impact of portrayals of fictional suicidal behaviour is not very impressive. A key study by Gould and Shaffer (1986) examined the impact of four made-for-television films on teenage suicide in 1984–5. Focusing on New York city metropolitan area, Gould and Shaffer found a significant impact of these films on the suicide rate. However, they recognised the limitations of their data and called for replications of their work outside the New York area. Subsequently Gould *et al* (1988) reported findings from a study across several United States cities which failed on the whole to replicate the results. Likewise, Berman (1988), Phillips and Paight (1987) and Stack (1990c) were unable to find evidence of an impact of these fictional suicides. Stack (1990d) concludes that the original findings were probably restricted to the New York area due to some specific contextual factor (e.g. a highly publicised suicide cluster).

The sole example of an attempt to test the imitation hypothesis where the stimulus event is parasuicide and the dependent variable is the frequency of parasuicide is reported by Platt (1987, 1989). Data were obtained on cases of deliberate overdosage treated in accident and emergency departments in 63 hospitals throughout Great Britain in the week following the televised overdosage (experimental period) and the week prior to the television programme (control period). Data for equivalent weeks in a control year were also sought. Overall, there was no significant change in the experimental period, nor for any age x gender subgroup except persons aged 45 plus years. Trends in overdoses were negatively related to viewing figures i.e. the greater the proportion of households watching the programme in a particular region, the less the impact on the frequency of overdoses. It was concluded that an imitation effect was 'not proven'.

The only study which reveals an imitation effect of fictional portrayals of suicidal behaviour is that of Schmidtke and Hafner (1988). They examined the effects of screening a six episode television series in Germany which featured the railway suicide of a nineteen year old male. Following the first (and subsequent) broadcast of the series there was a rise in the number of railway suicides which was most marked for the age and gender categories closest to the model, while no significant changes among older men and women were found.

Phillips's work: theoretical issues

Having considered methodological problems in Phillips's work, we turn to an examination of theoretical issues, which give additional grounds for scepticism about the alleged Werther effect. The main problem is that Phillips's (and others') theory of media-inspired imitative violence is inadequately developed. Researchers tend to explain increases in mortality following media violence in terms of imitation or social modelling. But a theory of imitative violence that would explain the kinds of increases in suicide which Phillips claims to find would have to do three things:

1   delineate the **properties of media stimuli** that influence the magnitude and duration of imitative behaviour;

2   specify clearly **the set of behaviours** that qualify as imitative responses; and

3   articulate the **process** that evokes imitative responses in a falsifiable way (Baron & Reiss, 1985a)

At present no aggregate study imitative violence proposes a theory satisfying these three prerequisites. Rather, aggregate research has done its theorising primarily by drawing analogies to studies of imitative modelling conducted at the individual level. These analogies rely on evidence documenting experimental instances of imitative aggression and, implicitly, on accounts of 'copycat' violence that are occasionally publicised by the media. However, researchers have not demonstrated convincingly that similar eliciting stimuli, behavioural responses, and mediating processes are involved at the individual and aggregate levels (Baron & Reiss, 1985a, b).

One further problem can be raised here. Although sociologists like Phillips never articulate their understanding of the processes involved in imitation at the individual level, it is fairly obvious that they work with an oversimplified and unidirectional model of the pathways between media violence and real-life aggressive behaviour. While research suggests that media-activated ideas and feelings may give rise to an open display of aggression, media exposure alone is not enough to make a person behave aggressively. For aggressive behaviour to occur, a number of factors – dispositional, cognitive, cultural and situational – must converge (Huesmann & Malamuth, 1986b). Even proponents of the established view (that media violence is causally associated with real-life violence) state their position most circumspectly. Thus, Turner *et al* (1986) state: "Television violence is *one* factor increasing the *likelihood* of aggressive behaviour, but this violence *does not produce a simple unidirectional casual effect* on aggressive behaviour" (emphasis added). In fact, the direction of causality in many field studies is unclear. It may be that violent viewing stimulates aggression (causal hypothesis), or individuals with an aggressive predisposition might prefer to watch violent programmes (reversed causal link, or self-selection), or certain characteristics of the environment may make aggressive behaviour and television violence viewing more likely (a third factor leading to a spurious association between viewing habits and behaviour). Reverse causation and third factor explanations are extremely difficult to rule out (Freedman, 1984).

The future

I should start by stating my belief that it is worth pursuing this topic: it is theoretically important, since it could help us to understand more about the sociology and psychology of suicidal behaviour; it is practically important, because of its implications for the freedom of the mass media and suicide prevention. In my view a mass media effect of non-fictional reporting of suicide cannot be ruled out, but needs to be considered as one (possibly weaker) independent variable in the complex set of factors leading to suicide. Evidence for an effect of fictional representations is very weak, but the specific impact reported by Schmidtke & Hafner (1988) cannot be lightly ignored. Although our research endeavours require considerable improvement before the case against the media can be said to have been proved beyond reasonable doubt, editors and journalists should (continue to) act with great circumspection when dealing with suicide stories and storylines.

How, then, should research on this topic proceed? With one important exception researchers are agreed that the way forward lies with . . . people!

Phillips and Paight (1987), for example, believe that psychological processes linking media suicide and real life suicide are best studied by micro-investigations, i.e. small numbers of subjects, large amounts of information per subject. By interviewing close relatives and significant others of the deceased, a psychological case history is assembled and the aetiological significance of the suicide story can be assessed. Suicides occurring after a publicised media suicide can be compared to suicides occurring at other times, in order to tease out the effect of the media story. Stack (1987) notes the clarion calls for more micro-level research but sounds a word of warning. Trends in violence may best be detected at the aggregate level, he contends, since laboratory experiments or self-reports are impossible or impractical. In the case of suicide, the victim cannot be interviewed. Even the psychological autopsy of significant others is marked by important barriers. Stack instead urges us to think of more sophisticated models (non-linear, non-additive), include more control variables (eg divorce rate), construct a better index of media coverage, devise alternative ways of differentiating media stories, all within the context of aggregate time-series regression analysis.

I do not believe that more and better of the same will get us much further. We certainly need to bring people back in, but also to recognise the enormous practical and methodological difficulties of micro-level research to which Stack alludes, and the fundamental weakness in this research tradition caused by the poverty of theory. In their paper, Baron and Reiss (1985a) suggest three courses of action:

1 refine imitative theory so that its predictions are more specific and falsifiable;

2 develop new methods to study behavioural modelling directly; and

3 employ a conservative and consistent set of testing procedures in gauging imitative effects.

The distance we have to travel before the micro-level approach attains even the relatively limited sophistication of current aggregate studies can be assessed by examining a statement by Gould and Shaffer (1986). Having shown a statistical link between fictional deceptions of teenage suicide and real life suicidal behaviour among teenagers, they note that the hypothesis that imitation led to the increase in suicidal behaviour is supported by the fact that one of the persons who died after a broadcast employed the same method as depicted in the movie.

The subject was reported by parents and friends to have seen the movie. However, Berman (1988) quotes the case of a boy who died by carbon monoxide poisoning in his garage soon after the broadcast of the film "Surviving" which depicted a dyadic carbon monoxide suicide. He left a diary in which he wrote extensively during the last two years of his life. The diary documented considerable suicide ideation during this period, as well as a prior suicide gesture and one other failed attempt at suicide by carbon monoxide well before the television broadcast. Significant rage toward his absent father and conflict with his mother subsequent to their divorce was expressed. Most importantly, he wrote of his confusion and pain related to questions of sexual identity. Of "Surviving" he wrote, "I loved that film." However, of another television movie, "Consenting Adults", which was aired shortly before "Surviving" and dealt with the topic of homosexuality within a context of lack of family support, he wrote: "...the movie reminded myself of me 100% ... I feel exactly about males as he did. I feel like I'm lying to myself". If Berman had not been able to get hold of the boy's diary, he might have reached a very different conclusion about the role of the film "Surviving" in the boy's suicide.

References

Bandura A (1973). *Aggression: A Social Learning Analysis.* Prentice-Hall, Engelwood Cliffs, New Jersey.

Baron J N and Reiss P C (1985a). Some time, next year: aggregate analyses of the mass media and violent behaviour. *American Sociological Review, 50,* 347–363.

Baron J N and Reiss P C (1985b). Reply to Phillips and Bollen. *American Sociological Review, 50,* 372–376.

Berman A (1988). Suicide in television films and imitation effects. *American Journal of Psychiatry, 145,* 982–986.

Bollen K A and Phillips D P (1981). Suicidal motor vehicle fatalities in Detroit: a replication. *American Journal of Sociology, 87,* 404–412.

Bollen K A and Phillips D P (1982). Imitative suicides: a national study of the effects of television news stories. *American Sociological Review, 47,* 802–809.

Durkheim E (1952, originally, published in 1897). *Suicide.* Routledge and Kegan Paul, London.

Freedman J L (1984). Effects of television violence on aggressiveness. *Psychological Bulletin, 96,* 227–246.

Gould M S and Shaffer D (1986). The impact of suicide in television movies. Evidence of imitation. *New England Journal of Medicine, 315,* 690–694.

Gould M S, Shaffer D and Kleinman M (1988). The impact of suicide in television movies. replication and commentary. *Suicide and Life-Threatening Behavior, 18,* 90–99.

Hammond J L (1973). Two sources of error in ecological correlations. *American Sociological Review, 38,* 764–777.

Hawton K (1978). Deliberate self-poisoning and self-injury in the psychiatric hospital. *British Journal of Medical Psychology, 51,* 253–259.

Horton H and Stack S (1984). The effect of television on national suicide rates. *Journal of Social Psychology, 123,* 141–142.

Huesmann L R and Malamuth N M (eds) (1986a). *Journal of Social Issues, 42*(3) (whole issue).

Huesmann L R and Malamuth N M (1986b). Media violence and antisocial behaviour: an overview. *Journal of Social Issues, 42,* 1–6.

Irwin L and Lichtman A J (1976). Across the great divide: inferring individual level behaviour from aggregate data. *Political Methodology, 3,* 411–439.

Kessler R C and Stipp H (1984). The impact of fictional suicide stories on U.S. fatalities: a replication *American Journal of Sociology, 90,* 151–167.

Kessler R C, Downey G, Stipp H and Milausky J R (1989). Network television news stories about suicide and short-term changes in total U.S. suicides. *Journal of Nervous and Mental Disease, 177,* 551–555.

Phillips D P (1974). The influence of suggestion on suicide: substantive and theoretical implications of the Werther effect. *American Sociological Review, 39,* 340–354.

Phillips D P (1977). Motor vehicle fatalities increase just after publicised suicide stories. *Science, 196,* 1464–1465.

Phillips D P (1978). Airplane accident and fatalities increase just after stories about murder and suicide. *Science, 201,* 748–750.

Phillips D P (1979). Suicide, motor vehicle fatalities and the mass media: evidence toward a theory of suggestion. *American Journal of Sociology, 84,* 1150–1174.

Phillips D P (1980). Airplane accidents, murder and the mass media: towards a theory of imitation and suggestion. *Social Forces, 58,* 1001–1024.

Phillips D P (1982a).The impact of fictional television stories on U.S. adult fatalities. *American Journal of Sociology, 87,* 1340–1359.

Phillips D P (1982b). The behavioral impact of violence in the mass media: a review of the evidence from laboratory and non-laboratory investigation. *Sociology and Social Research, 66,* 387–398.

Phillips D P (1985). The Werther Effect. *The Sciences,* 33–39.

Phillips D P (1986a). National experiments on the effects of mass media violence on fatal aggression: strengths and weaknesses of a new approach. *Advances in Experimental Social Psychology, 19,* 207–250.

Phillips D P (1986b). The found experiment: a new technique for assessing the impact of mass media violence on real world aggressive behaviour. *Public Communication and Behavior, 1,* 259–307.

Phillips D P and Bollen K A (1985). Same time, last year: selective data dredging for negative findings. *American Sociological Review, 50,* 364–371.

Phillips D P and Carstensen L L (1986). Clustering of teenage suicides after television news stories about suicide. *New England Journal of Medicine, 315,* 685–689.

Phillips D P and Paight D J (1987). The impact of television movies about suicide. A replicative study. *New England Journal of Medicine, 317,* 809–811.

Platt S (1987). The aftermath of Angie's overdose. Is soap (opera) damaging to your health? *British Medical Journal, 294,* 954–957.

Platt S (1989). The consequences of a televised soap opera drug overdose: is there a mass media imitation effect? In: R F W Diekstra, R W Maris, S D Platt, A Schmitke and G Sonneck (eds). *Suicide and its Prevention: the Role of Attitude and Imitation.* E. J. Brill, Leiden.

Robbins D and Conroy R C (1983). A cluster of adolescent suicide attempts: is suicide contagious? *Journal of Adolescent Health Care, 3,* 253–255.

Robinson W S (1950). Ecological correlations: the behaviour of individuals. *American Sociological Review, 15,* 351–357.

Rubenstein, D H (1983). Epidemic suicide among Micronesian adolescents. *Social Science and Medicine, 17,* 657–665.

Schmitke A and Hafner H (1988). The Werther effect after television films. New evidence for an old hypothesis. *Psychological Medicine, 18,* 665–676.

Selvin H C (1958). Durkheim's Suicide and problems of empirical research. *American Sociological Review, 63,* 607–619.

Stack C (1980). The effects of marital dissolution on suicide. *Journal of Marriage and Family, 42*, 83–92.

Stack S (1987). Celebrities and suicide: a taxonomy and analysis, 1948–1983. *American Sociological Review, 52*, 401–412.

Stack S (1987). The media and suicide: a non-additive model, 1968–80: a research note Paper presented at annual meeting of the American Association of Suicidology, San Francisco, USA.

Stack S (1990a). Divorce, suicide, and the mass media: an analysis of differential identification, 1948–1980. *Journal of Marriage and the Family, 52*, 553–560.

Stack S (1990b). A reanalysis of the impact of non celebrity suicides: a research note. *Social Psychiatry and Psychiatric Epidemiology, 25*, 269–273.

Stack S (1990c). The impact of fictional television films on teenage suicide, 1984–85. *Social Science Quarterly, 71*, 391–399.

Stack S (1990d). Media impacts on suicide. In: D. Lester (ed) *Current Concepts of Suicide*. Charles Press, Philadelphia.

Turner C W, Hesse B W and Peterson-Lewis S (1986). Naturalistic studies of the long-term effects of television violence. *Journal of Social Issues, 42*, 51–73.

Walsh B W and Rosen P (1985). Self-mutilation and contagion: an empirical test. *American Journal of Psychiatry, 142*, 119–120.

Wasserman I M (1984). Imitation and suicide: a re-examination of the Werther effect. *American Sociological Review, 49, 427–436*.

16 The Coroner's Response
W.F.G. Dolman

I am very aware that I am the only member of the Judiciary who has been asked to speak at this conference among this distinguished medical company, so I have to speak not as a doctor, which I am, but as a lawyer in the Coroner's court, and will concentrate purely on the legal aspects and constraints on a Coroner relating to suicide and the suicide verdict.

And constraints there are, which have an over-riding influence on the verdict or conclusion that a Coroner or his jury may deliver. Of course, the verdict affects the statistics: I hope that I will be able to explain the difficulties facing the Coroner in his court when considering a verdict of suicide. I will be looking at the line of reasoning in some of the recent cases before the Divisional Court, and I will also take this opportunity of examining the figures in one of my jurisdictions in some more detail and out of curiosity look at the means by which people end their lives deliberately. Of course my comments refer only to England and Wales: as you know, elsewhere the system of dealing with sudden deaths is very different.

After a sudden unnatural death, for many people their first contact with officialdom is with the Coroner's Officer. The distraught relative may have found the body of a loved one at home, or perhaps even more frightening, the victim has simply disappeared, only to be found later, perhaps in a car with hose-pipe attached to the exhaust, in some car park or out-of-the-way spot. (In my experience people rarely choose a public or crowded area for such an act. It is usually done out of sight, in private.)

The relative next learns that the death cannot be registered straight away, that there will probably have to be a post-mortem examination and an inquest. It is not my province today to examine the family's feelings, guilt or distress, their reaction to the tragedy. Let me merely remind you that the Coroner and his officer have to tread a most delicate path, gaining information. The Coroner has to conduct an independent inquiry, an inquiry for the Crown, not on behalf of the relatives as they sometimes think or Health Authority or for that matter the Department of Health. The Coroner's officer, usually a serving Police officer, but increasingly commonly a civilian, has to act as a buffer between the family and the Coroner. It demands a very special type of person.

Again, in purely practical terms, the family cannot make funeral arrangements until the Coroner releases the body after examination. The inquest is opened fairly promptly, but the full hearing may not take place for some weeks, when the Coroner will be armed with as much information as he can gather, doctor's reports, toxicology, which always takes some weeks, psychiatrist's reports and Police statements, indeed any relevant material. It is for the Coroner to decide which witnesses are to be called and what documentary evidence to introduce.

It may sound very basic but not surprisingly most of the population has never been inside a Coroner's court and are unaware of the procedure. This goes for many doctors as well. The Coroner's court is a court of inquiry, the only court of its type in the English legal system, and one of the oldest, if not the oldest court in the land. I can't resist quoting the introduction to the 1957 edition of Jervis on the Office and Duties of Coroners.

> *Coroners are a good example of the English respect for tradition and their pragmatic approach to institutions. Coroners do not fit neatly into a logical system of judicial institutions. They have both judicial and executive functions... they straddle the domains of both the Police and the medical profession though they are separate from each.*

That has a wonderful ring to it. The truth is more mundane. We are dealing with distressed relatives, many of whom have, as I have said, never been in a Coroner's court, let alone any other type of court. It is no part of a Coroner's duty to increase a relative's distress but painful facts have to be adduced in evidence, and as in medical practice, diplomacy is required. Facts have to be established. We are a court of facts, not a court of conjecture. It is our task to be detached, to look into matters objectively. A Coroner's court is awash with emotion, sadness and anger. It has to be de-fused. This means that the Coroner has to handle his witnesses gently, with kid gloves. Evidence is taken on oath, and matters such as handwriting on suicide notes has to be proved.

I must have seen thousands of such notes in my career, ranging from the few scrawled words on a scrap of paper, even writing in emulsion paint on a living room wall, to pages of closely written narrative. The contents of suicide notes would be a profitable field for research. They range from expressions of regret, hopelessness, to angry outbursts, and vindictive comments. Some pathetically attempt to be testamentary documents, wills, but written without the due formalities they cannot be valid. You will understand then why such notes are not made public. They form part of the evidence and belong to the Coroner as exhibits with the court records. Out of courtesy the notes or copies of them may be given to the relative requesting them. It is my practice and the practice of most Coroners not to read out these notes, merely to indicate their contents. This is not a matter of hiding evidence. The Coroner has a discretion under Coroner's Rule 37(6) not to read out such documents and as I have already said, it is not our task to add to the distress of bereavement.

The Incidence of Suicide

I want to look at figures for the Southern District of London jurisdiction, which takes in the boroughs of Bromley, Bexley, Sutton and Croydon. Between the years 1988 and 1992 there has been a gradual increase in deaths reported to the Coroner, from 3020 in 1988, to 4181 last year, 1992. The total reported in that period was 17,961. That number refers to all deaths where the doctor couldn't certify, or perhaps for out-of England orders. About one in ten deaths reported ends up with an inquest, in fact 1642 in the period. Those are the deaths suspected to be unnatural, including the suicides. Dealing with suicide verdicts, almost twice as many men were recorded as having killed themselves as women. The figures were: 206 males, 104 females. The total of 310 represents 18.8 percent of inquests. And in that suicide verdict lies the greatest scope for error.

The Suicide Verdict   This is arguably the most difficult part of the subject, perhaps due in part to the fact that, until 1961 suicide was a crime. Let me quote from Sir John Jervis himself, in the first edition of his text on Coroners;

> *Self-murder is wisely and religiously considered by the English law as the most heinous description of felonious homicide, for as no man hath power to destroy life but by commission of God the author of it, the suicide is guilty of a double offence: one spiritual, invading the perogative of the Almighty, and rushing in his presence uncalled for, and the other temporal, against the King, who has an interest in the preservation of all his subjects.*

No one could pretend that that is an accurate representation of English law today but such sentiments do colour the law's attitude to suicide. At this point then, I should look at the line of reasoning in some of the recent decided cases. Coroners, like other members of the judiciary, are slaves to precedent. The higher courts rule us. As a direct result, the verdict of suicide is very limited and my main proposition is that the Coroner's verdict of suicide must represent an underestimate of the true incidence in the broad sense. There must be many true suicides for which a Coroner cannot give a verdict. What one can say with authority is that when a suicide verdict is delivered, that person did intend to end their own life and did so. The suicide figures I gave earlier must be the lowest estimate of the real incidence of suicide. But if we do not use Coroners' verdicts, where is our independent measuring stick? Can we be more accurate?

There is a long line of cases, in nearly all of which an aggrieved relative has taken the Coroner to a higher court on account of the suicide verdict. No doubt the shame and opprobrium of a verdict that N. killed himself is such that relatives don't want to believe it. Is it sometimes part of the grieving process? A sense of guilt perhaps? It takes time and money to apply for a review of a Coroner's finding. Let us follow the line of recent cases to illustrate my proposition that Coroners are hemmed in by the decided law.

A good starting point is the case of R v. Cardiff City Coroner, ex parte Thomas in 1970. The judgment made clear that it isn't enough that someone deliberately took their own life. The court has to be satisfied that the deceased intended the consequences of his own act. Judge James said:

> *Suicide is voluntarily doing an act for the purpose of destroying one's own life while one is conscious of what one is doing, and in order to arrive at a verdict of suicide there must be evidence that the deceased intended the consequences of his act.*

To the person in the street and the doctor in casualty the facts that someone has taken a large over-dose would seem to be good evidence that the victim wanted to end it all. But that's not enough for the Coroner's court. The 1975 case of Barber tells us what a Coroner is to do if he can't find the degree of proof needed for the verdict. The Lord Chief Justice Widgery said:

> *Suicide must never be presumed. If a person dies a violent death, the possibility of suicide may be there for all to see, but it must not be presumed merely because on the face of it it seems to be a likely explanation. Suicide must be proved by evidence and if it is not proved*

by evidence, it is the duty of the Coroner not to find suicide but to find an open verdict. I approach this case, applying a stringent test and asking myself whether in the evidence which was given in this case any reasonable Coroner could have reached the conclusion that the proper answer was suicide....

If there is no strict evidence the Coroner must bring in an open verdict. I don't know if you recall the Calvi case, the Italian bank manager found hanged under one of the City bridges. Didn't he have bricks in his pockets and his hands tied? You will recall stories of dark deeds and the Italian P2 Lodge. That was another case where the suicide verdict was overturned and an open verdict resulted. Perhaps researchers should investigate open verdicts cases as well as suicide verdict cases to gain a more complete picture.

One more curious fact concerning the suicide verdict. When is a suicide not a suicide? Let's go back to 1985. On July 26th seventeen year old Lewis de Luca went to a teenage party. There was a fracas of some sort. He returned home late, considerably agitated, having made some reference about killing himself. He locked himself in his bedroom and when his father managed to get in, he found his son lying unconscious on the floor, his airgun beside him, with a wound in his left temple. There was no dispute that he had shot himself. After neurosurgery, indeed a series of operations, he eventually died, some 13 months after his injury. The Coroner brought in a verdict that he killed himself while the balance of his mind was disturbed. The boy's father challenged the verdict and it was held that because the death occurred more than a year and a day after the wound was inflicted a suicide verdict was not appropriate. Before 1961 suicide was a crime and then, as in other forms of criminal homicide, the death had to place within a year and a day of the act being done. Suicide is no longer a crime but that rule of law remains.

Means of Committing Suicide

Here's just a snapshot of the means by which people take their own life. The figures come quite simply from my last 50 suicide inquests in the South London and Inner West jurisdictions. I don't make any claims about them. Because of the small numbers I wouldn't dare extrapolate from them. There were 14 women, 36 men in the sample. For women the commonest means of committing suicide was by overdose, usually with analgesics or antidepressants, nine women in total. One woman ingested bleach. There were two women who jumped from a height, one asphyxiated with a plastic bag over her head, and one with car exhaust fumes.

Of the 36 men in the series hanging oneself was the commonest method of committing suicide (11), and jumping from a height the next most common (10). Very much more aggressive acts than the women's deeds. 5 men took overdoses, one drank concentrated hydrochloric acid. 7 men fixed hoses to the car exhaust or a petrol generator and died of carbon monoxide poisoning. One man stabbed himself to death and one drowned himself.

References

Farmer RDT. Assessing the epidemiology of suicide and parasuicide. *British Journal of Psychiatry* 1988. 336. 22–43

Jervis on *The Office and Duties of Coroners* 9th ed. 1957 ed. WB Purchase and HW Wollaston. v and 228.

Nicholson, S. Suicide in North Devon: epidemic or problem of classification. *Health Trends* 1992. 24. 95–6.

S.I. 1984/552. Coroner's Rules 37(6).

R v Cardiff City Coroner ex parte Thomas 1970 1 WLR 1475.

R v HM Coroner for the City of London ex parte Barber 1975 1WLR 1310.

R v HM Coroner for Inner West London ex parte De Luca *Casebook on Coroners 1989 ed PA Knapman and MJ Powers 224.*

17 The Confidential Enquiry
W.D. Boyd

The prevention of suicide has always been an important concern for psychiatrists and the self-destruction of someone in the process of receiving active treatment for psychiatric illness has been a cause of particular anguish. The possibility of using the clinical network available through the Royal College of Psychiatrists to carry out a nationwide survey of the problem was being discussed a decade ago (Crammer J. 1983) but research interest remained restricted to individuals or to individual areas of the country. In particular, work in Bristol led to the development of a local project to identify and to gather information about in-patients in psychiatric units who killed themselves (Morgan H.G. & Priest, P 1991).

Another concern which came to the attention of workers in the psychiatric field and then of public and politicians was related to a number of homicides – very few – involving people who were clearly mentally disordered. At a time when hospitals were being closed and community services developed – and criticized – there was a special alarm that supervision and care might be breaking down.

Contact between Government and College led to agreement that an enquiry into deaths through homicide or suicide would provide valuable information which could help to discover whether there was any potential for changes in clinical management which might reduce the likelihood of deaths. Attention was paid to earlier enquiries (CEPOD, Maternal Deaths, etc) and it was recognised that any information coming to the Enquiry should be made anonymous very quickly.

Soon a remit for the Enquiry was prepared and a steering committee set up, the membership of the committee demonstrating the commitment to a multi-disciplinary approach in gathering information. The identification of homicides was made easy by the generous assistance of the Home Office. Files have already been examined and information sought from consultant psychiatrists. This survey will continue.

It had been hoped that the parallel identification of deaths by suicide would be equally straightforward, but it became apparent that Coroners or Registrars, no matter how helpful they might be as individuals, could not offer a nation-wide system which would allow the picking up of relevant cases. Fortunately a group of psychiatrists interested in research and audit had already been brought together by the Research Unit of the Royal College of Psychiatrists and this group covering most Districts in England has given encouraging support and is capable of providing information about the occurrence of cases throughout the country. It is important, of course, that psychiatrists should be familiar with the aim of the Enquiry and this had been done through clinical meetings and by publicity in the College papers (Boyd W.D. 1993).

The research plan has been changed dramatically by the publication of Health of the Nation with its emphasis on reducing suicide rates. Local audit plans have been formulated and there is a real risk that investigations by national and local teams could be carried out in ignorance of each other. However, it is encouraging that so much interest has been raised in the topic, and it is to be hoped that coordination between the Confidential Enquiry and local audit will develop.

Once contact is made with the psychiatrist who was looking after the patient prior to death, the completion of a questionnaire will be requested. This questionnaire based on the Bristol research questionnaire (Morgan H.G. & Priest J 1992) covers a number of areas relevant to the case.

1. About The Subject

2. The Suicide Event

3. Suicidal Ideation While Under Psychiatric Care

4. Events and Relationships

5. Problems of Supervision During Period Of Care

6. The Patient's Lifestyle

7. The Patient's Behaviour While Under Care

8. Your Reaction To The Patient

9. Review Of Case After Death

The very last statement on the form asks "Please tell me whether with hindsight, you consider there are any other ways in which the likelihood of this death might have been reduced." Here, we are trying to obtain the sort of information which might be of the greatest value to the Enquiry even though it has not been spelt out previously.

The emphasis on multi-disciplinary care has been mentioned earlier, and it is intended that members of professional staff who had close contact with the patient should be asked for their own confidential views about the case, using a modification of the questionnaire already described. Contact with these individuals will probably be made most readily through the psychiatrist first contacted, but this aspect remains to be decided.

We have also had proposals that families should be involved and this is an attractive suggestion, supported by voluntary bodies with the interests of families at heart. However, there is an equally strong view that this is an unnecessary and unacceptable intrusion, which will simply re-light feelings of distress and raise acrimony which had been put behind them. A decision on this has yet to be made.

What I have described above forms the standard part of the Confidential Enquiry. However, we have already been given access to a number of local Enquiries which have dealt with individual cases and which have reached conclusions and recommendations of great significance. It will be useful to incorporate such information into this Enquiry, providing alternative material to that gathered by ourselves. Furthermore, information of a more individual nature may be made available to us from other groups which have already indicated their support for what we are doing – examples include the Mental Health Act Commission, The Hospital Advisory Service and Mind – and from families who have written to us in considerable distress.

In conclusion, we can be optimistic that, even if we find ourselves unable to collect a fully comprehensive sample of cases, we will be obtaining a broad picture of the circumstances of deaths involving suicide or homicide falling within the remit of the Enquiry and, with the help of many colleagues, will discover whether there are general lessons to be learnt from the experiences of individuals. There is no doubt in my mind that sudden death involving a patient under psychiatric care causes much distress and soul-searching among those involved, and it is my hope that they will find it useful to share their concerns with the Confidential Enquiry, knowing that some general benefits should ensure.

References

Boyd W D. *Psychiatric Bulletin* (1993) 17, 165

Crammer J L. *Psychiatric Bulletin* (1983) 7, 1–2.

Health Of The Nation (1993) Mental Illness, Key Area Handbook Appendix 3, 4, 36.

Morgan H G. *Psychiatric Bulletin* (1993) 17, 135–136.

Morgan H G and Priest P. *British Journal of Psychiatry* (1991) 158, 368–374.

18a Local Audit
Paul Lelliott

In a survey conducted in early 1991, the College Research Unit collected information on psychiatric audit activity in over 90% of districts and health boards in the United Kingdom (Lelliott, 1993). Figure 1 shows the commonest topics for audit, in these mental health services at that time. Although nearly one-half of services reported that they were reviewing "adverse incidents" only about 5% stated specifically that suicide was a topic for audit.

Figure 1   *The Most Frequent Topics Considered by British Psychiatric Audit Groups in 1991 (expressed as a percentage of services responding to a national survey – Lelliott, 1993)*

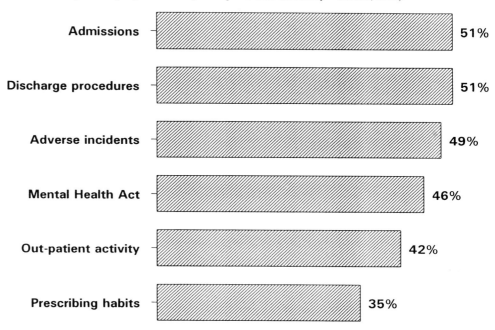

Hopefully if the survey was repeated today a very different picture would emerge. The inclusion of the reduction of the suicide rate, as a quantified national target, in the Health of the Nation White Paper, together with the continuing political, professional, managerial and financial pressures and incentives to audit make it difficult for a mental health service to justify not developing local suicide reviews. The Confidential Enquiry into Homicides and Suicides by Psychiatric Patients will give further impetus and will provide the opportunity for pooling of experience and comparisons between services.

Why should clinicians audit an event that has already occurred? Firstly they may identify deficiencies in practice or service provision that could prevent future suicides; secondly, using suicide as a "sentinel event", around which practice is reviewed, may lead to the development of better care for all patients using the service. The suicide of a patient, who may have been known by the service for years, can have devastating consequences for clinical teams. Working relationships between members may be seriously strained. At the same time as they are dealing with their own emotional reactions, clinicians have to respond to the needs of bewildered and often angry relatives and carers, give evidence at an inquest and sometimes deal with medico-legal complications. For these reasons careful attention must be given to the "ground rules" for suicide audit. These ground rules must ensure that clinical workers feel confident to participate, and also that the process is both sufficiently searching and rigorous to identify and act upon lessons for future clinical practice.

Below I shall briefly summarise what I see as being some of the issues and potential barriers, both local and national, that must be confronted and overcome for the establishment of widespread multi-disciplinary audit of suicides. These thoughts come both from my own experience in convening psychiatric audit in my own district, and participating in suicide reviews there, and also from discussions with audit convenors around the country who are involved in developing suicide audit. My intention is merely to pose some of the questions that need to be considered.

Case Identification

It is surprisingly difficult to identify even most of the cases of suicide within a catchment population. This is a problem particularly if audit is considered as part of a programme aimed at reviewing all suicides (ie. addressing the Health of the Nation target of reducing the **overall** suicide rate in the population) as opposed to reducing the rate amongst those with severe mental illness. The latter are much more likley to have been in contact with psychiatric services.

Sources of information that have been used include:

- **Word of mouth:** Most mental health services have an efficient "grapevine;" clinical workers usually hear of suicides of patients who have been recently in contact. A central point should be established to which any worker, who hears of a death, can report.

- **OPCS:** The data on death certificates is collated centrally and fed back to regional and district information departments. The process is slow however and the information is only as accurate as that on the death certificate; one region contacted had no data after 1991 and had recorded only 7 deaths by suicide in a district of 220,000 – less than one-third of the expected rate.

- **Coroner's courts:** Apart from the well-documented difficulty in identifying suicides from the verdicts passed at inquests, another problem is the inconsistent response of Coroners and their officers to requests for assistance in identifying cases and providing information. Some clinicians report full and enthusiastic cooperation others are not so fortunate. The response from three London Coroners illustrates the range: One agreed to provide information before the inquest was held; a second refused to do so until after the inquest; a third would give no information unless clinical workers undertook to inform him of the results of the audit review if they felt that it might have a bearing on the verdict.

- **Accident and Emergency Departments**

- **Pathologists** conducting post-mortem examinations prior to inquests will have a clear idea of cause of death and a strong intuition as to mode.

Timing of the Review

When deaths have been reported soon after the event, the suicide audit coordinator must decide the appropriate time to hold the review. If it is too soon for staff support issues to have been addressed those taking part may be unable to discuss events objectively.

Collection of Information and Conduct of the Review

Useful information about events surrounding suicides can be obtained from a variety of sources:

- **Case records:** hospital medical, general practitioner and community nursing notes may all contain information about preceding events. If the review is held too long after the death, notes may be difficult to retrieve.

- **Written reports** from clinical staff, transcripts of inquests and summaries of management inquiries.

- **Relatives and Carers**

Information from staff who were involved with the patient can be gathered either in written form, using structured pro-forma, or verbally through individual interviews or through meeting with the staff involved as a group. The latter has the potential advantage of clarifying issues of communication but requires a skilled facilitator to handle possible disagreements or recriminations between staff members.

Who to Involve?

Many patients with long-term mental illness who commit suicide have had contact with more than one clinical worker in the months before death. The review should include all involved with the patient and, where sectorised services are delivered by multi-disciplinary teams, consideration might be given to involving all members routinely in reviews. The same might apply to general practitioners given the frequency with which patients who kill themselves consult their GP before the event (Murphy, 1975a & b).

When developing local suicide audit the clinical team have to decide upon the role of managers in the process. Where services are arranged as clinical directorates, key managerial positions are occupied by clinicians; where this is not the case the involvement of service managers may still be useful, particularly when the patient was in hospital at the time of suicide.

What should be Recorded?

In the event of litigation a court could demand access to any report, produced as a result of a review. Those participating should be aware of this, but it should not become an excuse for not holding reviews. Whether a review is held or not any clinical worker could be called to give verbal evidence in Court, under oath. In the current climate clinicians are far more likely to face serious criticism for not holding reviews than to run into legal difficulties as a result of doing so.

It *is* important that participants are fully aware of what record will be made of proceedings. If the process is purely audit, and not part of some other procedure (see below), information or recommendations emanating from reviews should not allow for the identification of individual patients or workers.

Who has access to Findings and Recommendations

The purpose of audit is to improve clinical practice. Much of the benefit from suicide audit is likely to come simply from giving clinical workers the opportunity to reflect on their actions and perhaps decide that, if a similar situation arose again, that they would act differently.

It is likely however that where recommendations are not disseminated beyond those involved in the review a valuable opportunity is being missed. Lessons learned from audit are likely to be applicable to all clinical workers within the mental health service. If changes are required in the behaviour of clinical teams and practice guidelines are to be generated, the results need to be fed into the specialty audit group and perhaps into the district audit committee. If recommendations relate to issues of service delivery eg. management of referrals, or communications between departments, facilities or workers then operational managers within provider units need to be involved.

Purchasers of services need to assure themselves that appropriate mechanisms are in place to ensure quality improvement in clinical care. At present, in many services this is confined to ensuring that a proper audit programme is in place. It is likely that in future they will ask for more specific evidence that clinicians are reviewing their practice. In psychiatry, due to Health of the Nation, this will probably include evidence that a thorough and searching mechanism for suicide audit has been established. From the clinicians' perspective, effective dialogue with purchasers, on audit issues, has potential benefits in that it allows an opportunity for them to feed their priorities into Contracts as the clinical component of quality standards.

Relationship to Other Procedures

When participating in suicide audit, clinical workers have to be fully aware of the purpose and remit of the review. This is particularly true of reviews including different professional groups that may have their separate line managements or even cross agency boundaries. When junior doctors are involved in reviews with consultants; junior nurses with senior nurses and social workers with their team leaders; the relationship of the review to any possible disciplinary proceedings needs to be very clearly spelt out.

Likewise if a service decides that a suicide warrants formal investigation, or if it gives rise to a complaint, a decision must be taken as to whether the investigation should replace the suicide review for that death, whether the review should provide information for the investigation or whether it should occur in isolation from the investigation as a parallel process.

Conclusions

Local audit of suicides requires the willingness of clinical workers to critically review their practice during the aftermath of these distressing events. Its success however depends upon the commitment of the entire service to the process. All disciplines, including managers, must agree and observe the "ground rules" particularly those relating to confidentiality. Clinicians and managers must ensure that an efficient system is in place for identifying cases and also that recommendations are enacted. Purchasers have a right, indeed an obligation, to satisfy themselves that the process is effective.

References

Lelliott P T (1993). *Clinical audit in psychiatry.* Hospital Update. In Press.

Murphy G E (1975a). The physician's responsibility for suicide. I. An error of commission. *Annals of Internal Medicine, 82,* 301–304.

Murphy G E (1975b). The physician's responsibility for suicide. II. Errors of ommission. *Annals of Internal Medicine, 82,* 305–309.

The Health of the Nation: A Strategy for Health in England. Cm. 1986. HMSO: London.

18b Local Audit
John Lambourn

In the South Western Region we have taken both medical audit and suicide very seriously, and with experience of several different approaches to the problem already being tried, we were overjoyed by the timely arrival of The Health of the Nation. Within our regional working party there was unanimous agreement that the targets set for psychiatry are achievable. However with limited resources, it is essential that these are not squandered upon well intentioned intervention born of conviction alone, and we agreed that the first step must be a region-wide audit of all suicides and open verdict cases.

The audit should:–

1. Produce a sufficiently large and reliable pool of information on a range of reputedly or potentially predictive factors, for these to be used in the production of targeted risk assessment schedules.

2. Dispel the doubts of those who still believe that suicide is not a problem in their service, and that there is nothing worthwhile to be done.

3. Provide evidence of which interventions lack efficacy, or even increase risk.

4. Ensure that every district and trust had a uniform approach.

5. Build a sense of ownership of the pooled data.

It is also anticipated that this audit will improve standards of clinical practice by encouraging a more critical approach.

A further bonus of this audit lies in the fact that it can not be carried through by psychiatrists in isolation. It will necessitate working with others, and thus improve integration of services and mutual understanding.

There is already sufficient evidence to suggest that family practitioners are well placed to influence the suicide rates within their populations (Seager & Flood 1965), and it is extremely important that this be verified and reinforced to them, along with any immediate practical guidance which our audit will reveal. It was therefore looked upon as essential that we enlist their assistance and provide them with feedback later. Along with this was a commitment to offer them any assistance they might require when they too become interested in performing their own audits in this field. I must stress that in no way do we see it as our intention to audit what our GP colleagues are doing, rather we need their help in working out what is happening.

The coroner has jurisdiction in the cases which we are considering. It is therefore vital that we enlist the assistance of our coroners and their guidance to ensure that we do not in any way interfere with justice. The coroner also has "Coroner's Officers" working for them doing the job of seeking, receiving and collating much of information we need. With the coroner's blessing we can ask the coroner's officers for a photocopy of their initial reports to the coroner, and they are also the people who are best placed to provide us with the inquest verdicts once the coroner has decided.

The importance of multidisciplinary audit has been stressed; at the same time it is essential that nobody should feel threatened or suffer a need to be economical with the truth. The way round this problem has been the adoption of "cascading audit of sensitive issues" prototyped in Torbay. As soon as we hear of a suicide in a patient being treated by a multidisciplinary clinical team, the responsible consultant holds a meeting with their team. The primary function of the meeting is peer support for team members, but in reality a multidisciplinary audit takes place at the same time with the facts openly discussed, and lessons learned. At the next medical suicide audit meeting, the consultant is able to present facts stripped of emotional overtones, in the same way as members of other disciplines can relay back to their immediate peer group.

A local audit along the above lines has been in operation in Torbay for a couple of years. Its main strengths are its inclusion of all suicides and possible suicides, along with its involvement of general practitioners. Its simplicity and proven achievability in one trust, should guarantee a successful outcome when it is extended to a whole region. The weakness of the Torbay prototype has been its lack of in-depth investigation of cases known to the psychiatric service. For that reason it has been resolved that for these cases, the clinicians involved in their care should be strongly encouraged to complete a proforma from the "Confidential Enquiry". The best return rate and maximum benefit would be achieved at a regional level, by taking an active role in facilitating the national "Confidential Enquiry", while reaping the benefit of being able to extract from it, at the time when we most need it, the information on our own patients.

The process

Having acknowledged the value of the central initiative, we are convinced that unless the process is carried out at a local level, it will not work, and the results are unlikely to be acted upon. In order to overcome this, within each district and trust the consultant psychiatrist who coordinates medical audits will be responsible for setting-up and maintaining the audit of suicide.

Once a month the audit coordinator or their assistant approach their local coroner's officer for copies of the reports which have been prepared for the coroner in all cases where there is a possibility of an "open" or "took own life verdict". It is extremely important that we make our requests to GPs for information before the patient's records are returned to the FHSA, as retrieving them from there can lead to delays, and sometimes they are lost. Care must however be exercised in cases where the coroner has requested a report from the general practitioner, it is important that we do not approach the GP for information until he has completed the report for the coroner. The coroner's officer will know if everything is in order. At the same monthly meeting, the coroner's officers will also be asked for inquest verdicts on the cases from previous months.

In the case of patients known to the service it is probable that the clinical team which was responsible for them, either in hospital or in the community, will already be aware of the death. If not they need to be informed by the audit coordinator, and the cascade audit process is set into motion. The local audit coordinator will in addition to the standard proformas already referred to, hold a supply of the three different "Confidential Inquiry" forms for the audit of cases who had received psychiatric treatment. The appropriate form will be issued to the responsible consultant who will be encouraged to complete them as soon as possible after the meeting with their team. The results of the local cascade audit process, stripped of the emotional overtones, will also be conveyed back to the local psychiatric medical audit meeting, which will deal with suicides and other undesirable outcomes three or four times a year.

Although it is most certainly not our role to challenge the coroner's findings, there are cases of open verdict or even accidental death, where it is possible for those involved in their care to feel reasonably strongly that death was by suicide.

Once a month, the local audit assistants will send copies of completed anonymous data forms, along with all completed "Confidential Enquiry" forms to a central point for entry onto d-base format data base of all cases in the South Western Region. An audit assistant will be employed centrally, one day per week for both this task and to act as a reference point to the other audit assistants. Once the information has been added to our database, the "Confidential Enquiry" forms will then be forwarded on to the national audit.

Interim findings

An important finding is that GPs respond magnificently when approached properly and given a brief and pertinent questionnaire to complete on an important issue. So far we have a 100% return rate.

The project has now been running for 2 years, and in that time the coroner's officers have supplied us with 62 coroner's reports, and 60 subsequent verdicts. The official inquest verdict of "took own life" was recorded in 42 cases. There were also 15 open verdicts, in 11 of which the medical audit concluded that suicide was the most likely explanation. Thus we have 53 cases for interim analysis. With such small numbers, only major trends can be commented upon at this stage.

The first observation concerns suicide reduction and resource targetting. as more than half (28) of the cases were known to the local psychiatric service, a 30% reduction of suicides in this group will produce better than the 15% reduction for the population as a whole.

Table 1 Suicide Verdicts: 42

	Known to local psychiatric service 21				Not known to local psychiatric service 21			
Last saw GP	<1 Month 12		>1 Month 9		<1 Month 10		>1 Month 11	
Gender	M	F	M	F	M	F	M	F
	8	4	7	2	7	3	11	0
Previous Suicide Attempt	3	2	5	1	0	0	1	0

Division of the cases to those having seen the local psychiatric service at some stage, and whether or not they saw their GP within the previous month, produces four groups of similar size (Table 1). the last group, which is exclusively male and contains 5 of the young, car exhaust victims, being the one with the least potential for meaningful intervention by the medical profession.

Eight of the 12 known both to psychiatry and who saw their GP within 30 days of suicide, actually complained to the GP about being depressed. A further three who were unknown to the psychiatric service, but who saw their GP within a month of death, made similar complaints. These must be the groups most easily targeted for suicide prevention purposes.

Suicide risk scales must be made appropriate to the group of people to which they are being applied. A history of parasuicide is a risk factor identified in studies of psychiatric patients (Rorsmann, 1973; Myers & Neal, 1978; Roy, 1982) but it is dangerously misleading when applied globally. While in keeping with previous studies half of the victims known to the psychiatric service had a history of at least one previous "attempt", only one of the 21 who were unknown to the psychiatric service had a history of previous parasuicide. That negative finding on a well known indicator might well have given the GPs a false sense of security in the 10 such patients which they saw within a month of death.

Table 2   Method of Suicide

	Total	Male	Female	Age <50
Overdose	10	5	5	3
Hanging	11	9	2	6
Car exhaust	13	12	1	12

Overdose is no longer the commonest method, overtaken by hanging and poisoning, by car exhaust fumes. Suicide by overdose is equal in both sexes, while hanging and the use of car exhausts is a male prerogative. There is also a clear age difference with only three of 10 overdose victims under 50, while 12 of the 13 car exhaust victims were under 50. Replicating the suicide reduction attributed to the elimination of coal gas, by making catalytic converters compulsory for all vehicles may well be possible.

Table 3   Overdose of Medication

TRIPTAFEN
BENZODIAZEPINE & TRICYCLIC
BENZODIAZEPINE
BARBITURATE
BARBITURATE
PARACETAMOL
CO-CODAPRIN
CO-DYDRAMOL
CO-PROXAMOL
ASPIRIN

Looking at the medication taken in successful overdoses (Table 3), it is clear that despite advertising campaigns for SSRIs, playing on the lethal potential of tricyclic antidepressives, these latter preparations, though commonly prescribed, are not that commonly used as a method of committing suicide. If we are to influence suicide rates by limiting the availability of medication, then the focus of attention should be upon the analgesics, many of which are available on an over the counter basis.

The pilot study already shows many other suggestive clues. Larger numbers are needed before these can be safely commented upon, but the prospects are exciting.

References

Myers DH and Neal CD (1978) Suicide in psychiatric patients. *British Journal of Psychiatry*, 133, 38–44.

Rorsmann B (1973) Suicide in psychiatric patients: a comparative study. *Social Psychiatry*, 8, 55–66.

Roy A (1982). Risk factors for suicide in psychiatric patients, *Archives of General Psychiatry*, 39, 1089–1095.

Seager CP and Flood RA (1965) Suicide in Bristol, *British Journal of Pyschiatry*, 3, 919.

Part 4

Implications for Policy

19a Implications for Purchasing
Sian Griffiths

The inclusion of suicide targets within the Health of the Nation has not been uncontentious. There are many who were critical that it focused attention on the extreme of the mental health/mental illness spectrum. However, listening to the presentations at this conference has demonstrated that there are things we can do.

The importance of suicide as an important cause of avoidable years of life lost, particularly because of the young people who choose to die, set us a particular challenge. We know from presentations made earlier in this conference that suicide accounts for 1% of all deaths. We know something about people who commit suicide, eg. 25% are psychiatric outpatients and that suicide rates are higher amongst young men and in immigrant communities. These facts are now thought of as well known. I would suggest that they were not so well known before the publication of the health strategy.

By focusing our minds on suicide as a target, Health of the Nation has made progress in increasing our awareness of suicide. The production of the handbooks has increased our knowledge and understanding of suicide information. Very much welcomed is the initiative to improve information about suicide, which will be provided by the national suicide audit, and the local action it has stimulated in many places. There is not a region across the country which does not know its pattern of suicide deaths; or the differential pattern within the region. Thus, purchasers now understand the baseline from which we start.

It is not that the publication of HoN initiated action in an area of inactivity, more that it has provided a focus. For example, in North Lincolnshire a scheme was started in 1987 to ensure that all patients admitted to hospital as a result of deliberate self harm undergo full psycho-social assessment by an appropriately trained professional. Other initiatives, such as the establishment of a joint working party between the DHAs in West Sussex and the FHSA to look at information needs and areas for action, started more recently.

I would like to look more closely at three areas where progess is being and will continue to be made. These are: (1) healthy alliances (2) health strategies (3) managerial responsibilities.

1 Healthy Alliances Although HoN was published for the nation and is seen as transcending the barriers between government departments, the documentation included in the handbooks has been distributed via the NHS.

Yet as we have heard at this conference, suicide is inextricably linked to the environment in which people live and life events which befall them. There are not many people who would pretend that the NHS alone can be responsible for those. **Thus, the first implication is that the NHS purchasers**

cannot work alone and need to create healthy alliances. Geraldine Strathdee has described in some detail the sorts of healthy alliances needed at a local level. I would just like to add that healthy alliances can be at different levels and we all need to be involved in making them:

at national
   regional
      local levels.

To take just one example, we have already heard about the high rates of suicide amongst certain groups including farmers. It was at the Health of the Nation conference in South West Thames that the Minister announced £20K was available to support initiatives with farmers. At a national level, I know the National Farmers Union has contacted the DoH about this. There have been discussions about firearm legislation since guns are the commonest method. At a regional level, the directors of public health who have rural populations are discussing what they might do. In other parts of the country there are local support groups emerging. Given that debt is a major stress factor there has also been suggested some work with local bank managers on their attitudes to those with problems. Thus, 'healthy alliances' are being established at national, regional, local levels between the NHS and a wide variety of other agencies and people. This **advocacy role** is an important role for the purchasing authority to play.

2   Creating healthy strategies to prevent suicide is the second important task for purchasers. These need to be informed by scientifically based evaluation of the size of the problem, what are effective interventions and to include evaluation of the success in preventing suicide within population. I would suggest three key stages:

Evaluating the size of the problem: Given the Public Health Common Dataset, all health authorities are able to look at their current rates of suicide. Looking across South West Thames Region the figures for 1992 show variation between districts. Using the confidence intervals shows how difficult it is to make much sense of individual figures, but trends give additional information, and the predicted prevalence figures of the handbook enables us to estimate likely numbers with out populations. All of this was possible before. I would suggest it is now expected.

Effective Interventions: As we begin to understand better who might be at risk of suicide in the community and what might be done to prevent them, purchasers need to use the channels available to them to do all in their power to ensure that effective action is taken. Two examples where purchasers may wish to ensure effective intervention are mentally disordered offenders (MDO's) and primary care.

MDOs are at greater risk of committing suicide. They are often inappropriately placed in prison rather than a health care setting. We heard about suicide in prison yesterday – and the need to see prison as part of our community. Purchasers have a responsibility to ensure **appropriate placement** within secure facilities for such patients. They also need to ensure **appropriate treatment** is given which involves working with the providers to agree standards of care. Consideration needs to be given to interventions such as court diversion schemes.

We have mentioned the importance of the primary care setting throughout this conference. Across the country local purchasers are working with multi-disciplinary groups at local levels to develop effective preventative strategies. In Kidderminster there is a scheme which follows up each suicide attempt with a visit from a trained counsellor. At St Helier Hospital in Sutton an SHO and liaison psychologist have specific responsibility for drawing up clear policies for the treatment, review and follow up of all patients presenting after an incident of deliberate self harm. A similar scheme is being introduced in East Suffolk.

GP fundholders are purchasers and this year they have the capacity to buy community-based services. This includes counselling and the services of community psychiatric nurses. One of the responsibilities of GP fundholders must be that they need to consider reducing suicide risk when selecting services to purchase. Ensuring effective counselling is available, including support for counsellors, is one element that can be looked for in practice plans.

Monitoring outcomes: We have already referred to the introduction of suicide audit and efforts to improve information. I would support those who believe we need regular, systematic audit of suicides to continually learn what it is we can do to prevent unnecessary loss of life.

3 Managerial responsibility. Understanding risk factors and local populations is one thing, ensuring appropriate action another. The introduction of the mental health targets for reduction in suicide have increased awareness *and* the need for NHS managers to make sure that steps are taken to prevent suicide. It is worth referring to the management processes that will increasingly be used to ensure that efforts to reduce suicide are in place. These are:

Corporate Contracts

Purchasing Plans

Practice Business Plans

Making sure it happens involves linking the different levels to ensure that the regional contract with the NHSME includes a commitment to suicide prevention as well as in the contracts between the region and the health authorities within it.

I do not believe it would have been truthful to say all these mechanisms were in place and relevant to suicide prevention last year. I also believe that the discussions at this conference have helped clarify not necessarily the answers but the questions about what purchasers need to do to ensure appropriate policies for suicide prevention.

19b Implications for Purchasing
Hilary Stirland

The DHA Perspective

The aims of purchasing are to improve the health and well-being of the population for whom the "purchasers" have received resources. In the case of suicide prevention, fulfilment of these aims implies obtaining the most appropriate local balance among three main tasks, namely,

- identifying the distribution and then reducing the risks of self harm within the population

- detecting and treating effectively the illnesses that predispose towards self harm

- maintaining sensitive follow up contact with people who have long term illness (particularly people with mental illness but also those whose main disorder is chronic physical disease).

The tools that the purchasers can use to achieve their aims include:–

- Assessment of the health problems relating to mental health and suicide in the local residents and identification of potential strategies to alleviate these

- Direct provision of health promotion services to the general population, high priority groups and to local "caring" agencies (eg social and health care providers, schools, community self help groups, youth programmes etc)

- Contracting with a suitable range of providers of health care for prevention, treatment and continuing care services which are designed to meet the health problems in a way which is acceptable to the various local cultures, races and socio-economic groups

- Indirect (catalytic) influence with both statutory and non-statutory health and social care providers, other local authority departments eg housing, environment, leisure and amenities, voluntary organisations, community groups, self help groups and individual residents in order to enhance the social and physical environment, reduce societal pressure and increase the perception of self worth of the individual.

The unique role (or added value) of purchasers includes the ability to:–

- Take a broad population view of the problem and hence consider the range of provision, the requirements of each service and the best balances between different solutions eg between–
  i)   type of care – prevention/treatment/support,

  ii) focus of intervention – society/patient/carer

  iii) type of service provider – statutory/non-statutory/informal carer/self help.

158

iv) level of care – primary/secondary/tertiary

v) setting for care – hospital or other residential/daycare/outpatient/community

- Make the patient/client perspective central to both the needs assessment and the purchasing strategy for reducing self harm within the local population

- Act as a change agent to improve service effectiveness and responsiveness through a positive partnership with health care providers and encouraging better collaboration between primary and secondary care

- Work directly with and provide practical support to vulnerable groups of the population and enhance the capacity of these communities to identify and respond to specific local needs

- Negotiate broad, local health goals for the improvement of local health

Who are the purchasers and What do they do?

I want to cover three issues: the aims of purchasing; the tools that purchasers have to help them carry out their responsibilities; and the added value that purchasing can bring to the prevention of suicide within a population. I will be speaking from the perspective of a District Health Authority, but what I have to say could equally well be applied in principle to the other purchasers of care, that is Family Health Service Authorities, GP fundholders and Local Authority Social Service departments. If we are to make any headway in reducing suicide rates it is crucial that all purchasers work closely together to develop at least complementary, and preferably joint strategies so that individuals do not fall into service gaps and they cannot see the "joins" in service delivery.

What can purchasing achieve?

In Wandsworth, we believe that the aims of successful purchasing are to help people become healthier, to improve the lot of those who are sick and to reduce premature deaths.

In the context of suicide prevention, this means that we will be looking for strategies to help our residents handle stress and compensate for the effects of social disadvantage. We will also wish to negotiate for the range of interventions that will help to prevent suicide, and for continuing support to reduce the risk of relapse in people with severe mental illness.

The art of successful purchasing lies in striking the right local balance of effort and expenditure among reducing the risk of suicide within the population, detecting and treating pre-disposing illness and supervising effectively those with long term illness. Ways in which we might reduce the level of suicide risk in the population include:–

- working with parents, teachers, youth workers to enhance the self esteem of young people and equip them to make better and more informed decisions about their health and lifestyle

- helping people to cope with adverse life events and social circumstances

- identifying and then offering advice/guidance/support to those at increased risk of developing mental distress or illness

159

- improving the knowledge of parents, teachers and the general public about mental illness to reduce the stigma and encourage troubled people to seek help before they reach crisis point.

- **Important pre-disposing conditions** include depression and para-suicide behaviour. Purchasers will need to ensure that their health care providers are sensitive to warning signs and are able to respond appropriately and without prejudice.

- **Effective supervision** of people with long term illness requires realistic care plans for the severely mentally ill and a service that is flexible enough to plug in assertive outreach work when necessary. The risk of suicide in physically disabled people should not be forgotten. Depression in people with stroke is often undiagnosed, especially when there are communications difficulties. Carers can be very helpful in pre-empting crises if they are adequately trained and supported.

How can purchasing influence health?

The tools that purchasers have at their disposal are health needs assessment; direct provision of health promotion; contracting for services; and a catalytic influence on agencies whose main business may or may not be health, but whose actions certainly can influence health.

To assess local health needs we need to talk with local service providers, users and carers and learn from experience elsewhere so that we can come up with the most appropriate local solutions to the local health problems. In painting the local picture we can make use of both routinely available data like mortality rates, information about socio-economic characteristics and service use data. We can also undertake specific enquiries, for instance into deaths where self injury played a part. In Wandsworth, we have found:–

- significant variations among the electoral wards in social deprivation and in overall death rates

- suicide death rates that are 20% higher than the South West Thames Regional average but 45% lower than the neighbouring district of West Lambeth

- considerable random year on year variation even in the 3 year average standardised suicide death rates making it difficult to demonstrate whether or not the Health of the Nation targets are being achieved

- In 1991, half of the people in whose deaths self harm was believed to play a part were known to the mental health services and in 45% substance misuse was involved.

Direct provision of health promotion is intended to:

- dispel the myths surrounding mental illness and increase the level of understanding of a wider range of people

- give local community representatives the skills and abilities to help each other, for example via projects like Home start or Newpin

- help local communities improve their living conditions and lifestyles.

Contracting for services should result in:

- specification of a full range of services and choice of provider to suit different needs and provide different modes of access

- partnerships with voluntary organisations and the introduction and evaluation of innovative methods of service delivery

- better collaboration between hospital and primary care services

- gradual improvement in quality and outcome of service provision through the agreement of targets and staging posts towards these.

Indirect or catalytic influence on other people or agencies could achive:

- an improved physical environment which enhances the feeling of well-being through working with housing, environmental services and technical services departments of the local authority

- access to meaningful day time occupation through partnership with education, social services and local employment agencies

- access to interesting and stimulating leisure activities through working with the leisure and amenities department, and local voluntary and self help groups.

Is there an added value of purchasing:

There are a number of beneficial changes which have come about since the advent of purchasing. Although it is theoretically possible that these would have occurred anyway, the fact remains that purchasers can act like the grain of sand in the oyster shell which starts the growth of the pearl! Examples of the ways in which purchasers can uniquely contribute to the prevention of suicide are:–

i) by taking an overall view of their populations' needs, relative priorities and service opportunities, they can identify gaps and needs which are poorly met. Thus they are better placed to choose the best service balance and to lever changes to introduce effective interventions and to make sure that preventive action is not forgotten. Choices will have to be made in the following areas

- type of care – prevention, treatment, continuing care/support

- level of intervention – society, patient, carer

- type of care giver – statutory, non-statutory, informal carer, self care

- level of care – primary, secondary, tertiary

- setting of care – hospital, community, patients home

ii) by raising the profile of the patient and carer and ensuring that services are easy and safe to access and are sensitive to their beliefs and values, it is more likely that they will seek help and stay in touch with the support they require to avoid a tragedy. Empowering service users and their carers implies informing and educating as well as listening to their own perceptions of need and desired outcomes. There are a number of ways of obtaining user participation in decisions about health care, including focus discussion groups, formal patient and carer surveys, informal meetings with existing groups, patients councils, befriending and advocacy schemes.

iii) by asking questions and offering a fresh perspective purchasers can act as a change agent. For example, there is an increasing body of evidence that good community care improves the probability of a favourable outcome of treatment for mental illness and prevention of self harm. A positive partnership between purchasers and providers of health care can facilitate the shift from hospital to community based care by stimulating and supporting change. For example, in Wandsworth, we have generated a health gain initiative fund by selected disinvestment in order to pump prime innovative schemes to improve health. One project is to enhance the numbers and skill mix of community mental health teams to fulfil specific health objectives. The success in achieving these objectives will be monitored and further changes made as indicated.

iv) by working directly with vulnerable communities and pump priming new initiatives, it is possible to enhance their own coping skills and sense of being more in control of their lives. In Wandsworth, we are starting on a community project on one of the poorer council estates which was initiated by the local vicar. One of the aims of this project is to support isolated young mothers and others living alone in order to reduce their chances of becoming severely depressed.

v) by focussing attention on health outcomes instead of bodies in beds or attenders at outpatients clinics, it is possible to become more positively selective in choosing the right treatment modality and support package for the individual.

20 Implications for Education: Prevention of Youth Suicide
David Shaffer

Introduction – A Model to work with

Suicide prevention strategies should be informed by a coherent and hopefully accurate model of causation. The large literature on the risk factors for suicide and the smaller one on the changes that occur prior to the event, although not definitive, allow us to develop such a model (see Figure 1). The basis for the assumptions that have gone into the model are described and documented more fully by Shaffer (1988).

The model assumes that the majority of adolescent suicides are drawn from a large, but definable pool of at-risk individuals. Risk is increased by a variety of psychiatric illnesses or character disorders including depression; alcohol abuse; aggression/impulsivity; and anxious, perfectionistic, and rigid behaviours. Although only a small proportion of the individuals who bear such risk will eventually commit suicide, very few individuals who are not drawn from the pool will ever do so.

Figure 1

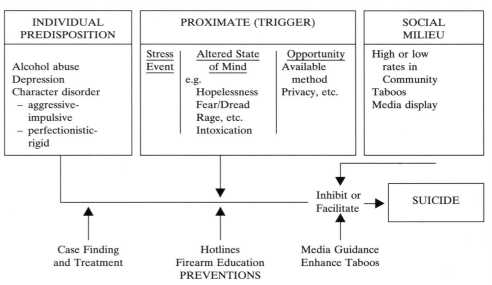

Stressful events occur commonly within hours or days of most adolescent suicides (although this is less true of suicide in depressed teens). They are not, in themselves, uncommon, e.g., a dispute with a boy- or girlfriend, an arrest, an impending examination or recent examination result, and many seem to be a consequence of the disorders that characterize the at-risk group. As far as we can reconstruct from psychological autopsy studies, the state of mind of the potential suicide immediately prior to their decision to suicide is usually disturbed, often, but not always, as a consequence of these recent stressors. Disturbed affects include alcohol intoxication, feeling enraged, being in a state of anticipatory anxiety or dread, or feeling hopeless. The occurrence of a stress event and an altered mind state in a vulnerable individual may still not suffice to lead to suicide and some culturally acceptable or known method has to be available. This will vary from community to community.

Finally, the likelihood that a pre-suicidal individual will proceed to attempt or commit suicide will vary as a function of their cultural milieu. Individuals living in communities with consistently high suicide rates will likely know and be familiar with others who have attempted or committed suicide and this will make it easier for them to engage in the behaviour at times of stress. Suicide will be a less common outcome for adolescents who live in communities or belong to cultures in which suicide is rare and unusual.

Primary prevention

Primary prevention could operate to reduce the number of at risk individuals and reduce their access to lethal methods.

1) Treatment of Mental Disorder

Because most suicides suffer from a mental disorder at the time of their death, the availability of mental health services or the introduction of an effective treatment should, reduce the burden of mental illness and, by extension, also reduce the suicide rate. This proposition was studied by Walk (1967) in Sussex and Nielson and Videbech (1973) in Denmark. Neither study found a change in the suicide rate after a community psychiatric service was introduced. However, neither study was controlled and it is possible that the stable suicide rates that were observed might have increased had the services not been introduced. Furthermore, both studies took place before the widespread use of antidepressants and lithium. Recent studies on the impact of lithium treatment on suicide rates among adult patients with bipolar or recurrent mood disorder (Coppen et al, 1991; Schou & Weeke, 1988) have not been conclusive.

Alcohol abuse has been shown to be an important risk factor for suicide for both teenagers and for adults (Robins, 1959) and reducing access to alcohol might be expected to reduce suicide rates. The suicide rate in the Baltic Republics declined significantly between 1984 and 1988 (Varnik and Wasserman, 1992). This was a period that coincided with both the introduction of democratic institutions and also, perhaps more importantly, as far as suicide is concerned, with strict limitations on the sale of alcohol. The decline in suicide was particularly marked for males falling from approximately 55/100,000 to 37/100,000 (Varnik, 1991). The more striking effect on males suggests that the restriction of access to alcohol could reduce the suicide rate.

2) Restricted Access to Methods

In young people, suicide is often impulsive. An impulsive suicide requires ready access to an acceptable method and so it is not unreasonable to expect that some suicides could be prevented by limiting access to commonly used, easily accessed methods of suicide. The most persuasive example of how reducing access to a method of completing suicide can impact on suicide rates is the so-called "British experience" of the 1960s. In 1957, self-asphyxiation with domestic cooking gas accounted for over 40% of all British suicides (Hassall and Trethowan, 1972; Kreitman, 1976). At that time, the mean carbon monoxide content of domestic gas in Great Britain was 12%. By 1970, through the introduction of natural gas, the mean carbon monoxide content of domestic gas had been reduced to 2% and, over the same period, British suicide rates from carbon monoxide asphyxiation declined steadily. By 1971, suicides by this method accounted for fewer than 10% of all suicides and the overall suicide rate had been reduced by 26% with most of the decline being attributed to the decrease in deaths by domestic gas asphyxiation. There was no compensatory increase in suicidal deaths by other methods, although there was an increase in the incidence of suicide attempts by overdose during this period. It is implausible that all individuals who would have committed suicide by domestic gas asphyxiation would not have tried another method. It is more likely that the suicidal population, no longer having access to one universally available, non-deforming and non-violent method turned to another i.e., self-poisoning. However, during that time this alternative method became progressively less dangerous. This was in part because of restricted access to highly toxic barbituates and in part because of improved methods of resuscitation. What is most notable is that British rates of suicide remained at the new, lower level (Farberow, 1985) for many years. While the detoxification of domestic gas also occurred in other European countries, the base rate of self-asphyxiation from domestic gas was much lower in these countries than in Great Britain and it was not associated with a similar reduction in suicide rates.

A somewhat similar but less dramatic phenomenon has been seen in the United States. The introduction of automobile emission control systems which reduce the carbon monoxide content of automobile exhaust has coincided with a decline in suicide rates due to asphyxiation (Clark & Lester, 1987).

Most suicides in the United States are committed with firearms and it has been suggested (Boyd and Moscicki, 1986) that increases in U.S. suicide rates can be attributed to the increased availability of firearms in that country's households. However, this argument, which is subject to the ecological fallacy (Selvin, 1958), is not entirely convincing because there have been similar increases in youth suicide rates in a number of European countries where there has been no marked increase in the availability of firearms. Nevertheless, it would be sensible to deny firearm ownership (most suicides by firearms are committed with legally registered firearms kept for sporting purposes) to those who share a household with a young male who falls into an at-risk category or discourage parents of high-risk teenagers from keeping firearms in their homes, except under the most secure conditions.

3) *Alter Social Milieu*

Evidence relating social and/or media influences to suicide appears elsewhere in this volume. Despite methodological flaws and some expected inconsistencies, taken together, the evidence is persuasive. Ecological studies such as those conducted by Phillips and his colleagues (Bolin and Phillips, 1981; 1982; Phillips, 1974; 1979; 1986; Phillips and Carlsenson, 1986) have shown that prominent display of news about a famous suicide in

Figure 2

39) During the past 3 months, how much of a problem have you been having with feeling **unhappy** or **sad**?

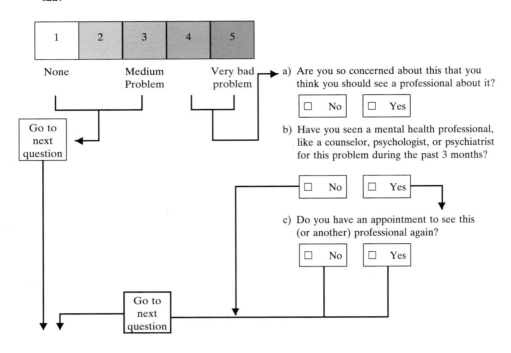

46) During the past 3 months, have you thought about **killing yourself**?

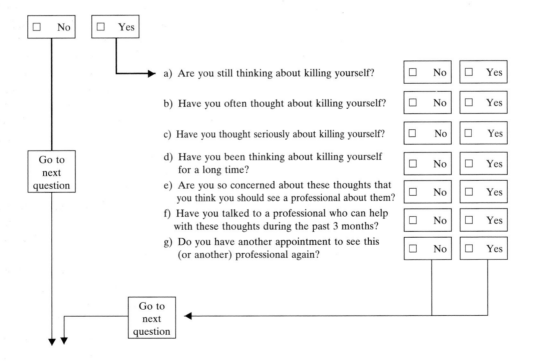

newspapers is associated with a significant increase in suicides during the one to two weeks following the news display. Other ecological studies on fictional representation of suicides (Gould and Shaffer, 1986; Schmidtke and Hefner, 1986; Gould et al., 1988; Schmidtke, 1988) are complemented by documented anecdotes of copycat suicides (Shaffer, 1974) and the documented occurrence of suicide clusters (Gould and Davidson, 1988; Gould, 1989). The effects of minimizing these influences have not been researched but providing guidelines for newspapers and television services and carefully reviewing educational curricula that could affect attitudes to suicide have a common sense appeal. More specifically, media could be encouraged to downplay the reporting of suicide. If suicide is to be the topic of a news story, reporting should not, out of misplaced compassion, minimize features of mental illness that might have been present in the suicide; ill-informed acquaintances who provide a romantic, but erroneous, formulation of a suicide should not be relied upon; and accurate details of the method should not be portrayed. Finally, news stories about suicide could be accompanied by messages indicating how to access sources of help.

| **Secondary prevention** | Secondary preventions identify and provide help for those who are already suicidal. |

Last-Minute Interventions – Hotline and Crisis Services

Intervention with people who are on the verge of suicide could be a potentially efficient strategy. This is the final common period for a variety of risk groups that might escape other interventions. However, systematic research on the efficacy of last-minute or crisis interventions is not encouraging (See Shaffer et al, 1988 for a review). There appear to be several reasons for this. First of all, there may be a general tendency for the groups at risk not to use hotlines. In one study, teenagers were significantly less likely to know about hotlines (Greer and Anderson, 1979). Men, who account for most completed suicides, also seem reluctant to call for help and constitute only a small minority of crisis service users. Presumably ignorance about hotlines and gender-related resistance could be overcome by specially designed advertising campaigns.

A second reason for the apparent failure of crisis services is that the advice given to callers is often inappropriate. It may be stereotyped and insensitive to the specific needs of the caller (Bleach and Clairburne, 1974; Apsler and Hodas, 1975). Other faults include operators who are dogmatic and give hasty advice and those who are overly directive, and gave advice prematurely before receiving adequate information (McCarthy and Berman, 1979). Hotline responders are also less skillful than professionals in eliciting relevant past history and integrating caller information (Hirsh, 1981). In summary, hotlines are highly sensitive to the skills of answering personnel so that within a service that has a uniform policy and training procedures, caller compliance will vary with different telephone operators (Slaiku et al., 1975). Although these vulnerabilities can be reduced by training – Elkins and Cohen (1982) showed that volunteers who had received preliminary training improved their performance with experience – an effective crisis service clearly needs frequent review and retraining so that, even if the most vulnerable group could be encouraged to call, this is not a robust mechanism.

Casefinding

Identifying people who fall into "at risk" groups and treating their condition is an alternative but potentially less accurate secondary prevention strategy. However, the cost can be reduced in adolescents because casefinding exercises can be conveniently carried out in high school students where a large population can be surveyed rapidly by relatively few personnel.

Case finding activities can be grouped into procedures in which information about suicidal risk status is obtained *directly* from the youth and those where it is obtained *indirectly* from third parties such as peers, teachers or parents.

Direct Casefinding

The most commonly used method of direct casefinding in school-based suicide prevention programs is to discuss and describe suicide in such a way as to encourage suicidal adolescents to refer themselves for treatment. Taboos about suicide are down-played and there is an expectation that any suicidal youth who might be in the class would be encouraged to declare their presence (in confidence) and then seek help. It is our observation that a commonly used component of this destigmatization element program is to dissociate suicide from mental disturbance. Suicide is presented as an understandable, but foolish and short-sighted response to stress. Videotapes, often of attractive and articulate survivors of past suicide attempts may be shown in which the previous attempter describes a past suicide attempt. The behaviour is explained as a response to a stress event that will be familiar to the teen students. We have never encountered a videotape that shows a clearly disturbed adolescent. One brochure prepared for adolescents that has been distributed world-wide, indicates that it is a "myth" that suicides have mental disturbances. On *a priori* grounds, this approach to destigmatization could make adolescents' view suicide as a more normal behaviour and although this has never been demonstrated, reducing such negative attitudes to suicide could remove attitudes that may be serving to inhibit potential suicides.

Indirect Casefinding

Indirect casefinding exercises in schools provide descriptions of symptomatic features, most commonly of depression, to students, teachers and parents along with suggestions about how to refer at risk youth to a treatment agency. Some of the problems with this approach are a) only a minority of suicide victims are depressed; b) many adolescents who are at risk do not have symptoms that are visible to others; c) conversely, many of the symptoms of depression such as social withdrawal and/or irritability occur commonly in adolescence, are not specific for depression, and in only a few cases presage suicidal behaviour and d) it is very difficult for teenagers or teachers to intrude unasked into the activities of non-kin who have not voluntarily requested help.

Evaluation of Curriculum-Based Suicide Prevention Programs

To investigate the safety and efficacy of suicide prevention curricula we undertook an elaborate controlled longitudal study of three broadly similar school-based suicide prevention programs (Shaffer, et al., 1990, 1991;

Vieland, 1991). 1,312 students in six high schools situated in urban, suburban, and rural communities who had received a program were compared with 2,012 students in control schools who had not been evaluated. Demonstration and control schools were matched for ethnicity, size and proportion of households in the school district falling below the poverty level. A 48-item, self-completion questionnaire that inquired about attitudes to suicide, warning signs of suicide, and attitudes to seeking help for emotional distress was administered between 1 and 3 days before the programs were implemented, and re-administered 1 and 18 months later. The same two-stage procedure was followed in the control schools, with no intervention being given between administrations. Co-operation rates were generally good. Analyses were performed on students for whom pre- and post-test surveys could be matched. Students were divided into groups on the basis of baseline responses, and were then examined for change at post-test using chi-square tests (Fleiss, 1981). Separate analyses were carried out on teenagers who admitted at baseline to having made a previous suicide attempt.

Two-thirds of the students found the programs helpful and fewer than 10% found them upsetting or knew someone who had been upset by the program. Most students agreed with the program's tenets before receiving the program. Not surprisingly, before any intervention was given the overwhelming majority held the view that suicide is not a reasonable solution to problems and that if you are thinking about suicide it would be a good idea to get help. It followed that the programs could only have their intended effect among a small subgroup of students who were deviant in their initial responses. Previous attempters' attitudes to suicide were significantly more likely to be deviant. Unfortunately, the programs were ineffective in changing the unwanted attitudes in the small group. Indeed, among students who, at pre-test, indicated that suicide could not be a solution to problems and, who felt that suicide could be a reasonable solution, a small, but statistically significant change in the opposite direction was noted. The programs also resulted in small and generally non-lsignificant changes in adolescents' knowledge of treatment resources and at the 18 month follow-up there was no evidence that the programs had been effective in inducing adolescents to seek help for their own emotional problems (Vieland, 1991).

Direct Casefinding Without A Suicide Curriculum

There is no obvious reason why identifying at-risk individuals by unskilled observers is better than doing so through direct inquiry. Symptoms of depression and anxiety are inherently more likely to be known to adolescents themselves than to outside observers (Weissman et al., 1987) so that a feasible alternative to asking friends and relatives to look out for depressed or suicidal teens is to ask the teens directly through systematic screening to identify themselves directly. This approach carries the advantage that it is not conveying information that could be misunderstood or applied in a paradoxical way.

We are currently testing a screening instrument and procedure for this purpose in the New York City region. The screening instrument includes items about physical, as well as mental symptoms and we hope that, by embedding the emotional distress items among physical health items, the former will be less conspicuous, and that it will promote disclosure of feelings. The questions about depression, suicide ideation and behaviour, anxiety, and alcohol use and abuse are phrased in a global way to optimize sensitivity. However, in order to reduce the burden of screening staff, positive answers to these global questions are followed by contingent questions on severity, need for and previous and current history of help (See Figure 2).

14-to-18-year-old students complete a 15-minute questionnaire in class. The questionnaires are reviewed to determine screen status and high-risk students who have indicated suicidal ideation within the past 3 months and/or lifetime history of previous attempt(s) or who indicate concern over mood symptoms or alcohol are then interviewed. The first stage of the interview procedure can be performed by unskilled assistants using the highly structured computerized Diagnostic Interview Schedule for Children (DISC) (Shaffer et al, 1993) that determines the criteria for a range of common psychiatric disorders including those that are known to be associated with suicidal behaviour. Immediately after completion, it prints out a summary of all positive symptom criteria and diagnoses. A clinician then reviews the questionnaire and DISC interview summary and, where appropriate, conducts a clinical interview of the subject. Students deemed to be in need of mental health services are assisted by a case-manager, who connects the child to a clinical service, maintains contact with the student, and continues to offer support for a period of six to nine months following the screening exercise.

Preliminary analyses confirm our expectation that adolescents with troubling suicidal preoccupations will identify themselves. 15.5% of 1,548 students screened at 5 schools reported suicidal ideation during the past 3 months, and 6.1% reported having made at least one previous suicide attempt. As in Great Britain, we have found that Asian students had significantly higher rates of both suicidal ideation, and previous suicide attempts.

Preliminary validation studies have compared questionnaire responses to scores on the Beck Depression Inventory (BDI). Screen identified high risk status by virtue of ideation has shown a sensitivity of .59, and specificity of .90 compared to a BDI score of ≥16 and a sensitivity of .27 and specificity of .97 with students considered at-risk because of one or more previous suicide attempts (excluding the BDI item on suicidal behaviour). The low sensitivity of the BDI in these situations suggests that our questionnaire is a more appropriate measure.

Up to 7% of students were deemed suitable for referral. The method also appears to identify teenagers who others did not think were disturbed. Without knowledge of screen status, professionals within the school were asked to identify which of the students screened were known to them as having emotional problems. Initial analyses regarding the unique value of the screen have indicated that approximately half of 299 students were not known to school psychologists or social workers as being in need of help, and may therefore have gone undetected had the project not been implemented.

Given the narrow risk factor profile uncovered by previous research (Gould et al., 1988), we suggest that it is not unreasonable to view casefinding for suicide risk as a sound, empirically based and attainable goal. The self-report method provides an inexpensive and relatively easy way to identify students who may be at risk, and to then inform, and enlist the help of parents when applicable, and to facilitate entry into mental health treatment, where appropriate. Preliminary results have shown that the screen is effective in identifying students at risk by one, or more criteria, and that the screen appears to be reasonably accurate. As approximately half of the students identified at the first round of schools were unknown to relevant school staff as being in need of help, this method greatly enhances the potential of the school as an effective site for preventive work. Students who were referred for mental health services represent a group who may not have been referred, even after parents were informed of the need for services. The method is hopefully safe, cost-effective, and easy to administer.

Bibliography

Apsler R and Hodas M. Evaluating hotlines with simulated calls. *Crisis Intervention. 1975;* 6; 14–21.

Bleach G and Claiborn W L. Initial evaluation of hotline telephone crisis centers. *Community Mental Health Journal. 1974;* 10: 387–394.

Bollen K A; Phillips D P. Imitative suicides: a national study of the effects of television news stories. *American Sociological Review;* Dec. 1982; 47(6): 802–809.

Bollen K A and Phillips D P. Suicidal motor vehicle fatalities in Detroit: a replication. *American Journal of Sociology;* 1981; 87(2): 404–412.

Boyd J H and Moscicki E K. Firearms and youth suicide *American Journal of Public Health;* 1986; 76(10): 1240–2.

Clarke R V and Lester D. Toxicity of car exhausts and opportunity for suicide comparison between Britain and the United States. J. of Epidimiol. *Community Health.* 1987; 41(2): 114–120.

Coppen A, Standish-Barry H, Bailey J, Houston G, Silcocks P and Hermon C (1991). Does Lithium reduce the mortality of recurrent mood disorders? *Journal of Affective Disorders,* 23: 1–7.

Elkins R L and Cohen C R. A comparison of the effects of pre-job training and job experience on non-professional telephone crisis counsellors. *Suicide and Life-Threatening Behavior.* 1982; 12(2): 84–89.

Farberow N L. Mental health aspects of disaster in smaller communities. *American Journal of Social Psychiatry.* 1985; 5(4): 43–55.

Fleiss J L. *Statistical methods for rates and proportions,* (2nd ed.). New York: John Wiley; 1981.

France K. Evaluation of lay volunteer telephone workers. *American Journal of Community Psychiatry.* 1975; 3(3): 197–218.

Genther R. Evaluating the functioning of community-based hotlines. *Professional Psychology.* Nov. 1974; 409–414.

Gould M S; Davidson L. Suicide contagion among adolescents. In: A R Stiffman and R A Feldman (Eds.) *Advances in Adolescent Mental Health, Volume III:* Depression and Suicide; 1988.

Gould M S; Shaffer D. The impact of suicide in television movies: evidence of imitation. *New England Journal of Medicine;* 1986; 315, 690–694.

Gould M, Shaffer D and Kleinman M. The impact of suicide in television movies: replication and commentary. *Suicide and Life-Threatening Behavior.* 1988; 18: 90–99.

Gould M, Wallenstein S and Davidson L. Suicide Cluster: A Critical Review. Special Issue: Strategies for studying suicide and suicidal behaviour. *Suicide and Life Threatening Behavior.* 1989; 19(1): 17–29.

Greer S and Anderson M. Samaritan contact among 325 parasuicide patients. *British Journal of Psychiatry,* 1979; 135: 263–268.

Hassall C and Trethowan W H. Suicide in Birmingham. *British Medical Journal.* 1972; 1: 717–18.

Hirsch S. A critique of Volunteer- staffed suicide prevention centres. *Canadian Journal of Psychiatry.* 1981; 26: 406–410.

Kalafat J, Boroto D R. and France K. Relationships among experience level and value orientation and the performance of paraprofessional telephone counsellors. *American Journal of Community Psychology.* 1979; 7(2): 167–180.

Kreitman N. The coal gas story: United Kingdom suicide rates. *British Journal of Preventitive Social Medicine.* 1976; 30: 86–93.

McCarthy B and Berman A. A student operated crisis center. *Personnel and Guidance Journal.* 1979; 49: 523–528.

Nielson J; Videbech T. Suicide frequency before and after introduction of community psychiatry in a Danish island. *British Journal of Psychiatry;* 1973; 123: 35–399.

Phillips D P. The influence of suggestion on suicide: substantive and theoretical implication of the Werther effect. *American Sociological Review;* 1974; 39: 340–354.

Phillips D P. Natural experiments on the effects of mass media violence on fatal aggression: strengths and weaknesses of a new approach. *Advances in Experimental Social Psychology;* 1986; 19: 207–250.

Phillips D P. Suicide, motor vehicle fatalities, and the mass media: evidence toward a theory of suggestion. *American Journal of Sociology;* 1979; 84: 1150–1174.

Phillips D P: Carstenson L L. Clustering of teenage suicides after television news stories about suicide. *New England Journal of Medicine;* 1986; 315: 685–689.

Robins E, Gassner S, Kayes J [and others]. The communication of suicide intent: a study of 134 consecutive cases of successful (completed) suicide. *American Journal of Psychiatry;* 1959; 115: 724–733.

Schmidtke A; Hafner H. Die vermittlung von selbstmordmotivation und selbstmordhandlung durch fiktive modelle: Die folgen der fernsehserie "Tod eines Schulers". (Transmission of suicide motivation and suicidal behaviour through fictional models: The consequences of the [German] TV series "Death of a student"). *Nervenarzt;* 1986; 57 (502–510).

Schmidtke A and Hafner H (1988). The Werther Effect after Television Films: New Evidence for an old Hypothesis. *Psychological Medicine,* 18: 665–676.

Schou M and Weeke A. Did manic-depressive patients who committed suicide receive prophylactic or continuation treatment at the time? *British Journal of Psychiatry.* 1988; 153: 324–327.

Selvin H C. Durkheim's *Suicide* and problems of empirical research. *American Journal of Sociology,* 1958; 63: 607–619.

Shaffer D. Suicide in childhood and early adolescence. *Journal of Child Psychology and Psychiatry;* 1974; 15: 275–291.

Shaffer D, Garland A, Fisher P, Bacon K and Vieland V (1987). Suicide Crisis Centers: A Critical Reappraisal with Special Reference to the Prevention of Youth Suicide. In (eds. Goldstein, Heinicke, et al.) *Prevention of Mental Health Disturbance in Childhood.* APA Press.

Shaffer D, Vieland V, Garland A, Rojas M, Underwood M and Busner C. Adolescent Suicide Attempters: Response to Suicide-Prevention Programs. *Journal of American Medical Association;* 1990; 264(24): 3151–3155.

Shaffer D, Garland A, Vieland V, Underwood M, Busner C. The impact of curriculum-based suicide prevention programs for teenagers. *Journal of American Academy of Child and Adolescent Psychiatry;* 1991; 30(4).

Shaffer D and Gould M. *Study of completed and attempted suicides in adolescents, Progress report:* NIMH Grant# MH38198, (1987). Hyattsville, M D.

Shaffer D, Garland A, Gould M, Fisher P and Trautman P. Preventing teenage suicide: a critical review. *Journal of American Academy of Child and Adolescent Psychiatry;* 1988; 27: 675–687.

Slaiku K A, Tulkin S R and Speer D C. Process and outcome in the evaluation of telephone counselling referrals. Journal of Consulting and Clinical Psychology. 1975; 43: 700–7.

Varnik A and Wasserman D. Suicides in the former Soviet republics. *Acta Psychiatrica Scandinavica,* 1992; 86(1): 76–78.

Varnik A. Suicide in Estonia. *Acta Psychiatrica Scandinavica,* 1991; 84(3): 229–232.

Vieland V, Whittle B, Garland A, Hicks R and Shaffer D. The impact of curriculum-based suicide prevention programs for teenagers: an 18-month follow-up. *Journal of American Academy of Child and Adolescent Psychiatry;* Sept 1991; 30(5).

Walk D. Suicide and community care. *British Journal of Psychiatry;* 1967; 113: 1381–1391.

Weissman M M, Wichramaratne P, Warner V et al. Assessing Psychiatric Disorder in Children: discrepancy between mother's and children's reports. *Archives of General Psychiatry;* 1987; 44: 747–53.

21 Implications for Training of Health Professionals
Eugene Paykel

In this paper I will look briefly at the training of health professionals and others in suicidal behaviour. I will try to survey the situation asking four questions. Who needs to be trained? What training do they get? What should be the content of training? What are the implications?

Who needs to be trained?

Broadly speaking, all health professionals need to know something about suicidal behaviour: there are very few aspects of health care on which this does not impinge. For some years, at St. George's Hospital Medical School in London, I taught medical students jointly in a topic teaching session on suicide with a physician, who dealt with management of overdose, and with a pathologist, who dealt with the fatal outcomes which, one way or another, reached him. We could have been joined by a toxicologist, a general practitioner, or any number of specialists to whom atypical and masked depressives might present.

Table 1 lists some of the people who need training. There are four groups. Mental health professionals are the obvious targets. However, the most important message is that the need extends well beyond them.

Table 1   Who needs to be trained?

Mental Health Professionals	Other Health Professionals	Other Professionals	Volunteers
Psychiatrists	Medical students	Social Workers	Samaritans
Psychiatric nurses	Hospital doctors	Counsellors	Citizens Advice
Psychologists	GPs	Sheltered housing staff	Bureaux staff
	General nurses		Others
	Practice nurses		
	Community nurses		
	Health visitors		

Equally obvious but more difficult is the need to train health professionals who are not mental health specialists. This includes all the professions. All doctors need it, and at a variety of levels, starting with medical students. Hospital specialists and specialists in training of all kinds need it. Nowadays, doctors on medical wards and in accident and emergency departments are expected to assess suicidal patients and they treat patients who take overdoses, and other suicide attempters, every day. Really all hospital doctors need to be skilled in detection, assessment and management of suicidal risk, since it may present almost anywhere. The association of suicide with physical illness highlights the need for good detection of depression and hopelessness in these circumstances.

Again among doctors general practitioners clearly need skills in relation to suicidal behaviour. Depression is common in general practice. A considerably larger proportion of suicides have seen a GP than a psychiatrist in time periods shortly before the suicide. Barraclough (1974) found that two thirds had seen a family doctor in the preceding month, but only 18% had seen a psychiatrist. Figures presented by Dr. Vassilas for general practice contact at this workshop are, however, considerably lower, particularly for young males, and point to a problem which professional education cannot solve.

Equally, nurses need training. In hospital the suicidal patient may be resented as consuming much needed time and resources, and cues may therefore not be picked up. In the community, the same applies to practice nurses, district nurses and other members of the primary health care team. It is also true of health visitors. They come into contact with a particularly vulnerable group, postnatal mothers, where depression is common and intervention has been shown to be effective (Holden et al, 1987).

Once we move away from the mental health specialist, we come across another problem which must be acknowledged. The needs are many and diverse; suicidal risk is only one problem encountered and an uncommon one. There will be a conflict between the effort needed to develop fully this skill, and the extent to which it will be deployed.

There are two other large groups who are not health professionals but are shown in the table. The first comprises professionals in non-health areas. Among this group social workers are particularly important. For those who act as approved social workers under the Mental Health Act, suicidal risk is one circumstance under which compulsory admission may be indicated. Others who come into contact with suicidal problems are sheltered housing staff, and professional counsellors.

The second group comprises volunteers. The Samaritans have made particular contributions not only to services but to thinking out the needs for training and supervision of volunteers, and I will touch again on this aspect in due course. There are many other groups. My sister, who is a musician but has worked for a few years in a Citizens Advice Bureau, has described to me how she frequently comes into contact with depressed people in crisis. Suicide is associated with a number of life situations and problems, particularly, in young males, unemployment and imprisonment. Implications for prevention and training reach far outside the sphere of health professionals.

What training do they get?

What training do people currently receive, and what are the gaps? In the training of psychiatrists and other mental health professionals, there is much theoretical emphasis and much practical experience in everyday work, of suicidal risk and behaviour. For psychiatrists, whose training I know best, assessment and management of suicidal risk is something to be acquired and refined as part of basic training in skills and knowledge, at SHO and registrar level, in lectures, seminars and clinical experience, and it is tested in the MRCPsych examination. In higher training at Senior Registrar level, the pre-consultant trainee acquires more experience in special problems, particularly relevant to his or her own more specialised area – adult general psychiatry, psychogeriatrics, mental handicap, psychotherapy, forensic psychiatry, child psychiatry.

Psychiatric nurses also receive training in suicide, and live with the problem in a close way in their work. Experience, with good supervision, is in my opinion a key aspect of training for mental health workers. Clinical psychologists get less training in this area, but overall, for most mental health workers, although not all is perfect, I do not think there are major gaps: it is more a question of the blind spot that living with the risk every day engenders.

When we move to other health professionals, the situation becomes progressively less satisfactory. Medical students receive only a limited exposure to psychiatry but that applies to the other medical subjects as well and in most medical schools there is parity in a specialist year in time allocation between psychiatry, paediatrics, and obstetrics and gynaecology. The teaching always does include some didactic education in suicidal behaviour and it is usually one of the better taught aspects of the psychiatric medical curriculum. The subject is seen as important, because of the risk to life. It lends itself to a factual approach and to structured clinical training in assessment, and it has specifics which can be examined. In Cambridge, our students are told that if they omit to ask a depressed patient regarding feelings of suicide in a clinical examination, they will fail it.

Somewhat forgotten is the training for non-psychiatric hospital specialists. As far as I am aware there is usually little training in this area other than in physical aspects of managing the consequences of the attempt. Again, for GPs, while there is some recognition of the need to interview for depression and suicidal feelings, and to refer the actively suicidal patient, the amount of training and skill acquisition may vary, and may not be high where a psychiatric SHO post has not been held.

For my two other groups in the table, training experience varies. Those social workers who act as approved social workers for the Mental Health Act receive special training for it. For others suicide may not rank so high. Psychiatrists complain about the extent to which the content of some social work courses and nursing courses seems influenced by sceptical social construction views of mental illness, and not well applicable to the real situation.

I will discuss the excellent training of Samaritans shortly.

What should be the content of training?

There have not been many attempts to formulate explicitly the content of desirable training, and one learns mainly from what is actually taught.

My own experience is mainly in teaching medical students and psychiatric trainees. For medical students the usual knowledge and skills include basic epidemiology of suicide and suicide attempts, some understanding of the complex motivation in suicidal acts; knowledge of the methods particularly for overdose, their lethality and methods of treatment – this is really medicine rather than psychiatry, but suicidal behaviour is an excellent topic for integrated teaching. A good grasp is needed of how to assess suicidal risk in depressed and other patients, and of the full assessment of the suicide attempter, and this needs to be accompanied by as much practical experience as possible. There needs to be some knowledge of management of the suicidal person, and a good deal of knowledge of the management of depression.

For psychiatrists, the fundamentals are the same, the detail different – much more knowledge including much more that is theoretical and psychodynamic, much experience of assessment and management in complex and difficult cases and situations. For other health professionals, the needs are not very different, although again the emphases and extent differ.

In the voluntary sector, in this country the Samaritans have the largest experience of training in relation to suicide and their training structure is a model for professionals as well. Material on training has kindly been made available to me by Simon Armson, the Chief Executive, and by Joan Guénault, National Director of Training. Nationally, the rate of loss necessitates training 8,000 potential new volunteers a year. Typically the initial training comprises 6 evening sessions and a full day, followed by about 6 months probationary period with 4 further training sessions. Beyond this there is further training on a regional basis in 1–2 day meetings. Some are on general topics, some on special subjects; some for all volunteers, some for more senior people. There is also more senior national training. There is a very careful supervisory structure for the hour by hour work at the approximately 200 branches and centres. There are of course many topics for training, of which suicide is only one. I have seen an excellent handout around which an experiential training session can be built, and an extensive resource pack on suicidal behaviour, including details of how to assess suicide risk and lethality, scripts for role playing, audiotapes, taking the telephone befriender through a variety of difficult suicidal callers, and including some thinking regarding one's own feelings about them. This is most excellent practical training.

An attempt at constructing a suicidology curriculum was undertaken by the NIHM Centre for Studies of Suicide Prevention at the beginning of the 1970s. It included theoretical and practical aspects. I was at the time working at Yale University and took part in an evaluation of it, but little seems to have been heard of it since.

An important issue here is just what needs to be taught. Increased suicide risk accompanies a number of psychiatric disorders and problems, most notably depression, alcoholism, personality disorder, schizophrenia. It accompanies major life crises. Training solely in suicide itself, without training in the wider recognition and management of these disorders and problems, will only help to a limited extent.

What are the implications?

What conclusions can one draw from this? It is tempting to believe that more and better training might be the answer to the problem of suicide. I am in favour of better training, and it would help but we need to be realistic. First, there is no good evidence at present that any substantial proportion of suicides results from failures in training. If it does, we do not know what aspect is at fault. This seems to require some research on what the failures are. Second, we will always be up against the problem that suicide is a comparatively rare event. Much effort may make little impact on suicide itself: its rarity will mean that the main impact will be on something else which is associated with it, but is more common. This is the problem that underlies many efforts to improve prediction of suicide and to prevent its occurence. Thirdly, a substantial number of suicides have not had any contact with the services. Training of professionals is unlikely to help with these.

It is worth while to distinguish two groups of suicides and to think separately about them. The first comprises suicidal people with major mental illness who are in contact with or have been in contact with the psychiatric services. Here training is already extensive. Staff are very aware of suicidal risk, and usually greatly upset when a suicide occurs. Although such patients are at much greater risk of suicide than the general population, and worth targeting for preventive efforts, I am sceptical whether more formal training courses would change the situation. In my own affective disorders unit suicidal behaviour is always a risk but suicide is fortunately rare. When I think back on those patients we have lost, it was often those on whom we had tried hard, but whose problems, whether of illness or personality, were not very amenable to current therapeutic techniques. If I had more resource, I would rather concentrate it on better aftercare, for the many incompletely remitted patients with persistent symptoms and risk of major relapse, than on increasing training for what are already well trained and experienced staff. Good supervision is important. So is audit of suicides, and it is a form of training. Care is needed to support staff in the process.

The second group includes people who have never, or not for a long time, had contact with the psychiatric services: the endogenous depression in middle age which first clearly declares itself in suicide, the young person in a major crisis, the elderly and physically ill. Here the target professional group for education is that of primary care workers. A secondary target is non-mental health hospital workers. Here training has not been extensive, so that increase is likely to be beneficial. It can include cues to recognition of depression and suicidal risk and the management of depression. The Defeat Depression Campaign of the Royal College of Psychiatrists currently has education of GPs and other health professionals as a major aim. In collaboration with the Royal College of General Practitioners two consensus conferences have been held, on recognition and management of depression (Paykel and Priest, 1992) and much educational material has been prepared. This is partly modelled on the American DART Campaign. There is also an aim to educate the public to recognise depression in themselves and family members.

However, I am still haunted by a nagging doubt. Suicide is such a rare event: very roughly it will arise once in every 5 years for the average GP. It is hard to make an impact in such a situation.

Clearly what is required is evaluation. Michel and Valach (1992) found that a seminar increased GPs' knowledge and attitudes regarding suicide, compared with giving of written information. There is one study evaluating the further impact of education, the widely quoted Gotland study (Rutz et al, 1989, 1990, 1992). In this Swedish island of 56,000 population, an intensive educational programme of 20 hours of lectures, discussions and videotape presentations, comprising 3 days in all, was targetted at GPs. It covered a wide variety of aspects of depression, including suicide. Effects were evaluated by study before, during and after the programme. There was a reduction in suicide from a baseline rate of 19.7 per 100,000 in 1982 to 7.1 in 1985, but the actual numbers were quite small and the difference was not significant. Prescribing of antidepressants increased, while use of tranquillisers, and sedatives, tended to decrease. Admissions to hospital for depression decreased, as did the amount of sick leave for depression. Unfortunately, in a further evaluation in 1988, 3 years later, most of these measures had returned to baseline.

This illustrates both the potential benefits and the potential problems. It seems that education can have an impact. Also targetting education on general practice and on depression rather than just suicide is worthwhile. It is also important to accept that such an educational campaign should be evaluated in terms of improving treatment of depression, rather than necessarily in terms of suicide reduction. However, given the other pressures, the variety of kinds of illness, and the need for skills in all the areas of general practice, the situation will slip back without reinforcement. The originators of the campaign recommended repeating it at 2 yearly intervals (Rutz et al, 1992).

References

Barraclough B, Bunch J, Nelson B and Sainsbury P (1974). A hundred cases of suicide: clinical aspects. *British Journal of Psychiatry, 125,* 355–373.

Holden J M, Sagovsky R and Cox J L (1987). Counselling in a general practice setting: a controlled study of health visitor intervention in the treatment of postnatal depression. *British Medical Journal, 298,* 223–226.

Michel K and Valach L (1992). Suicide prevention: spreading the gospel to General Practitioners. *British Journal of Psychiatry, 160,* 757–760.

Paykel E S and Priest R G (1992). Recognition and management of depression in general practice: consensus statement. *British Medical Journal, 305,* 1198–1202.

Rutz W, Wålinder J, Eberhard G, Holmberg G, von Knorring A-L, von Knorring L, Wistedt B and Åberg-Wistedt A (1989). An educational program on depressive disorders for general practitioners on Gotland: background and evaluation. *Acta Psychiatrica Scandinavica, 79,* 19–26.

Rutz W, von Knorring L, Wålinder J and Wistedt B (1990). Effect of an educational program for general practitioners on Gotland on the pattern of prescription of psychotropic drugs. *Acta Psychiatrica Scandinavica, 82,* 399–403.

Rutz W, von Knorring L and Wålinder J (1992). Long-term effects of an educational program for general practitioners given by the Swedish Committee for the Prevention and Treatment of Depression. *Acta Psychiatrica Scandinavica, 85,* 83–88.

22 Some Aspects of Economic and Social Policy
Alan Maynard

Introduction

The Health of the Nation initiatives in mental illness and suicide are to be welcomed. However they must be implemented with care and evaluated thoroughly. What do we know about the cost effectiveness of the programme interventions to reduce suicide? Will the policies set out in Health of the Nation ensure that performance targets for suicide are met? In 1991 there were 5,567 deaths from suicide and undetermined injury in England with "a worrying rise in younger men". The HoN targets are

i) to reduce the overall suicide rate by at least 15 per cent by the year 2000 (ie from 11.1 per 100,000 in 1990 to no more than 9.4), which is equivalent to saving 835 of the lives lost in 1991.

ii) to reduce the suicide rate of severely mentally ill people by at least 33 per cent by the year 2000 (from the estimate of 15 per cent in 1990 to no more than 10 per cent).

The HoN Key Area Handbook for mental illness lists a range of interventions to reduce suicide and all of them are potentially significant but of unknown cost effectiveness. They are: improvement in the management of depression in primary care; developing more local services; and changing the availability of means to suicide.

The authors of HoN recognise that the causes of mental ill health and suicide are multifactoral and that enhancements in health and social functioning will reduce suicide rates. Durkheim emphasised that suicidal behaviours are affected by society, in particular the individual's feelings of isolation and exclusion from the community which are often precipitated by life events.

The proposed Government policies to achieve the HoN suicide targets will be reviewed and other areas of potential policy relevance examined. The latter will include alcohol and drug use, penal policy and policies towards income distribution and poverty. For all interventions there is a need to identify their costs and effects because, in a world of scarce resources, interventions will have to be prioritised.

An Appraisal of the Proposed Suicide Interventions

Management of depression in primary care

(a) depression

Suicide is associated with depression and the extent of this condition is very large. Perhaps 50% of people visiting their general practitioner have depressive symptoms and of these about 5% will have symptoms of major depression (for a review see Freemantle et al (1993)). Freeling and his colleagues (1992) argue that only about 50% of patients with major depression are recognised by GPs. Others have found higher detection rates (eg MacDonald (1986)).

The HoN Key Area Handbook on mental illness (p17) notes that 90% of people who commit suicide have some form of mental illness, that 60% have consulted their GP in the last month and 40% have consulted their GP in the last week. However whilst suicide rates are closely associated with depression, with 40–50% of suicides committed by patients with undiagnosed and poorly treated depression, the general practitioner cannot predict which depressed patients are likely to commit suicide.

The Department of Health hopes that suicides can be reduced by better training of GPs so that they both recognise depression and likely suicides more efficiently but also intervene more appropriately. This hope is based on a Swedish study in Gotland which showed that GP training not only reduced suicides, it also improved other indicators of care quality and produced resource savings (in hospital and drug costs) which more than met the cost of the training programme. (Rutz et al 1992(a) 1992(b)).

It is debatable whether this Swedish result can be used as a basis to inform English policy other than generally. The Swedish suicide rate is much higher than in England with potentially less scope of change, and the design of the study (with no matched controls) is such that the effects of the intervention may be due to factors other than better GP training.

However even if the Swedish GP training results could be replicated in the UK, it is necessary to recognise that GP involvement in, and compliance with, such policies may have to be encouraged with incentives. In this respect it is regrettable that recent changes in the GP contract have failed to exploit the potential of incentives to affect GP behaviour and depression and suicide rates.

In the late 1980s both policy makers and politicians began to focus on the twin attributes of general practice: large variations in practice (eg referrals) and ignorance about what GP services were provided by GPs. The GP contract was general – to render those services that the average GP provides. This contract, in John Wayne speak, "a GP's got to do what a GP's got to do", had strengths and weaknesses. The Government found it wanting and replaced it unilaterally in 1990.

The new GP contract defined certain core activities and related performance to payment for these tasks (eg differing levels of attainment in immunisation, vaccination and cervical cytology). Many of these activities were of unknown cost effectiveness (see eg. Scott and Maynard (1991)). A nice example of this was the payment for health promotion clinics. There was little regulation of such clinics and, as a consequence, some strange activities were reimbursed (eg a Sheffield GP claimed a health promotion clinic fee for showing a Jane Fonda workout video!).

Criticism of this aspect of the new contract led to its revision from April 1993. In future there will be three "bands" of health promotion activity. The selection of the activity areas in these three bands is curious. Surely they should reflect the "burden" of disease and the scope for cost effective intervention? In 1977 Douglas Black (Black (1977)) used a variety of indices of sickness burden to create an index of the burden of diseases. This was revised by Robert Anderson in DH-EAO four years ago. Both sets of authors came to the same conclusion: the illness which created the greatest burden was mental ill-health.

Table 1   GP Health Promotion Targets

Band 1	Programmes to reduce smoking
	: use an age sex register : identify smokers and prioritise : advise and intervene
Band 2	Programmes to minimise mortality and morbidity of patients at risk from hypertension, or with established coronary heart disease or stroke
	: band one criteria plus : identify raised B.P. with regular checks of 15–74 year old population : maintain a register of patients with hypertension, CHD and stroke : manage those on register with practice guidelines, seeking to intervene on lifestyle where appropriate
Band 3	Programmes offering a full range of primary prevention of CHD and stroke
	: bands one and two plus : collect information on BP, smoking, alcohol, body mass index, family history and monitor diet and physical activity in target population : advice, interventions and follow-up in relation to local factors and practice guidelines : prioritise, reach non-presenters

Why is it that the illness which creates this great social burden is omitted from the new GP health promotion contract? It seems that one part of the Department measures the burden and another part of the same Department ignores colleagues' work! Why have the architects of the new GP targets focused on cardiovascular disease, offered no justification in terms of relative cost effectiveness for the policies they have negotiated with the trade union, and ignored mental ill health in general and suicide in particular? The cardiovascular targets might perhaps be achieved more efficiently by fiscal action on smoking in excess of mere index linking to inflation and involving indexing to reduce consumption as proposed in the last White Paper on health targets (Department of Health and Social Security (1977)). The mental illness and related suicide targets might be a more appropriate area for the use of GP incentives, particularly if Gotland – like initiatives can be shown to be cost effective in the UK.

(b) Alcohol and tobacco

Table 2   Alcohol and tobacco consumption

	Alcohol Consumption		**Tobacco Consumption**	
	Litres of Alcohol etc	Expenditure in 1980 prices £ million	Number of Cigarettes (1000 million)	Expenditure in 1980 prices £ million
1960	5.6	4750	110.9	5051
1965	6.2	5686	112.0	4842
1970	6.9	7073	127.9	4934
1975	8.8	9350	132.6	4995
1978	9.3	9930	125.2	4982
1980	9.3	9954	121.8	4822
1982	8.7	9370	102.5	4128
1984	8.9	9983	100.0	3944
1986	9.0	10297	95.0	3731
1988	9.5	10854	97.3	3728
1990	9.3	11080	97.6	3790

Sources: HM Customs and Excise, Central Statistical Office.

Table 3   Alcohol and tobacco use

	Prevalence of Heavy Drinkers* (Age Group)			Percentage Smoking Cigarettes (Age Group)		
Males	16–24	25–44	**Total**	16–24	25–44	**Total**
1978	28	21	17	41	48	45
1980	25	19	15	39	46	42
1982	22	16	13	37	40	38
1984	20	16	13	36	39	36
1986	22	16		36	37	35
1988	18	18	14	33	37	33
1990	18	18	14	33	35	31
Females						
1978	6	4	3	39	43	40
1980	6	4	3	37	43	39
1982	6	4	3	36	38	35
1984	6	4	3	35	36	34
1986	7	4		35	34	33
1988	7	4	4	33	35	32
1990	6	4	4	36	33	30

* Heavy drinking is defined as more than 35 units of alcohol per week for males and more than 25 units of alcohol per week for females.

Source: General Household Surveys (1978–1990).

In the last 20 years the consumption of alcohol has grown rapidly whilst the use of tobacco has fallen. Use of these substances amongst young men, a group where suicide rates have risen, is shown in Table 3. These data show that tobacco use has fallen, except for women aged 16–24 years. Heavy use of alcohol amongst young males also appears to have fallen significantly.

Are alcohol and tobacco risk factors in suicide? Two studies from the USA, where suicide rates amongst young men have also risen, indicate that they may be. Hemenway and his colleagues (1993) describe a close response relationship between the quantity of cigarette smoking and death by suicide in a prospective longitundinal study of a large group of mostly white middle class nurses. Garrison and her colleagues (1993) found a relationship between suicidal behaviour and cigarette smoking, aggression, alcohol and substance abuse in teenagers.

It is unlikely that there is a direct causal relationship between suicide and tobacco use: confounding factors are always a problem in epidemiology (see eg Davey-Smith and Phillips (1992)). Hemenway et al outline three alternative causal mechanisms. Firstly the suicidal outcomes may be produced by tobacco induced malignant diseases. Secondly the antecedent to suicide is depression and smoking may be used by the depressed to mitigate their condition. Thirdly smoking may be a marker for some other illness.

The Garrison et al results, for 3764 teenagers, undermines the first explanation. It is known that alcohol and tobacco use are correlated and that alcohol use and suicide are related. Thus it seems tobacco is a marker for alcohol use and alcohol is a marker for suicide. With aggression in these

South Carolina adolescents being related to alcohol use, and depression not measured in this study, the appropriate policy intervention may not be only to identify and treat depressed young people, but also to influence aggressive adolescents with patterns of high alcohol use.

It might be asserted that the GP health promotion targets may encourage practitioners to monitor lifestyle. However this requires GPs to adopt all three bands (in Table 1). They are being advised, (see Slingsby (1993)) that band three looks like being "hard work" unless the practice is superbly well organised and that band two is a better choice "particularly if you can find a less demanding source of compensatory earnings" (p74). The discussion of these targets seemed to focus mostly on GP income and not on health and whilst the enthusiasts have HoN targets in mind, many may "go through the motions" in order to ensure remuneration.

Thus whilst the new contract's health promotion targets might result in better monitoring of tobacco and alcohol, band 3 activity may be ignored by GPs. All GPs, as part of their conditions of service, will be required to collect lifestyle statistics from July 1993. However this activity does not appear to be well focused on mental health.

(c) GP management of mental ill-health and suicide: overview.

The incidence of mental illness in general practice is high and there appears to be scope for improved management of primary care resources. However this needs to be carefully evaluated as the cost effectiveness of GP interventions on suicide risk marker areas such as alcohol and tobacco utilisation and depression is poorly evaluated. Identifying what works is only part of the problem. The other challenge is to change GPs' behaviour both in screening and intervention practice. It is remarkable that this issue has not been incorporated into the reformulation of the GP contract for health promotion activity. Might it not be more cost effective to deal with cardio-vascular and stroke targets by banning advertisements and using fiscal policy to raise tobacco prices radically, and use the GP contract to reduce mental ill-health and determine whether this affects suicide rates?

Development of local services.

The focus of this work is the development of a "local picture" and the assessment of the needs of the local population. However this is only one of the tasks of the purchaser. The purchaser is also required to identify the cost effective means of local needs. Does a more 'local' service facilitate the achievement of suicide targets? Is such an achievement the product of better management or better resourcing? There appears to be no published UK evidence to inform purchaser choices: the HoN Key Area handbook cites an Italian study and unpublished British data.

There has been speculation, prior to the new Community Care arrangements from April 1993, that the system is under-funded and that management effort is focused unequally on care of the elderly rather than other groups such as the mentally ill. Whilst community care funding is "ring fenced", funding for alcohol and drug treatment is not. These activities are unevaluated and there is Ministerial criticism of their management, but they may be of particular importance for young suicides.

Changing access to the means of suicide

The switch to North Sea gas removed an important means of committing suicide but the data indicate that there was a substitution to the use of car exhaust fumes. Recently introduced changes (Jan 92) in controls over the car exhaust systems of new cars together with the fitting of catalytic converters in new cars from January 1993 will reduce cumulatively another route for suicidal people. The decrease in suicides by poisoning with solids and liquids may be due to manufacturers making substances which induce vomiting or are non-toxic (eg the SSRI drugs used to treat depression). The cost effectiveness of these changes is not always evident e.g. tricyclics are more cost effective than SSRIs (Song et al (1993)) and the use of SSRIs buys lives (ie avoid suicides) at a very high cost ie it may be cost ineffective to use high priced SSRIs.

The increased number of suicides in males, noticeably in the young males, from strangulation may be a product of the prison system. Given the extraordinary crowding in prisons with confinement to cells for 23 hours a day in some cases, fearsome companions and the Government's sloth in reforming the legal system, this cause of suicides seems unlikely to be curtailed in the near future. The cost effectiveness of policies of prison reform in terms of suicide avoidance has not been investigated.

Sociological issues

The exploration of links between suicide and economic and social trends, is contentious. Do unemployment, poverty, increasing inequality in the distribution of income and wealth, poor education and other socio-economic influences such as increases in divorce and single person households create the feelings of isolation and hopelessness which induce depression and suicide? Are these factors the cause of depression and suicide, or does the depressed state lead to unemployment of vulnerable groups and enhanced suicide risk? The direction of causation and the problems of compounding factors are neither well understood or adequately researched. Would policies such as compulsory membership of "job clubs" by the unemployed reduce isolation, mental ill-health and suicide? What are the possible interventions and is anything known about their costs and effects?

High unemployment rates (e.g. 13.8% and 18.7% for 16–19 year old females and males respectively, and 9.4 and 15.3 per cent for the genders in the 20–29 year olds group in 1992 (Central Statistical Office (1993)), together with disguised unemployment in training schemes and higher education, substantial redistribution of both wealth and income in the 1979–91 period from the bottom quintile to top quintile (eg for net income after housing costs the share of the bottom quintile fell from 9.6 per cent to 6.9 per cent, and the share of the top quintile rose from 35.3 per cent to 41.1 per cent), and 10 per cent of males and 7 per cent of females leaving school with no qualifications may create an "under-class" but its definition and the evaluation of its effects are not without difficulty. Exploration of these risk markers will need sophisticated modelling of epidemiological and economic – social data which takes full account of the "redefinition" of factors such as unemployment over the 1980s.

In the USA the social pressure – disadvantage hypothesis appears to be confounded because suicide rates amongst black Americans is generally less than for the white population (Shaffer (1993)), although Durkheim would ascribe this to the greater sense of community amongst blacks. However despite evidence such as this and the difficulties of linking social disadvantage to suicide in the UK, it is likely that such factors are of importance. The Thatcher ethos with its denial of society and the emphasis on the virtue of individual endeavour, may have increased isolation for vulnerable groups and increased their mental ill-health.

Whilst such arguments are contentious it is important to distinguish between ideological argument and empirical evidence. The latter is incomplete but this is no excuse for deploying ideology to exclude it from consideration. If Mr Major's classless society is to be achieved, inequalities will need to be mitigated and this may reduce suicide rates.

Conclusions

1. The HoN targets for suicide are ambitious.

2. The policies to achieve these targets – improved identification and intervention in general practice, improved community care and removal of risk factors – are costly and their cost effectiveness is unknown. Resources to reduce suicide are limited: how will the demands of competing services be prioritised?

3. Government policy is incomplete and incomprehensible in some respects. The opportunity offered by the reform of the GP contract with regard to health promotion has been lost despite Ministers and officials emphasising the importance of mental ill health. Is the 'capture' of these changes by non-psychiatric medicine and the targeting of cardiovascular disease and stroke (from April 1993) a cost effective policy relative to investing these resources in mental ill health? The publication of the DoH's reasons (especially evaluative trial data) for its choice of priorities would be welcome and is overdue.

4. To ignore the impact of unemployment, increasing inequality, poor education, penal policy and other socio-economic factors on mental ill health and suicide is unwise. The links are unclear but this should serve as an incentive to explore them, particularly using longitudinal cohort studies such as those of the National Children's Bureau and the Medical Research Council.

5. As in all areas of health and social care, "needs" are increasingly well identified. However the enthusiasm with which this activity is being pursued needs to be tempered with agnosticism. The problem now is how to identify "what works" ie what is cost effective. In a NHS where growth resources in 1993–94 are practically zero, prioritisation will be a very difficult task given the deficiencies of the knowledge base and the pressures to fund acute medicine. If the behaviour of local purchasers reflects that of the reformers of the GP contract in the Department of Health, it is unlikely that mental health services will be resourced adequately and that the suicide target for the year 2000 will not be met.

References

Black D (1977). Priorities in research in C I Phillips and N Wolfe, *Clinical Practice and Economics,* Pitman, Oxford and London.

Central Statistical Office (1993). *Social Trends,* HMSO, London.

Davey Smith G and Phillips A N (1992). Confounding in epidemiological studies: why 'independent' effects may not be all they seem, *British Medical Journal,* 6856, 305, 757–59.

Department of Health and Social Security (1977). *Prevention and Health,* Cmnd 7074, HMSO, London.

Department of Health (1992). *Health of the Nation.* HMSO, London.

Department of Health (1993). *Health of the Nation: Key Area Handbook on Mental Illness.* London.

Freeling P, Tylec A (1992). Depression in General Practice, E S Peykel (ed). *Handbook and Affective Disorders,* 2nd edition, Churchill Livingstone, Edinburgh.

Freemantle N, Song F, Sheldon T, Long A et al (1993). The *Treatment of Depression in Primary Care,* Effective Health Care Bulletin 5, School of Public Health, Leeds University.

Freling P, Rao B M, Paykel E S et al (1985). Unrecognised depression in general practice, *British Medical Journal,* 290, 1180–83.

Garrison C Z, McKeown R E, Valois R F and Vincent M L (1993). Aggression, substance use, and suicidal behaviours in high school students, *American Journal of Public Health,* 83, 179–84.

Henenway D, Solnick S J and Colditz G A (1993). Smoking and suicide among nurses, *American Journal of Public Health,* 83, 249–51.

Rutz W, Carlsson P et al (1992(a)). Cost benefit analysis of an educational program for general practitioners by the Swedish Committee for the Prevention and Treatment of Depression, *Acta Psychiatra Scand.,* 85, 457–64.

Rutz W, Von Knorring L and Walinder J (1992(b)). Long term effects of an educational program for general practitioners given by the Swedish Committee for the Prevention and Treatment of Depression, *Acta Psychiatrica Scandinavica* 85, 83–88.

Shaffer D (1993). Suicide: risk factors and public health, *American Journal of Public Health,* 83, 171–72.

Slingsby C (1993). Action plan: health promotion, *Medeconomics,* February, 74–81.

Song F, Freemantle N, Sheldon T et al (1993). Selective serotonin re-uptake inhibitors: meta analysis of efficacy and acceptability, *British Medical Journal,* 306, 683–87.

23 Implications for Research and Clinical Audit
Keith Hawton and Gethin Morgan

Two specific areas concerning suicide prevention are in urgent need of further research. The first is an intensive study of young suicides and the second is an evaluation of an educational programme in primary care regarding the management of depression and suicide risk.

Young suicides

Several contributors in this volume have highlighted the increasing suicide rates in males in the United Kingdom. Suicides by both young males and females lead to very substantial premature loss of life. It is essential that this group should be one major focus for suicide prevention. However, we know very little about the characteristics of young suicides, except that as other contributors have shown, they appear less often to have had recent contact with health care professionals, especially GPs, than have older suicides.

A study is therefore required of younger suicides (under 45 years of age). Probable suicides, such as those whose deaths have been assigned to the undetermined category, must also be included. The study should use the method of psychological post-mortem or autopsy in which information is systematically collected from relatives, friends, hospital and GP records, coroners' inquest information and other sources. Modern assessment procedures must be used to establish facts about each individual, in order to provide an overview of a series of suicides.

The difficulties encountered in conducting this type of study cannot be overestimated. For example, a relatively large number of deaths should be studied both in order to provide reliable findings and to allow meaningful internal comparisons between and within sub-groups of subjects (eg males versus females, very young suicides). Carefully chosen methodology will be required, particularly with regard to identification of factors such as psychiatric disorder, current problems, and personality disorder. The greatest difficulty concerns the choice of appropriate control subjects. This will depend on which factors are to be examined – eg, psychiatric controls might be chosen if one wishes to examine the role of social factors, deaths from other causes if one wants to elucidate the role of psychiatric disorder, and so on. Finally, such a study has obvious difficulties with regard to potential emotional stress for both informants and research workers.

In spite of these difficulties this study is badly needed. At present, suggestions for prevention of suicide in the very young focus, for example, on making potential methods for suicide safe, education in schools, and pleas to Government to counter increasing rates of unemployment. This study, if properly conducted, should clarify whether there are other potential foci for effective prevention.

At a minimum the following factors should be examined in a psychological autopsy study of young suicides:

- Psychiatric and personality characteristics

- Problems and precipitants associated with suicide

- Relevant social factors eg divorce, social isolation, unemployment

- Role of substance (alcohol/drugs) abuse

- Contacts with GPs, psychiatric services and other agencies before death.

This study should also be designed so that the temporal sequencing of factors (eg family breakdown followed by school problems and then substance abuse) can be determined.

Educational programme in primary care about management of depression and suicide risk

The Gotland study, in which an educational programme for GPs on a Swedish island about management of depression was associated with a decline in the island's suicide rate, has been noted by several contributors. Reservations have been expressed about the study, particularly with regard to its relatively small size and hence validity. It must also be remembered that relatively few young suicides contact their GPs during the period immediately preceeding their deaths. However, management of depression, especially at primary care level, is an obvious focus for attention, not just for the possible consequences in terms of suicide prevention. Thus such efforts could have more widespread benefits for patients who present in primary care with emotional problems.

The content of an educational programme should be relatively brief in order to be appropriate to all the other demands faced by GPs. The type of programme being encouraged by the Defeat Depression Campaign would seem suitable, perhaps supplemented by more specific focus on suicide risk detection, assessment and management. The effects of the study might be evaluated in terms of several parameters, for example:

- Changes in participants' attitudes and knowledge regarding management of depression and suicide risk.

- Use of antidepressants and other psychotropic medication

- Use of psychiatric services

- Suicidal behaviour (both fatal and non-fatal) among people on GPs' lists.

This study should use a randomised controlled design, one group of receiving the programme and one not, at least initially. If the effects of the programme on actual suicidal behaviour are to be examined, the study will require inclusion of substantial numbers of GPs and hence a large patient population.

Clinical Audit

Clinical audit is essentially a review of clinical practice, carried out in such a way that various deficiencies in clinical procedures are effectively identified, and where possible remedied. There are several reasons why clinical audit is likely to be particularly useful in the case of suicide and its prevention. Research in this field is beset with many practical difficulties with the result that the clinical assessment of suicide risk is still a very uncertain matter. What risk factors have been identified are notoriously unreliable especially

189

in the short term, which of course is particularly relevant to routine clinical practice. Given this situation it is very important that we identify and standardise day to day clinical procedures in the assessment and management of suicide risk and this is exactly what clinical audit of suicide should help us to do. Furthermore it may lead to the identification of a whole new range of short term predictive factors, hitherto unchartered by conventional research. The whole process should enable and encourage healthcare professionals to look at what they do, thereby energising their will to achieve excellence in clinical practice.

It is important to acknowledge that not all suicides, given our present state of knowledge, can be prevented, however good the clinical service may be. The purpose is quite simply to optimise clinical practice so that preventable suicides are avoided. The clinical review needs to be systematic and comprehensive, and ideally should involve the use of a standardised questionnaire to include all aspects of the problem, otherwise the process merely tends to be selective, excluding difficult issues and perhaps merely leading to mutual reassurance.

The simplest approach is to review those unexpected deaths which have become known to healthcare personnel. However, any clinical audit which sets out to be comprehensive will also need to match mortality data (including HM Coroner's inquests) with attendance records within all components of the mental health service. These include hospital inpatient facilities, community mental health teams, day hospitals and outpatients. General practitioner surgeries will also need to be included in any comprehensive review. If it is to be fully efficient the matching process depends upon the reliability of all sources of data. Though the whole process may appear cumbersome it is nevertheless necessary to collect and match data in this way because there is good evidence that hospital based practitioners may be unaware of some unexpected deaths in patients within a year of discharge from their care. Clearly this means that in hospital practice, at least, the lesson learnt from day to day clinical experience regarding the assessment and management of suicidal patients may be unreliable. Effective audit should help to rectify this.

The Department of Health will soon issue detailed guidelines concerning audit into unexpected deaths. The process is inexpensive and can easily be developed under normal working conditions without the need for extra resources. Nevertheless it is a challenging task in coordination and persistence and it can be very helpful to identify a special audit coordinator who can ensure that mortality data are collected, disseminated, effectively checked with all components of the clinical service, and then arranging regular audit meetings. Ideally these should be be multidisciplinary in nature. In order to ensure that all aspects of the problem are reviewed it is desirable to utilise a questionnaire such as that used in the Confidential Enquiry into Unexpected Deaths. Indeed the same questionnaire can be used for returns both to the National Enquiry and for the purpose of local audit. If clinical audit of this kind is to help and encourage clinicians to learn from experience it should not aim at finding scapegoats or to apportion blame. Fears of medico/legal repercussions may also inhibit enthusiasm: such anxieties can be allayed by ensuring that documentation is in the form of lessons learnt together with actions to be taken, without reference in detail to individual examples of suicide which have been reviewed. Clinical audit will never succeed if it is in danger of being confused with enquiries into clinical practice which management may need to conduct under complaints or other procedures.

In view of the many hazards which beset the day to day care of suicidal persons the accumulation of lessons learnt through reliable clinical audit is a most important part of any service which sets out to be as effective as possible in suicide prevention. Clinical audit is not merely a way of implementing the lessons learnt from more formal research. It can identify the new ways of understanding the many pathways which can lead to suicide. Improving the process of care is an important theme in its own right as one approach to the challenging task of suicide prevention.

Coordination of intiatives

It has become apparent that many research and audit initiatives are occurring with regard to suicidal behaviour, clearly stimulated to a large degree by *The Health of the Nation* suicide targets. There is a danger of duplication of effort and lack of early sharing of experience in this field. Therefore it would seem sensible to find some means of coordinating these initiatives. At a minimum a register of people working in this area should be established, together with some indication of their specific interests and projects.

24   Creating National Policy
Jeremy Metters

I would firstly like to distance myself from those who are agnostic about the aim of suicide prevention. It is important to remember that this conference has been about what can be done to prevent suicide, not whether prevention of suicide is more cost effective than the prevention of early cardiovascular disease deaths. The conference has covered many different aspects of suicide and has increased our understanding of who commits suicide, what can be done to prevent suicide and perhaps more importantly how much we still do not know about the prevention of suicide. Alongside this has been a recognition of the training implications of the prevention of suicide, training for a wide range of disciplines in the primary care setting, as well as looking at the quality of care. How can we support workers in the aftermath of suicide? What support is needed for relatives? Answers to these questions are vital if we are to meet health promotion targets.

Three criteria were used to choose health promotion targets. Firstly, was the issue a major public health matter? Could anything be done about it? Can we measure what might be done about it? On these criteria mental health in general and suicide in particular were included in the Health of the Nation targets. Indeed, Douglas Black's burden of disease made the need for inclusion quite clear, however crude the measures.

In addressing my title, I shall attempt to review the processes by which some of the lessons learnt at the conference might be taken forward in a structured and accountable way in creating national policy. Health of the Nation targets cannot be achieved by the NHS alone. The framework is what we all can do, whether in the health service, education, social service, or as individuals. If we do not change our behaviour we will not meet Health of the Nation targets and this is as true for mental health targets and for cardiovascular disease.

Over the last two days, we've heard a range of people talking about many different aspects of suicide from different walks of life. All need to be involved. People who have attempted suicide, those who are at risk, relatives. Someone referred to cooperation of professionals with relatives of those who succeeded in taking their own lives because they have a lot to say. And we must listen to them. I haven't heard much about the voluntary sector. I think the organisations in the voluntary sector have a great deal to offer and we should build partnerships with them. Particularly important is the prevention of suicide among young men. Churches, social services, and prisons all have important roles. I was interested to hear earlier this afternoon what prison governors are doing about suicide prevention. Obviously the GP and the primary health care team have a lot to offer as have psychiatric teams, purchasers, government and the media. Now, the media, I think, need to be careful about the adventurous way in which they report suicide because copycatting, whether it be of suicide or putting foreign bodies in food in supermarkets, is a phenomenon of our time and it's one that as yet has not been regarded as sufficiently important that it's affected the way in which events are reported by the media.

Two particular points to raise are the benefits that can be obtained from a confidential inquiry and from local audit of suicide. In local audit we must also examine the cause of death for those registered as undetermined cases. How should this information, and other issues, be brought together to support and improve:

- a strategic approach to purchasing
- the development of close links with the authorities, trusts, local authorities, the voluntary sector
- the effectiveness of the multidisciplinary team
- research needed
- the creation of networks and health alliances?

To support purchasing the DoH commissioned and published First Steps for the NHS. The mental illness section in the report has many useful recommendations about the content of corporate contracts. I agree with Alan Maynard, we first need to review existing reports to see these have been properly evaluated and assessed. But if we don't put mental illness in the list and try to make progress we won't ever know what can be achieved. So we have to make a start.

Providers also have to look at what they are offering to the purchasers, to be sure that they are offering the necessary service that should be available to try and reduce the unnecessary toll from suicide. Community Care legislation is of fundamental importance to those who are discharged from long stay care, or even short stay care who must have an appropriate care programme available for them when they leave their residential accommodation. This brings me to the wider network. Poverty, homelessness, mental breakdown, are all issues that reinforce the need for joint working to be maintained between the statutory and voluntary agencies. This is absolutely vital if we are going to achieve targets.

On research and development, it's important to integrate the findings of research and development into service delivery as soon as possible. Under Professor Michael Peckham's R & D initiative, we will be doing more in the mental health field to focus, not only on biological and medical research, but also on evaluation of services and the interaction with the social research which the previous speaker mentioned.

I think this conference exemplifies the way in which the DoH has to listen to, work with, cooperate with, all the various professional groups involved. We need to work with you and we need to learn with you so that policy can be developed in a way that is user friendly for the providers but above all for the users. In this the Directors of Public Health, with their responsibility for assessing needs within their own district, play a fundamentally important role. Some are looking very carefully at how to provide a comprehensive mental health service that includes an emphasis on the prevention of suicide.

Education is not only for general practitioners and psychiatrists: it must provide for the needs of nurses, occupational therapists, psychologists and others. Wherever you look, some health care workers may be in touch with potential suicides. The nurse in A & E, the health visitor attending to a mother with post natal depression, or looking after an elderly person who has just lost a relative. All of these people need to have training that will help them better to identify those who are risk of suicide, and to see how they can actually prevent that happening.

I have discussed healthy alliances briefly, and noted the need for better cooperation between the DoH and Department for Education. There are already contacts with the Department of Transport over car exhausts emission and with the Ministry of Agriculture on the issue of depression in the agricultural community, particularly relevant after what was said about the prevalence of suicide in the rural areas of Holland. We need to improve contacts with the Home Office over the services of health care and mental illness services available in prisons. We are, currently funding some special care schemes run by the Samaritans and we hope these will reduce the high suicide rates in the rural community. That too needs to be evaluated. We need again to look at the networks and alliances that can outreach to young people. So what is the DoH doing to create a national policy? I think this has to be an ongoing iterative process. A single conference like this or an announcement will not take us very far. What is needed is a continuous dialogue, a development of partnerships between the providers, the experts out in the field, and central government. Not only the Department of Health but other departments that have an input to make. The DoH role is also to ensure that the management and monitoring of health authorities' activities and contracts pay due regard to the prevention of suicide and indeed of mental health services. We can stimulate activities such as the Confidential Enquiry and also we can see that audit is not developed with two dozen different models throughout the country.

The important thing is that we should foster willingness to work together in all sectors. I have been impressed by the shared vision expressed during the conference, and enthusiasm and commitment and new ideas that have come forward. I hope that we can remember that a lot of what is proposed is unevaluated without that dampening our enthusiasm for trying to do something positive.

I look forward in due course, to hearing more of your own many activities to reduce suicide, which must be our shared objective.

Printed in the United Kingdom for HMSO
Dd 297609   C25   12/93   13110